Hooligan Hearts

Hooligan Hearts

A Memoir

John G. Walters

LEGACY ISLE
PUBLISHING

© 2022 John G. Walters

All rights reserved. No part of this book may be reproduced in any form or by any electronic or mechanical means, including information retrieval systems, without prior written permission from the publisher, except for brief passages quoted in reviews.

ISBN 978-1-948011-87-7

Library of Congress Control Number: 2022914320

Design and production
Angela Wu-Ki

Legacy Isle Publishing
1000 Bishop St., Ste. 806
Honolulu, HI 96813
Toll-free 1-866-900-BOOK
info@legacyislepublishing.net
www.legacyislepublishing.net

Printed in the United States

Dedicated to the people
who helped a *kolohe* kid from Ka'ū
grow up to be the man I am today

Ron and John at Honomalino.

Contents

	Introduction	9
CHAPTER 1	Cultural Conundrum	11
CHAPTER 2	"Who are these guys?"	14
CHAPTER 3	The Big Island	22
CHAPTER 4	Volcanoes	32
CHAPTER 5	Kaʻū	37
CHAPTER 6	South Point (Ka Lae)	39
CHAPTER 7	Pāhala	43
CHAPTER 8	Clothing	54
CHAPTER 9	The Plantation	61
CHAPTER 10	The Town	64
CHAPTER 11	Dolla' Tree Eighty	68
CHAPTER 12	The Hinged Board	72
CHAPTER 13	Obake	75
CHAPTER 14	The Gulches	79
CHAPTER 15	Killer Bees	83
CHAPTER 16	The Pool and Other Assorted Swimming Opportunities	88
CHAPTER 17	Caves	94
CHAPTER 18	Trees	98
CHAPTER 19	The Forest	107
CHAPTER 20	Learning the Hard Way	108
CHAPTER 21	Television and the Beginning of the End	115
CHAPTER 22	Kids, Don't Try This at Home*	116
CHAPTER 23	Games	125
CHAPTER 24	Gravity Has Its Way	132
CHAPTER 25	Kau Kau	135
CHAPTER 26	"Come eat, boys!"	142
CHAPTER 27	Animals	145
CHAPTER 28	Tina	148

CHAPTER 29	The Pugnacious Porker	155
CHAPTER 30	Stalking the Wild	158
CHAPTER 31	Glasses	160
CHAPTER 32	Kindergarten	162
CHAPTER 33	That Wasn't So Bad	165
CHAPTER 34	Catholic Interlude	172
CHAPTER 35	Come Dancing	183
CHAPTER 36	PSAT	187
CHAPTER 37	Da-vine Intervention	189
CHAPTER 38	Reading Class	190
CHAPTER 39	A Contender? I Think Not!	193
CHAPTER 40	The Knocks on the Door	198
CHAPTER 41	Motoring Madness	203
CHAPTER 42	Amusements and Diversions	209
CHAPTER 43	The Bicycle Built for Two Fools	211
CHAPTER 44	The Phantom Rider Is Out There	213
CHAPTER 45	"See you in court, kid!"	216
CHAPTER 46	Work	219
CHAPTER 47	Working on the Old Plantation	227
CHAPTER 48	Swimming Lessons	238
CHAPTER 49	Nīnole	240
CHAPTER 50	Fishing Fool?	245
CHAPTER 51	ʻOpihi	247
CHAPTER 52	Deep Divers and Surfing Fools	249
CHAPTER 53	The Eels	252
CHAPTER 54	Honomalino	255
CHAPTER 55	Cowabunga—the Exultant Cry of the Surfer	282
CHAPTER 56	Surfing Kaʻū	285
CHAPTER 57	Honoliʻi Pali	292
CHAPTER 58	Hāpuna	297
CHAPTER 59	So What Does It All Mean?	299
	Epilogue: Ron	302

Introduction

For all of my life, most of my relatives lived on the Mainland and I lived in Hawaiʻi. I never really knew them and as a result have very little in the way of family history and stories, or little sense of belonging to an extended family. But I have my own history, story, and place where I belong.

I wrote these vignettes to preserve and share memories I treasure. It's my hope that whoever comes into my family or reads these stories after I'm gone will enjoy them, and I will be able to share a little bit about the place, time, and way we lived—especially since that way of life has vanished along with Hawaiʻi's sugar plantations.

My upbringing was a little different. I know that and embrace it. I've always believed it's not about how we were raised; what's far more important is what we have done with our lives. I do have things I feel strongly about and a code I try to live by. We all should. But when I started writing these stories, I promised myself that I would be truthful, and that I wouldn't use them as a bully pulpit to inflict my personal views or beliefs on others, or to get revenge—at least that is my intent.

I've tried not to use people's names or otherwise identify them in my stories; this is intentional. This is my story and I'm putting it down the way I remember, which could be different than someone else's recollection. So be it—if anyone is offended by what I've written, that wasn't my purpose in sharing these memories. There are also things I left out. I felt that including them in this memoir would serve no purpose, and I didn't think they would add anything good or substantive to what I've written.

I've been sharing these stories for years. So far, I've only gotten one of two responses from most people. They either compliment me on my overactive imagination, or they ask if I had any adult supervision and seem to have a hard time believing it really was that way, back in my day. But looking back now, I wouldn't change a thing, even if I could. I've always believed I was damn lucky to have grown up on the Big Island of

Hawai'i back in those days, and my memories, both good and bad, mean a lot to me as I age. I'm grateful I was there and was a part of that way of life before it was gone.

Others helped build the memories I am sharing in my stories. Most of them are gone now, along with my chance to tell them how much I grew to value them, what they meant to me, and how much they contributed to the person I've become.

One more thing: I never saw myself as an instigator in those days, but you'll see from these stories that I certainly was a willing henchman and collaborator. I'll always be grateful that my older brother, Ron, included me in most of his adventures. He's gone now, but I'd like his memory to live on in these stories. I hope you can see what kind of a guy he was, and how much I valued and appreciated the memories we built together. He was my brother and my true friend; a better friend could not be found.

CHAPTER 1

Cultural Conundrum

For years when people ask what race or culture I am, I've replied, "purebred *poi*." After all, a poi dog is a mixed breed dog that combines all kinds of breeds into a new and unique being. I've always felt kind of like that when I think about race and culture, especially mine.

Take Europe, carve off Finland and everything east of Germany and below France, and there you have it, my racial heritage. I've written down what I know of my family elsewhere, but this isn't about my family, it's about what became my culture.

In the end I guess I took a little from everyone and packed it together inside me, both the good and the bad. I like being local; that's really who I am and that's good enough for me. The people I identify most closely with and look up to, and the values I try to live by, I would describe as "local."

Not your "chicken chest," truculent, "I'm-bigger-than-you-so-I'm-righter" stereotypical local. But the people of quiet strength and values, who have shown me by their example what it means to be part of a community. The people that showed me that if I met them halfway, they would nurture, support, and share their lives with me. I'm a better person than I would have been because of them.

When I had to explain what I believe is our shared cultural experience with some people who never lived here and did not have my perspective, I simply explained that I consider the overriding culture in Hawaiʻi to be "local" and everything else blends with, contributes to it, and at least for me becomes our shared cultural experience.

We do use words that some may find offensive, thus the reason for this long-winded and rambling explanation. Bear with me, this stuff is important, but not easy to put into words.

To put it into perspective, take the word *haole*. I was taught that the literal translation means "without the breath of life" or "white." But I'm not going into the historical context. I have no idea what they were thinking when they started using the word.

But I have been called haole all my life. Before you get upset, just realize that I'm not upset, so don't be offended on my account. To me, haole is just a word that describes people like me, neither good nor bad, just a word.

Once at a gathering of representatives of the Haida and Tlingit tribes, I used the word in my presentation, to describe myself. But someone, not a haole, and not from Hawai'i, took offense and challenged me for using what he considered a racial slur. I did try to explain how I felt about the word, but, unconvinced, he considered it a racial slur and unacceptable to use.

In the end I told him that haole is a description and not in and of itself bad. But there are circumstances where it could be bad, very bad. When he asked me what I meant, I explained if someone called me haole, or "haole boy" like they did for most of my life, no problem. Like the way most of the grown-ups in Pāhala only knew me as "Waltah boy," and couldn't remember my first name. That never bothered me, and with three Waltah boys it provided a little bit of anonymity and plausible deniability, in case of need, which sadly enough was frequently.

But it could be a problem, a real big problem. The tone of the word changes depending on any words used before and after the "haole." You can fill in the blanks yourself, or just think "expletive deleted." Almost as bad as saying, "What?" or "Why?" In those situations, with the wrong inflection and the wrong words, things usually got a little heated and sometimes ended badly.

The kids in my family all grew up here in Hawai'i without an extended family that could pass on any of our unique and plentiful cultural traditions or rich heritages. To me that meant that I never really had a single culture unique to my family that I could lean on to express my Viking, English, Irish, French, German, or whatever culture. So I became "local," not Hawaiian, Filipino, Japanese, Portuguese, Chinese, or haole. But a cultural mixture of all of the people I knew and the values and traditions they felt were important.

All in all, I feel fortunate. I never gave up anything I ever had, or missed anything I never knew. But I gained a lot more than I would have otherwise, and I treasure the perspective I gained from the people I've known.

CHAPTER 2

"Who are these guys?"

When I started writing, I realized that without a little background my reader won't know who I'm talking about.

I'm not going to go into a lengthy and boring discourse about my illustrious family history. One of my aunts once gave me a genealogy chart with a list of our relatives. It was pretty long and went back pretty far, but bottom line was that our relatives left Europe for America. She wasn't very happy when I pointed out that only desperate people with no prospects would have been willing to get on a leaky boat and sail across the stormy Atlantic to an unknown land with pretty much nothing to start a new and hopefully better life. I guess we were part of the flotsam and jetsam of Europe. Not a bad thing; at least they had courage, hope, and ability, otherwise we wouldn't have lasted this long.

I don't know what racial stock we came from. Depending on which parent I talked to, the purest strain we have is one-fourth Swedish or Norwegian. The rest is a smattering of Europe bordered by Finland, Spain, and the edge of Germany. So, I guess we really are purebred poi.

My father and mother were raised in South Dakota; my father in Brookings and my mother in Sisseton. My great-grandfather on my father's side, Sol, was a pretty successful businessman. But along the way he changed our name from Peterson, which he started with, to Walters, the one we have now. As the story goes at that time there were a lot of Sol Petersons in South Dakota and people kept mixing them up. So, after losing a big business deal, he got frustrated and looked in the phone book for a more utilitarian last name. I was told at the time there was only one Walters listed and he wasn't named Sol. So he trotted off and changed his name. He never looked back. I guess he got all his mail after the name change.

My grandfather on my mother's side, Harry, was the postmaster in Sisseton; my other grandfather, William, owned farms and ran a secondhand shop in Brookings.

Both my parents were raised during the Great Depression. My mother told me they didn't have it that bad; her father was a federal employee and they always seemed to have enough. That wasn't the case with Pop. As he told it, just before the Depression hit, his father, William, was involved in a big land deal and had sold five farms he owned to finance his next move. He took the money to the bank about a week before the crash in the 1929. His friend, the bank manager, tried to get him to keep the cash in hand, but he wouldn't. When the Depression hit, he lost it all, except the family home in Bruce and his secondhand shop in Brookings. It hit him hard, real hard.

Pop said that one day shortly thereafter, Grandpa packed the family car, told everyone he was going away for a while, and drove off. Nobody heard from him for about six months. Then he came back and drove up to the house with a new attitude and two small alligators he gave to the children. He never said a word about where he had gone or what he did when he got there. Pop said they kept the alligators in the basement and fed them a steady diet of chickens until the next winter when someone got tired of being snapped at and cleaning up after them and left the door at the top of the stairs open. They vanished and were never seen again; coyote bait, I guess. Grandpa kept wheeling and dealing from his secondhand store. He must have done okay; when he died, he owned seven farms near Brookings.

One odd thing: Long after my grandfather died, Pop showed me a pocket watch that had been passed down to him after Grandpa died. Of course, I unscrewed the case to look at the movement; those old watches are something else. When I got the cover off, I mentioned to Pop that Grandpa must have needed money pretty bad back then because he had hocked his watch in a pawnshop lots of times. Pop got offended, because that wasn't the way the family remembered Grandpa, and asked me how I knew. Inside the back cover were lots of three-digit numbers scratched into the case. I showed them to him and told him they were most likely put there by a pawnbroker to keep track of his inventory, but he claimed they must have been from a repair shop. He didn't get any happier when

I counted them—and there were a bunch—and I mentioned that if they were repair numbers, the watch hardly ever worked. He never agreed, but that's what it had to be. Later on, he asked me how I knew about the numbers, so I told him I had read about it in a Sherlock Holmes mystery. I still have the watch, but, to me, those numbers don't represent failure and hard times. To me, they represent tenacity and my grandfather hanging on to something that must have meant a lot to him.

But to continue: Grandma, Pop, and his brothers and sisters were pretty much on their own for a while. He told me they were only able to keep the home they lived in because my aunt, a schoolteacher who married an attorney and had moved to Hawai'i earlier, was sending money home. Pop helped out by hunting and fishing for food. He tried to make it sound grim, but I could tell he loved hunting pheasants and other game.

Eventually, thanks to FDR and the New Deal, he joined the Civilian Conservation Corps (CCC) making roads in the badlands of South Dakota. He sent all his earnings home to help the family. From what he said it must have been an uncertain time.

Much, much later I was browsing a local swap meet and a small ring caught my eye. I really don't know why. I like other kinds of stuff, but that ring called to me and I bought it for about a buck. I bought it because it had a CCC crest and I thought it would be cool to give it to Pop for Christmas. When I gave it to him, he opened the package and just looked at it for a long time without saying anything. I asked him if it was okay. After a while he said it was more than okay; he just couldn't believe what he was seeing. Then he told me that times were so hard back then that even though the ring only cost about fifty cents or so, he couldn't afford one. It was the only thing he wanted to remember his service in the CCC, and he couldn't spend the money to get one. He said he never thought he would see another one, let alone have one given to him. Must have been the universe moving in strange ways, but this time for good. A "chicken skin" (local goosebumps) moment. He treasured that ring until he died, when he bequeathed it back to me.

Moving on again. Pardon the digressions, my memories of our family history are a little fuzzy in places and I want to get it all in while I still remember anything. Just so you know I'm being as accurate as I

Pop on the rocks at Honomalino.

can, but no promises I got everything right. But I will be in the ballpark.

I guess things got better eventually; both Mom and Pop went to college. I don't remember where Mom went; she never really said much about college. Pop graduated from the University of Minnesota during World War II. Shortly after he graduated with a physical education degree, he enlisted in the Navy. The thing was, he enlisted as a chief petty officer, boatswain, and was assigned to recruit training at the Great Lakes training facility. Just so you know, that's pretty unusual; sailors mostly get to be chiefs after about ten years of service. But the war kind of speeded things up for Pop.

While he was at Great Lakes he applied for and was accepted into OCS to be an officer. He graduated as an ensign, and shortly after that he was promoted to a lieutenant junior grade (LTJG) and assigned to a destroyer escort, the USS *Wyman* in the Pacific campaign. He stayed on that ship out at sea for about three years during the war. He transferred to the Naval Reserve after the war and retired as a LTJG after serving twenty years.

While he was on the *Wyman* it passed through Hawaiʻi on its way to the war in the Pacific, and he had a chance to visit his sister and her husband in Hilo. While he was there, he got to spend some time in Kona. After that there was no looking back for him. He knew he had found his paradise and he was going to move to Hawaiʻi as soon as he could after mustering out of the Navy when the war ended.

He survived the war, got out of the Navy, married my mother, and they both moved to the Big Island and taught at Konawaena High School. He taught physical education and she taught English.

After a while Pop got a job as a bookkeeper in Hilo, and he and Mom moved from Kona to Hilo, bought a house, and started having children.

First there was Ron, then me, then three more, then they stopped. Everyone but me was born at Hilo Memorial Hospital. Lucky me, I was born in Sisseton, South Dakota. According to family history, my mother flew up to South Dakota, I was born about a month later, then a month after that she flew back. I could never figure it out. Why Sisseton? I kept asking with no answer, until finally one night after Mom had had a few vodkas she told me that she went to Sisseton because she wanted to have one of her children in her hometown. Back then Hawaiʻi was a territory and I guess she thought the others wouldn't be citizens or something; she never said. Anyway, I was born at a little hospital on the Wahpeton Sioux reservation, near Sisseton.

While we children were being born, Pop started working as a bookkeeper and office manager for several of the C. Brewer & Co.-owned sugar plantations. We lived in Hilo, Pepeʻekeo, Pāpaʻikou, and Onomea, and finally moved to Kaʻū in 1957, where we lived in Pāhala. That's really the place I grew up in and call home.

Mostly we were healthy; the plantation took care of their own in those days. But I must have been a challenge. You'd never believe it now, but I was a sickly child. No, I'm not kidding. As my mother tells it, I was not gaining weight after she gave birth so they put me in the hospital and fed me a formula of Karo syrup and sweetened condensed milk. Probably the reason I've fought to keep my weight under control my whole life.

But it didn't end there. She also told me that when I was four or five, I fell prey to polio and became paralyzed in both legs from the waist down. I remember that. I remember waking up and not being able to move my legs, then the men lifting me on a stretcher and taking me to the hospital. I really wasn't worried until they hit my ankle against the door frame and it didn't hurt; that freaked me out—it was supposed to and things weren't working right. They took me to the hospital in Hilo and from what my mother told me later they consulted with doctors on the Mainland, who told them their only chance to keep my legs working was to inject the Salk vaccine into my spine. The plantation flew in the vaccine and they gave it to me. What I do remember is being bent over a large section of log and tied down so I couldn't move while they slowly injected the vaccine into my spine between two of my vertebrae.

I can't describe the pain. There are no words that can do that memory justice. All I could do for an endless hour or so was bite on a towel they gave me and wait for it to end. But it did and a couple of days later I was lying in bed with my spanking new Davy Crockett flintlock pistol when one of the nurses brought me my morning dose of Cream of Wheat, which I hated, just like every other morning. But this time it was different. I was so mad at being in bed and having to eat food I didn't like that I just exploded and kicked it off the tray onto the floor. First, she was mad, but then she realized what happened and started to yell and cry, and hugged me saying it was a miracle. I still feel good when I think of how much it meant to her to see me well. But I have to admit I do feel bad about kicking that tray; she was a real nice lady who took good care of the kids in that ward. And especially when I think about how lucky I was. I knew lots of kids that didn't have it that good, with withered arms or legs and other problems from polio. Thanks again, Dr. Salk. You did a good thing. You certainly saved me.

But my problems didn't stop there.

Let's be clear, this isn't a pity parade. The things I went through as a kid shaped who I am now. Those physical challenges led me to make choices and do things that I am truly grateful for now, as I get older and look back on my life with the perspective of a lot of years behind me, and more to go, I hope.

The biggest challenge I had growing up was asthma, demon asthma. I had it bad; almost died several times. I just cannot describe how it feels to struggle for air with every breath, over and over, every night, with no relief and mostly with no hope it would ever go away. It got really bad when the volcano would erupt. I'm very allergic to sulfur fumes and when I got a whiff, everything would start to shut down. I used to wake up at night during the '50s and wake my mother up to tell her a volcano had erupted. After a while she knew I could tell, every time.

But there was relief, and again the plantation stepped up. It got so bad they sent me to Honolulu with my mother where they poked me with about a hundred substances on my arms and back. When the results came in, I knew I was doomed. The fates had not been kind. I was allergic to sugarcane tassels, dust, animal fur, and sulfur. O joy! Of course, that's all there was in Ka'ū.

But they had a plan, they would treat my symptoms with a little blue and yellow steroid pill to keep me breathing and administer shots for the things I was allergic to (two shots every ten days). That lasted for years. But it worked. Needless to say, I am not afraid of needles.

So my nightly routine back then was to lay down, then about an hour later when the wheezing started, I would get out of bed, go into the bathroom, and take a blue and yellow pill. Afterwards I'd go into the living room and sit in my father's chair until the pill took effect and I could breathe, then I'd sleep there for the rest of the night. Mostly, I didn't even wake up my parents. I just took care of it myself once I knew what to do.

Eventually it seemed to work (knock on wood) and as I got older the attacks pretty much stopped. But while this was going on, the one thing I could do any time, every time, was read. Reading distracted me and kept my mind on something besides my fears and anxiety. And since I wasn't doing anything radical mostly, I didn't have any trouble breathing when I was reading. So I read. I read everything I could get my hands on, since I wasn't able to run and play hard without provoking an attack for years. Even after I got better, I just kept on reading.

The reason I'm belaboring this point is because that's one of the things I got out of reading, along with values and examples of the kind of person I wanted to be as a grown-up. I'd also like to give something of value back to the people that helped me through that time. It's way too late to say thanks, but hopefully these stories will show what kind of people they were and how much they cared for others.

My mother really was a special person. Somehow, she made a life for herself in Pāhala and a rich life for her children. We were always doing something, from hunting for bottles or glass balls to picking liliko'i and guava to make jams and jellies, mixing up batches of donuts for everyone in the neighborhood, or making our treks to the beach every weekend.

Mom in Kona.

There were birthday parties, family gatherings, and other occasions. She always stepped up and I never once heard her complain, even when we committed one of our many acts of lunacy. Most of the time she would lecture us, patch us up, and send us off to figure things out as well as we could by ourselves.

She was the editor of the plantation paper and, to our repeated chagrin, the author of a weekly article in the *Hilo Tribune-Herald* called "Over the Back Fence," in which she shared her experiences with the rest of the Big Island. Many is the time I was accosted as a child by some woman who felt compelled to confront me with my dastardly behavior—and me with a saint for a mother, they'd say. Well, she wasn't a saint, but she was my mom and I will always be grateful for everything she did for me.

In 1964 someone threw a bomb into the family structure and blew it up—my parents got divorced. Ron and I stayed with Pop, but the rest of the kids went to Honolulu with Mom. Things just weren't the same afterward. We saw each other, but somehow looking back I think that after the divorce whatever family we had started to fade away, and things were never the same again.

CHAPTER 3

The Big Island

For most of my early years we lived on the Big Island. We lived in various towns and hamlets, which I'll tell you about elsewhere, but those were only a small part of the whole island. So, I'm going to take you on a short tour of the Big Island in the 1950s and early 1960s.

I guess a good place to start would be Hilo, which was and is the biggest town on the Big Island. It's on the east side of the island and flanks a large bay. There is a harbor in the bay protected by a long seawall made of huge boulders that protects the harbor from the ocean. As you look inland from the mouth of the bay, most of the town is in the center of the bay, right up to the waterfront. Off to the left is the harbor, while to the right is a bridge and cliffs that lead off to the Hāmākua Coast.

Hilo wasn't a big town, but it was the biggest we had, and it had more stores and services than any other town on the island. Most of the professionals like dentists and doctors preferred to live there instead of out in what we affectionately called "the sticks," which was pretty much every place else on the island except Kailua-Kona. Until we moved to Pāhala, we lived near Hilo and spent a lot of time in the town, usually at the Elks Club, my father's favorite watering hole. But while he was catching up with his cronies we could walk around town to nearby stores and sometimes get a cone at the Dairy Queen.

There were lots of stores, but the ones I remember best were the hobby shop where they sold plastic models and the pawnshop on Mamo Street where they sold knives and antiques. There was also a surplus store with bayonets, helmets, backpacks, and other kinds of military gear. We had no money, but the guys who ran the stores didn't mind if we looked, as long as we didn't make a mess or bother them too much. They knew we'd be back when we could afford something.

The first place I remember is Pāpaʻikou. We lived in a house that was on the road to the mill. I was young, so I don't remember much about the house. I do remember swimming in the ditches off the road and learning, along with Ron, that it's not a good idea to make little furrows in the dirt under the house, fill them with gas, and light them on fire. We paid for that one in pain.

A slight digression: When I was young, people believed in spanking kids who misbehaved. There were pretty much two kinds: "lickings" and "dirty lickings." I guess the best way to describe them is that "lickings" was discipline, but "dirty lickings" was revenge. Ron and I got spanked but I never got dirty lickings, and neither did Ron. But I know time-outs would not have worked, and reasoning with us wasn't in the cards. That's not how things were back then. But looking back I can't remember ever getting spanked when I didn't deserve it, being beaten unmercifully, or hit with an object or disciplined in front of anyone else. And when it was over, it was over with no bad feelings on either side. The trouble with spanking was that it just didn't work.

In any case, we knew from an early age what the rules were and there would be consequences if we stepped over the line. But at least for me, if I stepped over the line, I had thought about it and the risk was worth the fun. So if I got caught, tough luck. In that case I took the consequences without complaining and just moved on. That's what most of us did in those days. Those consequences never stopped us, but they did slow us down, and sometimes, just sometimes, they stopped us before we got in over our heads.

Ron and I had many discussions on the proper way to deal with punishment. Ron always believed that it was best to start wailing, even before the hand was raised for the first whack. I believed the stoic, "take it silently like a man" worked better. Whatever way we used, we both dealt with the punishment. Looking back, it helped us learn boundaries and understand the rules of conduct we needed to follow. Ironically, I ended up with a career in child protective services. It was always hard for me to deal with helping someone understand the thin line between physical discipline and punishment to get revenge. In my life, I tried not to use it raising my kid. It wouldn't have worked with her anyway, she's kind of like me that way. But what better way to spend a career than helping keep kids safe and happy.

From Pāpaʻikou we migrated to the Hilo Sugar Company and a house in town. Again, I was too young to remember much, but I do remember the porch around the whole house we used to ride our trikes on when we played, and the manager's pond with crayfish we used to fish for with stones. It was from that house that Ron and I used to walk down to the main road to ride the sampan bus to Catholic school in Hilo.

In 1957 we moved from Hilo Sugar to the Hawaiian Agricultural Company in Pāhala. That's where I lived for the rest of my time on the Big Island. But we still went to Hilo at least once a week.

Hilo was a booming metropolis compared with the rest of the island. What we liked about Hilo was the stores with toys—lots of toys—and lots of other places to go and things to do that were different.

John and Ron and a Hilo sampan.

Like going to the town square while Pop was hanging out at the Elks Club. For some reason, back in those days people were worried about a nuclear attack. I guess that's not so far-fetched for Hilo, based on the submarine attack in December 1941. That's when a Japanese submarine fired off some token rounds from their deck gun toward the piers in Hilo Harbor. What were they thinking? They hit a small boat and part of the pier and vanished into the dark. My uncle had a piece of the shrapnel from one round they found on the pier that he kept and showed us when he told the story.

But what he liked to remember and tell us about that night was the coastal defense fiasco. Seems like the powers that be had decided it would be a good thing for the good folks of Hilo to be able to defend themselves against just such nefarious attacks. So, they put a coastal artillery piece out on the point near Unc's house that could command the entrance to Hilo Bay. The placement was cleverly camouflaged by the surrounding coconut trees. When the attack came, the costal defense volunteers rallied at the gun. They went through their drill and after pointing the gun out to sea toward where the sub might have been, loaded it and let a round go. Bad idea—they were in such a dither they weren't wearing helmets. That made it kind of interesting when the muzzle blast knocked all the coconuts out of the surrounding trees, which rendered the entire crew *hors de combat*. My uncle was one of them and he chuckled about it for years. They should have trimmed the trees.

Anyway, back then in the center of town there was a real, live atomic bomb shelter. It was small, made of what looked like tin roofing, and didn't look like it would offer much protection, even underground where it was supposed to be. I always thought it looked like a big coffin and not something I wanted to hide in until the dust settled after a nuclear holocaust hit the Big Island. No wonder there were signs in the Elks Club bar that read: "In case of nuclear attack: 1) Finish your drink, 2) Pay your bill, and 3) Bend over and kiss your butt goodbye."

Luckily, Hilo was never targeted. Go figure.

But Pāhala wasn't safe either. It was a no-brainer. Obviously Pāhala was a target of prime strategic importance and would be targeted in any atomic strike.

There was some basis to that reasoning. It wouldn't be the first time Pāhala braced for an attack. At one time, long before I moved to Pāhala, somebody had dug out a bomb shelter with a tunnel system in a hill just above the camps on the lower side of the mill. It was a pretty shaky operation. When I played in them, the tunnels were lined with wood from crates that had dried out and rotted, so when we crawled through the small tunnels, dust kept falling on us whenever we touched the sides, while the wood lining the tunnels would break at the least bump or pressure. We didn't play there much. It was pretty spooky and after we went through the tunnels and picked up a stray army helmet or two it wasn't much fun crawling through the cobwebs and avoiding the rats and scorpions while worrying about cave-ins.

So nuclear Armageddon threatened the Big Island, no doubt the result of some kind of demented risk analysis during that time period. But wait, all was not lost; we had saviors step up in Pāhala. Because of the concern and the attention being given to bomb shelters, some enterprising lads in Pāhala decided it would be a real moneymaker if they made a huge bomb shelter. They were planning to presell space in it to people from Pāhala who believed the bomb would fall and who wanted to survive in a post-apocalyptic world. It was the talk of the town, so we all heard about it, and we kids all spent some time watching the work progress.

Everyone knew these young entrepreneurs. They had no money, and they knew they weren't going to get any unless they had something more than promises to show prospective customers. So, they dug a huge pit near their home to establish their credibility and intent. The dirt was fairly easy to dig and when I first saw it, the work they had done with just picks and shovels was staggering. It looked huge; it was about eight feet deep, I don't know how long, and in the shape of a very large room. I guess the plan was to finish it when people bought in, collect the cash, and finish the shelter. Then they would be the bomb shelter bosses when everything went to hell in a handbasket. Or, they could have a perfectly good bomb shelter they could use for other stuff if an attack did not materialize.

But that's not what happened. What happened was rain, lots of rain. Biblical rain, the kind that collapses pits in the ground and turns them into dirty, muddy swimming pools for the kids in the town. When that happened, we snuck in and happily thrashed around in the filthy water until it dried up and returned to its natural state. Needless to say there was much merriment in the town as this all unfolded, and the naysayers were very satisfied with the outcome, as it gave them something to bandy about.

Back to Hilo.

There was also Hilo Drug Store, a bakery, hardware stores, and markets. Compared to Pāhala, Hilo had it all. They even had a county fair with a circus every year that we attended religiously. There was wrestling and sports and something going on all the time.

Hilo also had a Kress Store. You have to remember that we kids had never seen many stores, so the Kress Store was the holy grail for us while growing up. They had toys and other things that kids lusted after, but rarely got.

Hilo also had some theaters. There was one on the waterfront until the tsunami of 1960, but the one we went to most often was the Palace Theatre, which featured a Saturday matinee. Like a faded beauty, the Palace back in those days still had a touch of old-time grandeur with its large lobby. We only went to the matinees on Saturday when we lived near Hilo. There was also Mamo Theatre on Mamo Street, Hilo's street of ill repute at the time. The Mamo was a similar venue to the Palace, with the addition of somewhat risqué movies they showed after ten at night.

There were hotels, but the only part of them we ever saw was the dining room at the Hukilau Hotel, and that very seldom. Mostly, we ate at home or, if we were really lucky, at the Dairy Queen.

Hilo had something else not so good. They got tsunamis. They got lots of tsunamis. There is something about the topography of Hilo Bay that makes it a tsunami magnet. There have been a number of tsunamis that hit Hilo right in the chops. I even watched one roll in around 1957 before we moved to Pāhala. We watched that one from the hills on the Hāmākua side of the bay. That one just rolled up the Wailuku River and covered the bridge at the mouth of the river without doing much damage. But there are two that went over the top. The first, in 1946, was terrible. It hit on April Fools' Day and people thought it was a joke when the word went out. Lots of damage and wreckage. Lots of people got hurt.

What I think about when I think of the 1946 tidal wave is a picture. It's one of those pictures that sticks in my mind and makes me wonder, *What if it was me?* As the story goes, there was a ship at the dock that was breaking loose and a longshoreman climbed down to the dock to secure the lines. But he got caught by the next wave and vanished. But before he disappeared someone got a picture of him standing on the dock, arms crossed, confronting the huge wave full of twisted wreckage that was just about to wash over him. I just know that man had dealt with whatever was going to happen, and was at peace with himself and the world for the time he had left. I hope that if I'm ever in a situation like that I can demonstrate the same presence and courage he did.

The second tsunami was in 1960. I was living in Pāhala then, but I did go to Hilo after it hit and saw what had happened. It was unbelievable. Hilo's bayfront was wiped out and swept clean. The only thing between the bay and the wreckage piled high above the waterline was the Hilo Theatre.

Funny story about that theater. This is what I was told after the tsunami. The theater looked like Noah's ark; it had a bow that faced into the bay and a stern like a ship that faced the shore. When the architect was asked why he made such a butt-ugly building, he explained that he was building it to survive the next tsunami. The theory was that bow would force the waves to go around the building with minimal damage to the structure. The stern would do the same as each wave receded. I can't verify the story, but when the waters settled, the theater was still standing, all alone, in one piece.

There were boulders as large as rooms in parking lots and everywhere we looked there was damage. The only time I ever saw anything even close to that amount of devastation was on Kauaʻi after Hurricane Iniki. If you're one of the guys that names hurricanes and are reading this: Please, no more Hawaiian names. Seems like those are the ones that hit.

That 1960 wave hit in Kaʻū as well. I was sick and out of school that day, watched over by the lady who sometimes helped my mother. When she heard about the tsunami and what was happening down near the shoreline, she got me dressed and said we were going fishing. Then she hurried me out to a friend's car and off we went. By then the tsunami was over and we were in no danger as we drove down to the Kaawa flat and the low spot in the road that always flooded in a heavy downpour. That time it worked in reverse. The waves had pushed lots of water, mud, and whatever was in the way about a mile up the shallow spot.

It was incredible. There were lobsters waving their antennas, huge eels slithering back and forth trying to figure out how to get back to the ocean, *tako* (octopus) laying low wherever they could find cover, and fish. Lots of fish. There were big fish, small fish, red fish, silver fish. Just a lot of everything. Way more than we could take with us or use. We waded through the hip-deep mud grabbing whatever was in reach. For me that was anything smaller than me that didn't look like it would bite me. We'd shove them in burlap bags and keep going until we were too tired to continue. Then back into the car and back to Pāhala to get cleaned up and pretend we were both there all day. Kind of sad really, all those fish dying, but at least they mostly didn't go to waste since people from both Pāhala and Nāʻālehu drove down and got whatever they could before everything got stuck in the baked mud.

After passing through Hilo, to the left, across the noisy bayfront bridge, we next hit the Hāmākua Coast. Like I said, we lived in several towns there before we moved to Hilo. Mostly the towns sit behind cliffs that lead down to the water below. I always felt a little afraid of the waters off the Hāmākua Coast. We never swam there and the couple of times I surfed there I spent more time looking for sharks than having fun. Never fun, not to be able to see what's under the board. When I went, we were lucky to have a foot of visibility.

There were sights to see like ʻAkaka Falls and Kolekole Park, one of the neatest parks on that coast. We liked it because it had a waterfall and an area to swim in fresh water right alongside the ocean. On up the coast was Kamuela, on the way across the Big Island to Hāpuna Beach, Spencer's Park, and a huge *heiau* near the ocean. We usually didn't go that far afield. Not much reason when everything we liked to do was more readily available closer to home.

North of Kamuela was the town of Hāwī and the North Kohala area, places I never visited until I got my own wheels. I don't know why we never passed through there. We went everywhere else on the island but never seemed to make it that far.

We usually came back from the Kamuela side via Saddle Road. Like most roads in the '50s, it was a winding, essentially one-lane road that wound between Mauna Kea and Mauna Loa and ended up in Hilo. Usually foggy and wet, it was not a road for the impaired or faint of heart, especially at night.

Back then, the roads were just about one and a half car widths wide, and there usually was a substantial shoulder on each side that we used frequently. The cars back then were sturdy and wide and there wasn't enough space on most of the roads for two cars to pass each other and stay on the road. So what usually happened was that when two cars met, both of them would slow down and ease over to their side with two of their tires on the road and the other two on the shoulder. The roads were halved with a line painted down the middle, which came in handy at night since it was easier to see where the road was and stay on it. After dark the routine was much the same except most drivers dimmed their lights before passing each other. If no one was around we always just straddled the line and drove until we saw another car approaching on the other side of the road. There wasn't much traffic back then.

Oh, one tip for you. If you are ever traveling Saddle Road in the evening and an elderly Hawaiian lady appears in the back seat of your car, be nice to her; it's probably the volcano goddess Pele and it's best not to upset her, or the least that will happen is your car will stop running. If you're nice, she will disappear, leaving only a flower behind. It never happened to me, but it happened to several people I know. People I could believe. There were also stories about the *puʻu* in the lava fields where land had been surrounded by lava during some of the eruptions. People said those were the places where the people who lived there honored Pele so she left them alone.

After arriving back in Hilo after transecting Saddle Road, we would turn right and travel down the main road through Pāhoa, Mountain View, Volcano Village, and back to Pāhala.

So that's a short trip around the island from the Hilo side. More on the specific places will come later in other tales.

Going the other way from Pāhala, first we would pass through Nāʻālehu, then up through Waiʻōhinu, then past South Point, Manukā Park, then the roads that peeled off the main road to Miloliʻi, Hoʻokena, Kealakekua, then through the small towns on the hill to Kailua-Kona.

Past the turnoff to Miloliʻi was Hoʻokena and Kealakekua Bay. Hoʻokena was a great beach with a wide sandy area with cliffs that circled around the beach. The water was clean and clear, and there wasn't too much current so we could swim pretty much anywhere we cared to in the small bay. Kealakekua Bay was where the "city of refuge" was located. Legend has it that if anyone had broken a *kapu* or was in real trouble, if they could reach the refuge, they would be safe as long as they stayed. The city of refuge was on the Kaʻū side of a huge bay, with tall cliffs in back and a low spot across the bay with a monument to Captain Cook, who was killed there.

Usually we didn't go further than the turnoff to Miloliʻi, but sometimes we would go to Kailua or stay with some friends near town. In Kailua we walked on the seawall that fronts the main street in the town, jumped and swam off the pier, and watched the charter boats coming in with their catches. There were some beaches further down the coast where we would bodysurf and dive, but we hardly ever got that far. In retrospect I can understand why; it couldn't have been easy to round up and transport five whining, arguing kids from Pāhala to anywhere, unless there was a good reason, and Hilo was closer and had more to do in town.

CHAPTER 4

Volcanoes

Normal is kind of funny; it changes and morphs from one thing to another with age, knowledge, location, and time.

Back when I was a kid on Hawai'i island, it was normal that every couple of years a volcano would erupt. Since Hawai'i is the newest island in the chain it gets most of the eruptions. The rift is a geological area that tends to get a little excited from time to time and occasionally blow its stack. It was one of the things that made living on Hawai'i special.

Until I left the island to join the Navy, I spent a lot of time going to watch volcanoes erupt. Because we didn't have television and the radio reception was nonexistent, there wasn't a lot going on a lot of

Kīlauea eruption, ca. 1950s.

the time. Every eruption, if it wasn't dangerous, was an entertainment opportunity.

Don't get me wrong, I know that many people lost a lot to volcanoes, in places like Kapoho and the old warm springs down in Puna that disappeared under a lava flow. I still feel bad about what happened to the people who lived in that area. I wish it could have turned out better. We lost some of the best of the Big Island back then. We did go to the town of Kapoho one day during the eruption, and it was not a good feeling to watch the cinder raining down and slowly engulfing the town while a line of trucks and cars tried to carry off everything they could before the end. It never happened to me so I don't really know how it feels, so just realize I mean no disrespect when I say volcanoes were a form of entertainment. Nobody I know, especially me, ever thought a disaster was entertaining. But not all the eruptions were disasters, and those are the ones I am writing about.

One place I especially miss was the Kapoho warm spring. I don't mean the little one that was left after the Kapoho eruption or the one they called the Queen's Bath—neither one of them is left either. But the one I remember best was the biggest of the springs. It was a magnificent place—a large spring with high cliffs and ledges over the deep water at one end and the shallow water at the other. It was way different from the normal fresh, or almost fresh, water that we usually swam in. It was exciting to climb up the cliff and jump into the clear, warm water, sinking much further than we would in the ocean. We swam among the many frogs and sometimes crayfish that made their home near the edge of the spring.

For me, volcanoes were a mixed blessing. On the one hand, we'd all pile into my mom's old Chevy or the family station wagon with plenty of provisions and drive up to the latest volcano from Pāhala. On the other hand, I always had to worry about the fumes. Luckily, or more likely by intent, we always set up our stuff upwind of the volcano so the fumes blew the other way and I was mostly okay.

Volcanoes all had their own personalities. There were the chunky ones with sharp lava and all edges (*ʻaʻā*), then there were the ones that flowed like molasses across everything in their path (*pāhoehoe*). We stayed away from the ʻaʻā flows because they flung lava into the air and it wasn't safe to be near them. We got a little closer to the pāhoehoe flows but still kept our distance. Lots of times they would cross roads and we could drive up pretty close to them and watch the rivers of lava move toward the ocean from a safe distance. The only time we got maybe a little too close was when a chunk of lava would roll or fall nearby. If we could see any red inside, we would drop pennies into them and watch them melt, then pick them up with sticks, cool them in water, and take them home.

I guess this is a good time to tell my readers who are not familiar with our local customs that you never, I mean never, take any rocks away from Hawai'i. Don't even think about it. They belong here, and here is where they want to be. Bad things happen if they are taken away.

One volcano I'll remember till I die is the 1959 eruption of Kīlauea Iki. When word came that it was erupting, the first Saturday we could, we got into the Chevy and drove up to the road over the crater, where we parked near an opening in the roadside brush to get a good view. We kids watched for a while, played, ate, napped, then played around again, while the grownups sat, had a few drinks, and talked story. Way better than TV. It was an interesting place to play—we were mostly out of sight of the adults and generally weren't bothered much, unless of course someone got into a tussle or got hurt and drew the attention of the parents. If that happened, they descended on us like a vengeful flock of geese and tried to sort out the truth while everyone was talking at the same time. When that happened, if I wasn't involved, I got as far away as I could till things calmed down. I didn't want to be collaterally in trouble. Sometimes it seemed the adults were more entertaining than the eruption.

Luckily, the wind blew mostly toward the south and carried most of the fumes away, or I would have been in trouble. Most of the time if we smelled sulfur we didn't go or I got left behind.

From our normal lookout we could look east toward the eruption, about a half a mile away. We could see the glowing red and yellow lava fountain reaching into the sky, then dulling from red to gray and finally black before dropping on to the huge cinder hill forming behind the fountain. The cinder cone was surrounded by, and covering, the skeletons of the 'ōhi'a trees that had been killed by the cinders.

There was a constant roar that provided a background to the conversations of the adults and the play of the children along the road that circled the crater. Along this rim, there was a railing and a network of trails hidden from the road that was bordered by ʻōhiʻa trees, ferns, and grass. It was great fun, and we stayed far into the night because everything was just better at night. All of the colors in the eruption showed up against the night sky brighter and bigger, so we all wanted to stay as long as we could.

There was one night that stands out in my mind. I still can't believe I was there when it happened. The volcano seemed to be fountaining a little higher than usual, but otherwise it was pretty much a "normal" volcano night. But there was a moment when everyone just stopped what they were doing and watched in silence. What we saw was the figure of a woman in the lava fountain dancing the hula. She looked to be about as tall as the fountain, and she danced for a couple of minutes before fading away. "Chicken skin" just doesn't cover it. Words cannot even come close to describing the feeling of awe at what could only have been Pele, not to mention the feeling of gratitude for her visit. Nobody got a picture, and hardly anyone that was there told many people about what happened. I guess for me it's always been kind of private, something to be shared sparingly and with respect.

There were other eruptions we witnessed, but one that we didn't happened in the Kaʻū Desert between Hawaiʻi Volcanoes National Park and Pāhala. This eruption in 1790 took place while a group of warriors were returning to Kaʻū from a battle they'd fought with the warriors of Kamehameha. On their way back, they were caught in the eruption and died, leaving only their footprints in the hot ash, footprints heading off to nowhere.

There were also several older craters that erupted frequently, not with a lot of damage, but incredibly beautiful. One of my favorites was Halemaʻumaʻu, a crater not far from the main road, so that it was easy to reach and watch an eruption up close from the observation platform at the crater's edge.

Once, long after I left Hawaiʻi, Ron gave me some photos he'd taken of one eruption. When I said I didn't recognize the location, he explained it was Halemaʻumaʻu. That was kind of odd because the pictures had been taken from the ground, and from that angle the only "ground" was inside the crater. Yup, he had rappelled into the crater during the eruption and taken those pictures. He said he wanted to get an angle nobody had ever taken. I guess he had, but it was nothing I'd ever do myself.

One other thing about Halemaʻumaʻu: Birds made their nests in the caldera, way above the lava. We called them crater birds and we could see them wheeling in pairs in the air above the crater. I've been told they nest in the crater walls and feed at sea.

Halemaʻumaʻu erupted often, and for a long time when we drove way up into the hills at night, far above the Kaʻū Desert, we could see it glowing in the distance, its plumes of fumes slowly rising into the night, lit from below by the eruption in the crater. Words just can't do it justice, but believe me, it was one of the most beautiful sights I have ever seen. It was even better when there was a full moon. On those nights the whole Kaʻū Desert could be seen by moonlight, with the crater outlined in red. Just amazing. We'd sit watching it for hours, just talking story and taking it all in.

When I left the Big Island to serve in the Navy, one of the things I missed was the volcanoes. But it sure was nice not to worry about breathing.

CHAPTER 5

Ka'ū

Ka'ū starts just after Volcano Village and ends around Manukā Park in South Kona. It extends to just down the road from Volcano Village, ending on the other side of Ocean View Estates.

It's the largest district on the Big Island, and probably had the least people back in the '50s. After all, everyone else on the island referred to us as "the sticks." There was a lot to see and do in Ka'ū, not very obvious to someone who didn't live there or know what was lurking beneath the obvious. It was a kid's paradise. Not everything was easy to get to, but it was all interesting; sometimes dangerous, but always fun.

Ka'ū has an essence all its own. Where else can you drive from a volcano, through a desert, up into a forest, then down to a beach in a couple of hours? We had it all.

The village of Nā'ālehu is just up the road from Pāhala toward Kona—up the hill above Honapu and the ruins of an old wharf. Before a tsunami destroyed the wharf, it was used to load cattle and sugar to be transported interisland. Nā'ālehu, like most of the small towns I visited on Hawai'i back then, had a theater and some stores. We usually didn't spend much time in Nā'ālehu, since we were usually just passing through on our way to Kona or South Point.

There were a couple of ranches, Kapāpala, near Pāhala, and Kahuku up the road from Nā'ālehu. Sometimes we'd go to the ranches and it was always a thrill to look at the jawbones from the boars the cowboys hunted nailed on the side of a shed. Sometimes they would give us a couple and we treasured them for trading material back in Pāhala.

Kahuku was a little different. But what I remember about Kahuku was George, the fishing *paniolo*.

George was the foreman at the ranch. I knew him well; he was a great guy, always willing to spend a little time talking story with me when I drove up on my motorcycle to see his daughter. One day I noticed a marlin tail nailed to the side of a shed in his yard. When I asked George about it, he grinned in a sly way and told me he'd caught it. But he and I both knew he never fished—not his thing. I asked him where he was fishing when he caught it. He replied he got it from outside the fence line by the shore near South Point. I had to hear more, so I convinced him to tell me the story. It didn't take much and it was a great tale.

Seems that while he was riding his horse along the fence line checking it out, he saw a fishing boat closer to shore than normal. Looking down, he noticed a big fish under the cliff along which he was riding. The fish was thrashing near the base of the cliff in shallow water. He got off his horse with his rope and was able to drop a loop over the tail of the fish and pull it tight. He then used his horse to drag the fish, a big marlin, up to the top, then cut the fishing line and rode off with the fish. He somehow got it home, cut it up, and gave everyone on the ranch a share. But he kept the bill and the tail as trophies.

I had a little trouble believing that one. I left wondering what he had been drinking or who really gave him the fish. But I had to eat crow later on.

A couple of months later when I visited, the tail was still there but now there was something else—a framed news clipping. In the article it told how an angler from someplace on the Mainland had hooked a huge marlin off a charter boat and fought it for a couple of hour, until the fish swam inshore, where a cowboy lassoed it, cut his line, and made off with the marlin. Finally, a good story that was true. George did say he knew those waters and if a shark didn't get the fish, those guys would never have been able to get far enough in to get it into their boat.

CHAPTER 6

South Point (Ka Lae)

Up the road from Nāʻālehu is Ka Lae, or South Point, which is what most people call it. But by whatever name you know it, it is one of the most beautiful places on earth.

We visited that area frequently. We'd leave Pāhala, drive through Nāʻālehu and up the winding narrow road past Waiʻōhinu to the road that meandered from the main highway out to South Point. Along the way we would run over metal guards placed in the road to keep the cattle in their pastures. Sometimes the cattle would wander onto the road and often they'd amble slowly in front of our car, ignoring the honking horn and screaming kids. Then we'd pass the house with the tree that leaned over because of the continuous strong wind, and later the tracking station that stood on the cliff for many years.

Then the view would open up; a huge cliff on the right side of the road leading to a small, almost invisible beach with lantana and dust on the other side, and jeep trails that left the main road for unknown destinations.

Usually we visited the cliffs before we moved further down the coast. We'd park and inspect the holes in the rocks that we had been told were canoe moorings, looking over the side to see the boats moored below, reached by a rickety steel ladder that led down to the water. Behind the ladder there were huge sea caves that seemed to breathe with every wave that washed in and out. The water was incredible; clear, blue, and deep. Later on, when I got older, we'd jump off the cliffs into the water and swim around for a while, but not too much. South Point was said to be kind of sharky.

Up on top there were wooden cranes they used to lower supplies and raise fish from the boats below.

One of the really cool things about the cliffs was the way people in Ka'ū fished from them. At South Point, the wind would usually blow offshore in the morning and onshore in the afternoon. For years the fishermen had taken advantage of this change in the winds. The big fish normally didn't swim near the cliff; they were further offshore over an underwater ledge where the shallows meet the depths. The ledge was too far out to cast a line from shore and too deep to anchor a boat.

But they figured out a way to get their lines in the right spot. Back in the day when they fished with canoes, they would tie a line to the mooring line and play it out with the wind at their backs until they were positioned correctly, then fish. Later when the wind shifted the other way, they would just pull the canoe back to shore using the line they were tied to with the wind at their back. Those guys had it figured out.

Fast-forward to when I lived there. Not everyone had a vessel they could belay to the fishing grounds. But the fishermen figured out a way to get their lines out to the grounds by making small wooden rafts with sails they could run out using the morning wind until they were positioned where they wanted. But they had to figure out a way to get the lines from the shallows to the fishing grounds without fouling on the bottom. This is where it gets good. Their solution was so simple and elegant, but it showed how in tune they were with their craft and knowledge of the wind and ocean. Once the rafts were positioned, they would wait a little while before yanking the line to deploy the *palu* (chum). The reason they waited was that their lines were coiled through Life Savers candy—yup, the ones that are shaped like a ring. After the raft was in position, they waited until the candy melted and the weighted line deployed to just the right depth. When the line was down, the bag of palu would open and lured fish to the bait.

It worked, and it worked well. Later on, I heard they used balloons and other things that would float, but the idea was the same.

After we visited the cliff, we would drive down to the point and jump off the rocks and swim for a while. Once, I had an epiphany while standing on the point. I yelled, "Ron, I'm the southest guy, the southest guy in the United States! Just me. Everyone else is in the US is north of me." When Ron got it, he pushed me off so he could be the southest guy—older brother stuff.

Further along down the coast toward Pāhala was a green sand beach—a beautiful but treacherous beach. On a calm day it was great. We'd slide down the green sand behind the beach and frolic in the shallows or play in the shore break. We didn't go out far there because of the currents. We'd been warned about them for years. When the surf was up, it was really scary. There isn't much beach and when the large waves broke all the way up to the hill behind the beach, it was best to stay away. But the sand was bright green and when the sun hit it just right it was incredible to see just how green it could be.

On down the coast was Kaʻaluʻalu Bay, a small inlet with a cattle ramp off to the left as you looked seaward. There was a short snappy left break off the reef and a smaller wave that broke in the middle of the bay. There were also shallows we could swim in safely. When usually we went there for a big picnic, Ron and I would sit for hours looking at the breaks and try to figure out how we could surf those perfect empty waves. But we didn't have boards, and the adults would never let us go that far out to bodysurf. Later, when I got a car, I did make it down and surfed there many times. I might have been the first—or only—one to surf there for years. I know I was always alone in the water with no one around except for my shark lookout. More to come on this in my surfing vignette.

One nice thing back then was that people trusted each other to do the right thing. I was taught by my father and other adults to leave any place I went to in better shape than it was when we arrived. That meant that before we left any picnic or camp we policed the area, picking up any trash that was lying around, even if it wasn't ours. Even now it seems like the right thing to do. Many of the places I've been are remote and hard to get to, but very much worth visiting, and it always seemed fair to make sure the next guy didn't have to visit a bunch of rubbish.

That went for gates as well. South Point had a lot of gates. Gates are kind of neat; not only do they keep people and animals in, they let them out. Back then a lot of places we went to had gates, because they were ranch property used to keep cattle in sections to avoid overgrazing. Not very many of them were locked; mostly they were there to keep the cattle in, not the people out. That was important because a lot of them were on roads or trails that went from the main roads to the ocean. Because the gates were unlocked, it was fairly easy, with the right vehicle, to fish, swim, and surf in some pretty lonely and remote places that would otherwise be out of reach. But using those gates meant that every time one was opened, it had to be closed after we passed. That meant that the people who needed the gate closed had to trust that everyone would do what was needed so everyone could use the gates. That also meant that everything needed to be squared away in the places we went. No rubbish, no fires left untended, and everything pretty much how we found it when we got there when we left. Looking back, I can't remember any time we found a gate open or a campsite or picnic area messy. As I've said before, we took care of each other back then.

South Point also had a fishing village that no one ever seemed to use and one other attraction: Back then, the Japanese used glass floats for fishing to hold up their nets, and frequently these would break off and the wind would push them to South Point, where we would harvest them. Lots of them broke on the rocks, but there were many that didn't, so we'd comb the beach and make piles of unbroken floats that we took with us or, if we had too many, just left whatever we didn't take for the next guy. The real prizes were those with writing on the blob of glass that closed up the float, or those with a little water in them.

When the fun was done, we would go to what they called Palahemo, a deep hole with brackish water away from the cliffs. We'd climb down and wash off the salt water. It was dark and scary and we were told it had no bottom and led out to an opening in one of the sea caves.

Then we'd go home. Five worn-out kids, but not too worn out to fight over who got to open and close the gates on our way out to the main road. We'd spend the rest of the trip sleeping in the back of the station wagon until we got home, when it was time to empty the car and clean everything up.

CHAPTER 7

Pāhala

I pretty much grew up in Pāhala. Pāhala will always be the place I'm from, but I knew early on that it wasn't going to be my home. I'm not sure why, I guess I've always known that's not where my life was going. But wherever I've gone, and whatever I've done, there's a part of me that will always belong to the place that raised me from a child to the man I am today.

We lived in Pāhala in varying numbers of family members from 1957 until Pop moved out sometime around 1969 or 1970. When we arrived in 1957, it was a small, sleepy town with nothing much going on. Today, it's a small, sleepy town with less going on. Sugar was king in those days. The island of Hawai'i was dotted with sugar plantations and just about everyone was supported by the sugar industry.

Pāhala is in the Ka'ū district, which is bordered by Hawai'i Volcanoes National Park on the Hilo side to the northeast, and the Kona district, which starts on the western side of Nā'ālehu. Pāhala is perched on the slope of Mauna Loa surrounded by forest and cane fields, just about fifty-two miles from Hilo. To get there, leave Hilo, turn right, drive past Volcano Village until the first mill stack, and there you are.

There wasn't, and isn't, much to the town. It always seemed like a place where people who didn't live there just drove past, rather than a destination. In the 1950s there was the obligatory main street that wound from the highway through town and back to the main highway again. Along the main street were the homes of the managers and supervisors of the plantation, and further down the hospital, plantation office, the post office, and shops and stores, followed by the mill, then a row of small stores, the theater, bank, and community hall, then you're out of town.

Peeling off from the main street were smaller streets, some of them unpaved, leading to the various camps that made up the town.

It seems that by either preference or more likely mandate, ethnic and cultural groups were clustered in mini-communities within the town. There were a Japanese camp, Portuguese camp, Filipino camp, Hawaiian camp, and Chinese camp scattered through the town, along with smaller outlying camps called Upper Camp and Lower Camp further outside of town. Most of the houses were small but well built, and very practical, with tin roofing, redwood single-wall tongue-and-groove construction, and plumbing on the outside of the homes for ease in repairs as needed.

In the upper section of town were the Catholic church, elementary and high schools, and houses along the roads leading up into the cane fields.

Along the lower section of town were Japanese, Chinese, and some of the Filipino camps, along with a barbershop, a short-lived restaurant, the Hongwanji Buddhist mission, and a couple of stores. Dirt roads passed through that section of town toward a slaughterhouse, the rubbish dump, and the main road.

On the other side of town where the main street met the highway was the old government road, which paralleled the main highway for about four miles toward Punalu'u, until they intersected and the old road disappeared.

Pāhala was situated among a number of gulches that were mostly dry, unless they ran with water when it rained in the mountains or when the snow on Mauna Loa melted. During the spring, the water was clear and very cold. Otherwise, it was a dark and dirty brown.

We lived in three houses in Pāhala, all on the main street, but most of the events I've recounted occurred in the upper house, the largest of the homes in which we lived.

Despite its sleepy appearance, there was lots to do in Pāhala and the surrounding area, and while many of our adventures seemed to get us in trouble, we still had lots of fun, and nobody got hurt.

We were policed in the '50s by a sheriff who was a big, husky guy. He lived in the town and knew everyone by name. I never saw him mad, and he always drove around in his wood paneled station wagon with his Irish setter. He always had time to talk to a kid and never seemed to brush us off or talk down to us. I heard later that he had a unique style of policing, like the way he dealt with speeders. His attitude was that if they were from out of town, the quicker they got out of Ka'ū the better; he wasn't going to chase them and if they got hurt, that was on their heads. But if the speeder lived in town, he wouldn't risk life and limb in a car chase, but later he would visit the offender at home and have a little talk about the error of his or her ways. I also heard that he attended all the illegal cockfights—not to gamble or bust people but to keep order and make sure nobody bet more than they could afford. Everyone at the cockfight knew that if he told someone to stop gambling, and someone took a bet from that person, the fights were over and someone was going to get arrested.

We regularly attended the Catholic church in town. It seemed like everyone in Pāhala went to church on Sunday and was pious and god-fearing for the allotted hour, then back to normal. This meant that for one hour we had to wear clean and neat clothing, including shoes, and behave, or there would be hell to pay when we got home.

Ron became an altar boy, which meant that he helped the priests serve the Mass. In those days it was in Latin and the altar boy spoke responses during the Mass. He was a great altar boy; he had it down. When he was up helping the priest, I would have been willing to swear I saw a halo above his head, just a little askew and somewhat dim. Kind of a Ka'ū halo, I guess. I always thought he must have figured that, with all the trouble he got into, being an altar boy gave people a reason to give him points on the good side of the ledger too.

I was sent by my mother to follow Ron into altar boyhood, but I was not destined for that fate. I never learned more than the most rudimentary Latin and had no motivation. I just didn't want to be there. But I guess God figured that out and put me out of my misery.

He did it by stepping in and miraculously demonstrating my unsuitability to the whole congregation one Sunday morning, by carrying my swear words—spoken in confidence behind the church in a momentary lapse of judgment—through the open windows and within earshot of the whole temporarily pious and God-fearing congregation. When I came back inside to serve the wine, I thought it was odd that everyone was looking at me like I was the son of the devil. Later I found out why. Inevitably I was dismissed by the priest, who told me I wasn't altar boy material, and suggested I "look into my soul." Well, I did—and my soul wasn't for sale.

I can still remember the priests, always dressed in black, no matter how hot it was. They all had their individual quirks, like the Belgian priest who stood way too close when he spoke to us, which was only a problem because he liked pickled herring and ate it accompanied by lots of beer. He was the one who would lift the chalice up when we were pouring the water into it, but lowered it when we served the wine, which resulted in a healthy dose of holy spirits. No wonder he always looked so happy.

We Catholics also had to go to catechism. Oh joy, that meant we had to sit for an hour or two on benches made in hell to punish children, under the priest's house in the afternoon heat of Pāhala, and listen to a nun drone on and on about God, behaving, and being good Catholic children. It got pretty intense, what with the collision of post-lunch lethargy and a nun who wanted our full and undivided attention. One memorable day I was nodding off and muttering to the kid next to me, as we all were wont to do as the lesson droned on. I guess I was a little too noisy, but I was tired and didn't want to be there. So she rang her bell—the bell from hell, the bell that she applied every time she wasn't happy—and proclaimed, "John, the little bell is saying, 'Be quiet.'" In a momentary lapse of judgment, or maybe insanity, I talked back. Worse, I replied that the bell wasn't saying, 'Be quiet." I could hear it plainly, and it was really saying, "Ring a ling, ring a ling." Bad move. I spent the next two weeks writing in a semi-legible hand on the blackboard, "I will be quiet when the bell rings." Just more fun and games.

Once in a while the church would hold a bazaar with games and prizes to raise money. Like every type of occasion in town, everyone went. What I remember best is the prizes we could fish for with bamboo poles. We had to hook little wooden fishes with eyebolts where there should have been mouths. When we snagged one, someone would read the number on the bottom and dispense the appropriate prize. The prizes were a little "different." They gave us things like straw hats with beer openers on them and labels that proclaimed, "I am an alcoholic. In case of emergency, open me a beer," and pocketknives with the Pope's face embossed on the scales and the like. What were they thinking?

There were other churches and temples in Pāhala and they had their celebrations as well. The Pāhala Hongwanji held a *bon* dance every year and, as with the church bazaar, everyone in the area attended. The men erected a large square tower in the Hongwanji yard, with strings of paper lanterns leading from the corners, which swung in the breeze and lit the ground below.

The Hongwanji members would dress in traditional outfits and surround the platform, moving back and forth and in and out to the sound of the music, the beat of the drums, and the instructions called from the tower. Sometimes I would strap on a headband and try to follow, but I was never very good at it, so I usually left the line before I was asked to step aside and let the real dancers do their thing.

Down in the graveyard, there would be offerings of food and *sake* left for the departed. Occasionally the less than reverent and respectful among us would dip into the sake left on the graves. Not me—I have more respect than that. The dancing would last for hours, far into the night, much later than we stayed out, but back home we would fall asleep to the sounds of the music and drumming in the distance.

There were other regular community events, including a police benefit that toured the island each year. Every kid in Pāhala got to attend every year that we lived there. Maybe it had something to do with the sheriff, who took it upon himself to make sure that all the kids got to go for free. I heard later that he offered his police benefit tickets at the illegal cockfights and that they sold quickly.

Those shows were kind of surreal. I always thought that the performers were at the end of whatever road they were going down, leading to some dismal end. Maybe it was just me, but they never seemed happy, even though they all had smiles plastered on their faces while they went through routines they could do in their sleep. Some of them sang, some juggled and cavorted, and once they brought in a guy who could balance four chairs on his chin—with a kid sitting on the top chair. Real valuable life skills. I always went but felt kind of sorry for the entertainers. Except for once. One time they brought in Tommy Kono, the weightlifter and Olympic gold medalist. It was truly inspirational; he did things like lift weights that looked bigger than he was and finished his act by blowing up a hot water bottle until it burst. But best of all he was a humble, down-to-earth, likable guy. Later on, when I was a marathon group leader, he worked for the city and I saw him a lot. He was always the same, polite and friendly, but with a presence. I truly liked and respected him as long as I knew him.

We also had school programs. The ones I remember the most were the May Day programs, field days, and Christmas plays.

May Day wasn't that bad. There were games and fun, so we ran around and participated in contests like the one where we picked up a marble lying on the ground with a smooth pair of chopsticks, ran about twenty-five yards down the field, dropped it into a Coke bottle, then poured it out, picked it up again, and ran back. Not that easy, but it can be done. I'm pretty good at chopsticks now.

And there was the Christmas play, that damn Christmas play. I've always hated plays. I spoke better English and wasn't as shy as some of my schoolmates, so a lot of the time I was forced to do something. Someone always thought it would be a good idea—not me, but someone. That meant rehearsing after school and wearing a hot, dusty costume that had been sewn several years earlier and had seen better days. What fun!

One fine year my mother was involved in the planning, so lo and behold, I was chosen to be Santa. To be clear, I didn't volunteer; I was dragooned into service. What an unlucky break. That meant that I couldn't fade into the background like I usually did, but instead everyone would be watching me. Santa, go figure, portly, white, glasses, and they already had the beard. Ho, ho, ho. Very poor choice—although for me it really wasn't a choice.

The worst part was that there was a girl who had been tapped to be a wise man who wanted the part. I liked her a lot; she was everything I wasn't. She was motivated; learned all the lines on her own and could do the part way better than I ever would. But nobody seemed to see what I did at our rehearsals. She would watch me flub my lines, mouthing the real lines perfectly. After a while, I just couldn't take it, and I offered to step down, but I was ignored and told to press on.

What could I do? Maybe what I did best: I went on a campaign to get kicked out of doing the Santa gig. After all, my self-esteem wasn't at risk and I really respected and liked that girl. Besides, shouldn't we all be able to get at least one thing we want in this life? Anyway, I really screwed it up, over and over and over. I still can't figure out why they kept trying to make me get it right. For a while I took some heat, but I had timed it so close that when they finally decided that enough was enough, and that I wasn't the chosen one, there was no time, no alternate Santa, and the show had to go on.

Finally, after getting chewed out for missing my lines yet again, I pointed at the right person and told them she could do it way better than I could. So they relented and tried her out. Damn, she was perfect. She had a flawless performance, and it was one of the best shows we ever had, at least for me. I was demoted to shepherd and happily got to twirl my broomstick shepherd's crook enough to drive the director crazy. I've never had any regrets or told anyone why I did so poorly; it was just the right thing to do.

Over the course of any given year, there were many parties, and some of them were huge. Seemed like everyone in town attended all these functions, and helped put them together and clean up afterwards.

There was a community hall that always seemed to have a wedding party, baby *lūʻau*, or dance going on, and we would sometimes sneak out after bedtime and walk down to the hall and watch the festivities from outside in the shadows. I really enjoyed just sitting there watching the grown-ups having a good time. Looking back, I really think that was one of the things that made our community strong. I knew that not everyone got along. That's life. But we did things together and there wasn't anybody in town who couldn't ask for a little help along the way if they needed it, and get it when it was most important. In the end we were all in it together and took care of each other. Not always what we wanted, but usually what we needed.

Once a year there was a rodeo in Nāʻālehu, Pāhala's closest neighbor on the Kaʻū coast. We were, and I still am, extremely partisan in our support of our respective towns. At the risk of offending those that had to live in dry, dusty and hot Nāʻālehu, I much preferred Pāhala, a veritable Garden of Eden and paragon of small towns. But we often went to and through Nāʻālehu and always attended its Fourth of July rodeo, when the town filled up with people from all over the island.

Pop would drive us in early and park the station wagon in a strategic location, with the tailgate right up against the fence so we could see everything from the car. Then he and the rest of the men would knock down a couple of cool and frosty beers and do man stuff while the kids played in the area around the car.

It was hot, dusty, and marvelous fun. We'd run around with the other kids until we got tired, then crawl into or under the station wagon for a little nap until it was time to get up and do it all again. All this while the roping, tying, riding, and rodeo type stuff was going on in the field in front of the car. Then when evening fell and the town emptied, we'd join the long caravan of cars driving through the twilight back to our home.

It was at the Nāʻālehu rodeo that I was first introduced to ice shave, a local tradition and delicacy. I know you're probably thinking I got it wrong, but back then it wasn't "shave ice," it was "ice shave." This was the Big Island in the 1950s, after all, and things were a little different than they are now. Ice shave cost a nickel, and for your nickel the vendor would take a hand scraper and shave chips off a block of ice into a conical paper cup. It really was ice chips, even if we called it ice shave. Then he'd pour a liberal dose of strawberry syrup on top and hand it over along with a small wooden spoon. I just can't tell you how good it tasted after running around in the sun for a couple of hours. We'd sit and chip away at the ice until we had a slurry of ice and syrup, then spoon it down, stopping only when the inevitable "brain freeze" hit us and we'd have to stop and stick our thumbs on the roofs of our mouths to defrost our frozen palates.

The American Legion had a clubhouse down at the shoreline near Punaluʻu Beach, where there were grand feasting opportunities whenever they held functions. The food they served was incredible. There was always all-you-can-eat steak fresh from the grill, accompanied by *kālua* pig, rice, chicken *hekka*, *poi*, shrimp, *sashimi*, and on it went. We would eat until we were stuffed, then sneak back to the closet where the slot machines hid. You know, the closet that wasn't there, with slot machines that were illegal that really weren't there? At least nobody who should have done anything about them seemed to notice them. We'd pop a couple of dimes into them hoping for a big score until an adult came in and told us in a loud voice that kids shouldn't be gambling. But I noticed that when we ran off, the adult stayed, and we could hear the arm coming down and the spinning of the wheels. I remember hearing once that they used the profits for good works and their functions, so I guess nobody really ever lost.

Pāhala wasn't overburdened by stores. There were a few clustered around the old post office, a couple down below the mill, and a row of them on the main street, ending with the now infamous Pāhala Theatre with the old bank at the end.

The stores were small, cramped, and filled with things to delight the heart of any child. There were comic books, soda and candy, and my personal favorites: pocketknives, corncob pipes, wire slingshots, balsa gliders, and cheap pocket watches. Whenever we got a little money, usually on our birthdays or for Christmas, off we'd go and spend it down in the stores.

We had a couple of markets, dry goods stores, a couple of barbers, and some general stores down in the camps. For a while there was a restaurant, but it vanished and I guess nobody wanted to take a chance on another one. There were no bars in or near the town and most everything else we needed was in Hilo.

The bank occupied an old house next to the theater. Not very secure, but easy to find and there was never a long line.

Growing up, I knew a bank robber. He wasn't your gun-wielding, masked marauder, but one of the kids from school who saw the bank safe standing open one night and slipped in through a window and dipped into it for a couple of bundles of dollar bills. We knew something was up when he started treating people to extra lunches and offered to take us to the store and buy us whatever we wanted. After all, none of us had money and a dollar was a fortune in those days. Sadly, he blew through the money he had in a single day. But wait, he knew where he could get more. That night he made another expedition. Same routine: Look inside to be sure the door to the safe was open, then climb in through an open window. I heard he was really surprised when, just after he grabbed some more money, someone grabbed him. He got into a little trouble, but common sense ruled. His family couldn't pay the money back, and I guess bank management figured the door should have been closed anyway.

And there was the Pāhala Theatre—the notorious Pāhala Theatre.

I don't remember it quite as it has been described elsewhere, but it did have its moments. When I lived there the theater had declined somewhat from its glory days and looked a little faded and tired. But it was a real movie theater with a false front, ticket booth, and a small concession that sold a limited selection of snacks at greatly inflated prices.

I guess that was okay. The movies cost twenty-five cents for a kid, fifty cents for an adult, and seventy-five cents for a seat in the reserved section. That was the section with the most padding on the seats. Otherwise it was pretty grim; those seats had been around the block and had lost a lot of whatever makes a seat comfortable. We learned which ones had holes with wires sticking out and avoided those sections. There was one seat that was reserved for one of our town toughs. That was the one behind the missing seat, the one he tore out and threw at the screen in a drunken frenzy one night. We left that one empty, just in case. Nobody really minded the section of the screen with the tape since most of the movies never reached that far down on the screen.

The movie schedule reflected the cultural mix in the town. As I remember the schedule and the way people described it, on Friday, Saturday, and Sunday it was haole movies, Monday featured Japanese *samurai* movies, Tuesday was an off day, Wednesday was haole movies again, and on Thursday they ran Filipino movies. So there was always something to see.

One other eccentricity was that for the whole time I lived in Pāhala and went to the movies, they played one side of the album *Blame it on the Bossa Nova* when the film wasn't running. I got awfully tired of singing and humming along to that music. I couldn't help it; I was programmed after all those years. The worse thing was that even after I left the theater that damn tune would be running through my head, and I would find myself humming it, even though I didn't like it. One day I walked down to the theater and offered to give them my sparse record collection so they could change it up once in a while, but nope, they told me they liked that record and had two or three more, just in case that one wore out or got broken.

Going to the movies in those days was a considerable investment in time. We didn't just dive into the main event. First there was the news, then two or three cartoons, followed by a couple of Three Stooges clips, then the previews, and finally the movie. The whole experience ran from about seven at night till ten or longer. There was an early movie on Saturday and Sunday; mostly those were the ones the kids went to. We really got our money's worth in those days.

Mostly we all got along and there wasn't much trouble at the theater. It was kind of neutral ground, and even people who didn't normally get along took a break and just enjoyed the movie.

But I did witness one disturbing incident. It started out like any other normal sweltering summer evening. The lady in the booth sat there with the back door open, fanning herself and selling tickets to the small crowd of people hoping for a little relief from the oppressive summer heat. Then one of the kids from school showed up. He was a teenager, about my age, and he had a mean temper so we always left him alone. When he walked toward the ticket booth we moved away. We did think it was kind of odd that he was wearing an army trench coat; it was pretty hot and the rest of us were in T-shirts and shorts. But pretty soon we found out why he was wearing the coat. He moved to the open back door of the booth and said in a very strange voice, "Come with me." The lady looked back and told him to leave her alone, she was working. Then he stuck his finger into one of the pockets and poked it into her back, saying once more, "Come with me." That time she lit into him and yelled at him to leave her alone. Nobody could figure out what was going on until the youth started screaming and threw himself on the ground. That's when we realized something more was happening. I guess the clue was that he was naked under the trench coat. I think we all got that one—no need for any "Colonel Mustard in the study"-type of deduction. We grabbed the kid and restrained him until one of our policemen took him away. I'm not sure what happened to him after that. I hope he got some help.

CHAPTER 8

Clothing

As kids we didn't have a large selection of clothing. Mostly we didn't wear shoes much; they weren't required and we didn't like wearing them.

I can still remember the annual torture session. We'd trek to Hilo and find a store that sold shoes. Then one by one, while the rest of us ran amok, the poor struggling clerk would try to fit us with shoes that, hopefully, combined the perfect compromise of price, Mom's taste, and the children's desires. Somehow the first two items on the list always prevailed. That actually wasn't so bad compared to the next part. You have to remember that we only wore shoes to church on Sunday and to a very few special events. Shoes in those days were built to shrug off any abuse a kid could give them and were pretty much indestructible, but they were never comfortable, especially kid's shoes.

Mostly my shoe selection was comprised of comfortable, barely worn shoes that Ron had outgrown (my preference) or brand new, rarely used Buster Browns, which never seemed to fit after that magical first moment in the shoe store, when they actually felt like they could be okay until the last day I wore them. Those two days were great, but the in between was filled with cramped toes, sweaty feet, and blisters—lots of blisters. It didn't help that by not wearing shoes most of the time we had apparently widened our feet and the shoes we always got seemed to be made for some narrow, mythical Mainland feet, so either they were just the right length but too narrow, or wide enough and way too long. Small wonder I still don't like wearing shoes.

So, I only wore shoes under duress, and as little as possible. I liked going barefoot a lot, but there were drawbacks. Living in the country as we did, there were lots of thorns; there were bougainvillea, lantana, burrs, and my personal plague: the *kiawe* tree. I've seen two types of kiawe, the killer one with thorns and the more benign thorn-less version. I guess the missionaries who brought them over from Africa picked the thorny ones to keep all the elephants and giraffes in Hawaiʻi from overgrazing them or something. Not like the cattle could climb them. What were they thinking? Whatever the reason, there were lots of kiawe trees. They somehow grew in the most inconvenient places, like beaches, where we spent a lot of time.

The kiawe thorn is special; stepping on one isn't like just stepping on any old thorn. This thorn is long, sharp, and has a nasty habit of working its way into your foot and being really hard to get out in one piece. Typically it would break off, leaving a small section at the tip to fester until it became infected and then, hopefully, could be squeezed out, along with all the pus. If not, it called for a trip to the clinic, where they dug it out and then stuck on a bandage that lasted about five minutes after we left the place—and we were free to step on another one. I spent many unhappy moments doing field surgery on my foot with a dull Scout knife.

Just so you know, the best way I found wasn't painless, but it worked most of the time if applied immediately after the puncture. The thorn has a small bulge at the wide end that is just big enough to get the blade of a knife under, then a quick tug and most of the time the thorn would come out in one piece. It hurt, but it was better than a festering sore. The only other way I knew—and only used if I couldn't stand to walk on the foot—was to cut a slit over the thorn and dig it out. Those were desperate times, and self-surgery was the only option when we were far from town and had to get back under our own power, no matter what. (No cell phones in those days, kids.) Out of sight meant that we were out beyond help, so we were pretty careful.

Consequently, whenever we headed anywhere we knew there was lots of kiawe, we tried to wear rubber slippers. We never wore shoes, just wasn't done. The slippers wouldn't stop the long thorns, but they slowed them down and made them easier to get out of our feet. The only real problem with rubber slippers was when they got a little worn and we snagged the front of one of them while walking and tore out the thong. Once that happened, the slipper was never the same, and no matter what we did the thong just kept pulling through the hole until we had to throw the slippers away. But there were people who kept them for years. I've seen rubber slippers that had to be only an eighth of an inch thick that were still up and running. But not mine.

When we were caught out without slippers, we learned other methods to avoid the thorns, like shuffling our feet along the ground instead of picking them up and putting them down, or nudging the thorns aside as we slowly made our way to safety.

We were also blessed with a black sand beach at Punaluʻu, or Nīnole as it is also known. You'll never know what hot is until you're barefoot on a summer day when you can see the heat waves shimmering above the gauntlet you have to negotiate to get from the car to the shoreline then back to the car. The black sand beach would blister your feet, it was so hot. We never wore slippers. We tried them, but when we stepped in the loose sand it would rise up further than the slipper and just burn the softer skin on the sides of our feet. So we used to get our feet wet and plaster them with damp sand and very slowly walk toward safety, until the sand dried and fell off, then we ran until we got to a shady spot. Sometimes, if it was really hot, we'd use our swim fins, moving and stepping on one after the other to make it from the wet sand to the car.

But despite the obstacles, barefoot was the preferred and most practical way to go. What could be better? No fuss, no bother, no socks or tying shoes, easy to clean, and appropriate in most social situations. The mighty foot.

We also didn't have to wear footgear in school until the seventh grade, so mostly we didn't. But there was one time that everyone in school wore something on their feet for about two months. In 1959 Kīlauea Iki erupted with huge fountains of lava. But as those fountains rose into the wind, small globs of lava were blown away from the main fountain. As the globs fell, they left behind little tails of spun glass that blew off in the wind until they hit something and stopped. They looked like glass spiderwebs, and they were so light that even a tuft of grass would halt their progress. Pāhala was downwind and full of obstacles. Pele's hair, as we called the spun glass, got into everything for one or two miserable months. It was so thin and clear that when it got into our feet it was almost impossible to get out until it festered and squeezed out with the pus. Tweezers were useless because the glass was invisible and even if you could locate it, the damn thing would break when grabbed. Worse yet was trying to walk when some invisible needle kept poking at the bottom of your foot—not much fun. So we suffered; men, women, and most of all children, barefoot children. After this plague started it wasn't long before everyone in town put something between their feet and the ground, including me.

Feet posed other interesting problems. Since we walked barefoot all the time, we grew callouses on the soles of our feet that sometimes were an eighth of an inch or more thick. I know because when the soles got too hard, the skin on the side of the foot would crack. We measured it once, it was an over an eighth of an inch thick at the edge, which made it real uncomfortable when the skin split, as we had to trim the edges right down to the deepest part of the crack so it would heal.

Other body parts also received special attention, like our hair. The standard hairstyle for our family was long for the girls, but for the boys it was different. Until I was about thirteen, I went to one of the two barbers in town. One was run by a Japanese lady in the Japanese camp, the other by a Filipino man with a barbershop near the post office.

Regardless of where we went there were only two selections: one finger and two fingers. For one finger, the barber would rest his or her clippers on one of his fingers and just mow everything above it until the hair looked kind of even. For the style conscious, there was the longer and more dashing two-finger haircut. Yup, same as the one finger, only two fingers high. We always told the barber we wanted the two-finger haircut, but she always threatened to call Mom to check, so I never got one. A haircut took about ten seconds. We'd sit in the chair with a towel around our necks and she would put her finger down and just mow everything off that poked up above it, row by row, very quickly until it was done. After our haircuts, we walked around looking like little marines who'd just gotten into boot camp, or victims. It wasn't all bad—when we were at the Japanese camp barbershop we could look at the *furo* or climb the mango tree and pick the fruit the barber couldn't reach when it was in season. When we did, she would give us pickled mango as a reward.

Our apparel was much like the town, simple but utilitarian. Mostly we wore jeans with T-shirts.

Let me tell you, there's nothing calculated to wake you up on a Pāhala winter morning like a quick dash in your underwear to the clothesline, grabbing a pair of jeans, and then trying to push your leg down through the strongly starched and well-bonded pants legs. The ripping sound that accompanied this feat seemed to ring out through the neighborhood in the cold mornings as other kids did the same. But wait, the worst is yet to come. Because of the starch, the pants chafed between our thighs and we ended up walking bowlegged or very painfully until it softened either from sweat or blood. No matter how much we complained, we always found the jeans on the line with those wire things that took out the wrinkles inside.

Funny, jeans never felt really comfortable unless they were dirty, and then, despite our best efforts to hide them and wear them repeatedly, they would disappear, only to rise again the next day ready for another torture session. The only thing worse was when our underwear was also starched, then double the pain.

Our clothes never lasted long; we were hard on them. I can't remember ever having a pair of jeans that hadn't had patches ironed onto the knees three or four times by the time they got shabby, or were reincarnated as cutoffs after I outgrew them.

Seemed like the only time we looked presentable was for pictures, church, or parties. But that was okay with me, I've always felt there is no need for any more clothing than a pair of shorts and a T-shirt, with my ensemble rounded out by a pair of good slippers.

The weather in Pāhala was mostly dependable. It would be cool in the morning and hot at midmorning, then clouds would cool things down in the afternoon until it got cold at night. But not always.

Toward the end of summer we suffered and sweltered all day. During the day the tar on the roads would melt and we would scrape it up and play with it. That's when we looked for any relief—some water or a cool spot that offered even a brief period of time when we weren't broiling. During the summer we spent a lot of time at the beach. But guess what? All that time we were slathering ourselves with coconut oil, hoping to get that perfect tan. For me that meant burn and suffer, peel and itch, over and over again.

One memorable day during the hottest summer I can remember, Ron called me over. He had an egg and a steel spatula in hand. He told me he had heard someone say it was hot enough to cook an egg on a car hood. What's a kid to do? The gauntlet had been tossed. So we went out to Pop's Pontiac station wagon where Ron selected a flat spot on the hood. He cracked the egg, and damn if it didn't start cooking. Not sizzling, but we could see the white change color as it cooked and moved through the egg white, then the yolk got solid. That was cool. What wasn't too great was when he tried to take the egg off the hood. No oil meant a very stubborn and sticky egg that he had to scrape off a little at a time, along with a good amount of paint. Pop was not happy. That was an almost new car and the hood never looked quite the same. Funny how that works. With a whole car to look at, somehow everyone who looked at the car immediately noticed the scrape marks. There was much comment and merriment at Pop's expense for a while. But he got over it and we proved it could be done. Science rules!

But wait, not only was it hot, sometimes there was rain of biblical proportions. Real Old Testament rain that isolated the town and brought water running down the main road three or four inches deep. Water that filled every depression in town and caused the gulches to run. But for us, rain was just another type of fun. When we were younger, we'd run around in the rain without shirts, soaked to the skin, splashing in every puddle we could find and having a grand old time. When we got older and had skateboards and bikes, we'd race them down the main road pretending we were locked into a huge wave, with the required surfing positions, of course. We did quasimodos, head dips, rode the nose, and whatever else we could imitate, all while racing through the flood with water spraying up all around us. Very fun, but it didn't rain like that often.

We even got hail. Hail, yes, we got hail. One day while we were in school and it was raining a lot, we heard loud pounding on the tin roof of the school. We were kept under cover, but we all ran out and watched a bunch of what looked like ice cubes falling from the sky. They melted pretty quickly and vanished into the water on the ground. But Pop, with admirable acumen and foresight, grabbed a bunch and put them into the office freezer to preserve for posterity. Too bad the cleaning lady let them melt when she defrosted the freezer while cleaning it. Pop never got over that one. But really, who would have known?

It got very cold during our winters. I loved that time of year. It was cool, there weren't many mosquitoes, and the gulches ran with crystal clear, really cold water. During the winter Ron and I had a ritual we followed every day as long as it was cold. During the night we would huddle under our blankets and try to stay as warm as possible. But first thing in the morning Ron would get me and we would strip down to our underwear. Then, gasping and hyperventilating, we would run out the door and stand in the yard, watching our breath, which was visible, each of us trying to be the last one to bail out. Then we'd run back inside shivering and shaking, the winner gloating and the loser vowing vengeance. As I said, small town, not much going on.

It was a great place to live, especially for a kid.

CHAPTER 9

The Plantation

Pāhala was a sugar town. Just about everything and everyone in the town was dominated by the production of sugar. Most of the adults in the town made their living in some way connected to the plantation. I never knew why it was called a plantation, which sounds kind of colonial, with panama hats, white suits, bosses on horseback with riding crops and funny pants, and lots of gin and tonic (for medicinal uses, of course). But our plantation was just a big farm that cultivated and processed sugarcane.

I regret not paying more attention to what happened there, especially now since that way of life has pretty much vanished. But it seemed pretty simple back then. Growing cane was a never-ending cycle of planting and harvesting in rotation with the various fields throughout the year.

First, workers wielding cane knives cut cane stems twelve to fourteen inches long, which are called seed cane. They were cut and stacked together tightly in bins, and when a bin was full the workers tied the seed cane together with wire and dumped the bundle out. A good worker could cut and tie about 125 bundles a day—about one every five minutes.

The bundles were then loaded into hoppers and dipped into a chemical to seal them and discourage pests and loaded again into one of the planters. The planting machine was a huge caterpillar tractor with two bins bracketing the operator and four men on top who fed the seed cane onto conveyer belts. As the planter moved through the field, the machine would plow furrows into the field, the belts would fed the seed cane into the furrows, and then the machine would cover the seed and fill the furrow.

The field would be weeded and fertilized until the cane was ready to harvest. Then the bulldozers would clear a section around the field and it would be set on fire. The burning killed all the pests, cleared the field, and sealed the juice into the cane stalk. I heard that burning the fields was discovered by accident when a worker dropped a burning cigarette into a field that was going to be harvested one day. After the fire burned down, they decided to go ahead and harvest anyway and discovered that harvesting was easier, cleaner, and they got more juice from the harvest. I wonder if that worker got fired for being careless, or got a bonus for making the job easier?

So often we had huge fires blazing at night. I think mostly they burned at night because it was easier to spot out-of-control sections and put them out before they became dangerous. And it did get dangerous. Our manager's father, it was said, had died in one of the fires trying to get some workers out who'd been surrounded by the blaze. They found a way out but he didn't.

After the fires went out, the caterpillars, cranes, and haulers descended on the field and loaded and transported the cane to the mill. The cranes were huge. They had hooks on the end that looked like dinosaur ribs, which grabbed bunches of cane that the caterpillars pushed into rows to be lifted into the haulers waiting in a line. We could hear the sounds of the engines day and night, as the trucks drove back and forth transporting the harvested cane.

Sometimes Ron and I would sneak out at night and catch a ride with a friendly driver. There was no passenger seat, so we would sit on a wooden crate or the floor and duck down when we got to the field so no one would see us. The trucks went fast and the roads were really steep. We could hear the sounds of the engines whining and the squealing of brakes as they came down through the town on their way to the mill. Sometimes the brakes would fail and the drivers would have to run their trucks off the road into a field, where the cane would slow them down and finally stop them. I don't remember hearing that anyone got hurt, but I heard about a lot of close calls.

The mill ran twenty-four hours a day during harvesting, which was mostly year-round. The town was never quiet. It wasn't loud, but the noise of the mill was always there in the background.

Our town was dominated by the mill stack, which stretched sixty or seventy feet, the highest structure in town. Legend had it that the stack was haunted by a riveter who died when he fell into it during construction.

It was said that his ghost continued to hammer on Sundays, and I can testify that every Sunday afternoon there was a loud clanging from the mill. Ron and I and some of his friends went to the mill several times to try to find out where the noise was coming from, but we never could so we always believed it had to be a ghost.

The mill was run by steam generated by burners at ground level. We'd sneak in to look into the red fireboxes and watch the flames until someone would see us and chase us out. The water used during the processing was cooled by passing through a series of fountains and pumped back through fittings that sprayed it into the air and into a cooling pond—a hot, murky, algae colored, but irresistible cement pond that (you knew this was coming) we loved to swim in. Generally, the workers looked the other way; after all, most of them had grown up in the town and played the same games when they were kids. They also knew we swam like fish and were in little danger of drowning. But we had to get out after the water was cooled and channeled into a flume that drained it downslope and out of town. We'd swim and climb up into the fountaining hot water until they chased us out.

One day Ron snuck in alone without letting the men know he was there and they started to drain the pond with him inside. Not good. When the water started draining the strong current began sucking him into the underwater grate. He was saved only because one of the mill workers took one last look and saw him being sucked in. Next time we showed up, big lecture, swimming hole shut down. As you can imagine, Ron was not our hero for a while. But I'm glad he was saved.

But I digress. Back to the cane. After it was unloaded, it was taken to the mill, cleaned, rolled, and turned into thick, dark, sweet molasses that was stored in enormous tanks below the mill, until it was spun into sugar in a device kind of like a cotton candy machine. This raw sugar was then shipped to California, where it was refined, packaged and sent back to Hawai'i and off to other places to be sold.

The plantation had everything a small working community needed: a mill, garage, offices, hospital, school, stores, and a couple of churches. It even generated electricity to be put into the islandwide grid—after which, my father told me, the electric company charged the plantation more to use than they'd paid the plantation for it.

CHAPTER 10

The Town

No account of my time in Pāhala would be complete without describing my first day in town and the events that unfolded as I adjusted to my new home.

As I've mentioned in other vignettes, Pāhala had a set of rules all its own. Bear in mind, these rules were unwritten and their application somewhat capricious and arbitrary. More often than not, this depended on who was deciding what the rules were and how they were applied at the moment, rather than any standard or consistent application of the unknown and unsaid.

With that said, here goes.

We moved to Pāhala in 1957 just after the school year started. I was seven years old. When we moved into our house, one of the first things I noticed was a small, well-used path through the backyard, up a short hill, behind some trees, and onto the school playground.

The playground was magnificent, but this isn't about the playground, it's about the kids in the playground. I realized I was from the city and a little different from what they were used to, but my first contact was a pretty good indication of how a lot of my time in the town would be going forward.

When I got to the playground there were a bunch of kids over near the swings, so I walked over and said hi. I figured that's what people normally do, but as usual it worked out a little different for me. When I said hello, the largest kid replied with a surly, "Eh, haole, you like beef?" I thought he meant the meat, so I said sure, and he punched me. There were many of them and one of me and they didn't look friendly, so I beat a hasty retreat back to safety and tried to figure out what had happened. I asked Ron who, as an older brother, was my advisor and fount of wisdom on all things that had to do with kids. No dice; he didn't know either. We both found out later that in Pāhala, if someone asked if you wanted to beef, and you said yes, there was a fight. Who would have thought?

But things became even more surreal when I went to school that Monday. Even though it was a lot different from Catholic school, it wasn't too bad. I had met some other kids who didn't feel they needed to welcome me to town with violence, and everything was going okay until I ran into the playground bully again.

More unknown, unwritten rules of engagement: We were passing in the hall when he bumped me with his shoulder and muttered something I couldn't understand. So, I asked him, "What?" He replied, "Why?" I asked again, "What?" Then he said, "After school." Not understanding what was going on, I said okay. That's where it stood until one of the other kids figured out I had no clue about what had just transpired and told me I'd agreed to fight the bully after school. That didn't go down really well with me. Here I was, new in town, on my first day in school, and I'd already been punched and had now agreed to a fight after school. All without a clue what was going on and how all that had all happened. That's what I told the good Samaritan, but he said, "You have to go. If you don't, he'll never stop picking on you." That turned out to be pretty good advice and the Samaritan turned out to be a pretty good friend.

The bully's seconds made sure I knew where the arena selected for the fight was located, and I duly walked alone down to the field under a tree by the Mormon church. I knew it was the right tree because there were a bunch of kids under it.

When I got there, I was not comforted. There were about ten or fifteen others there besides the bully, and I didn't know any of them except the kid who'd told me earlier what was going on. But there was nothing to do but square up opposite my opponent to the cheers and jeers of the crowd. You know, there's never an adult around when you need one.

Then the bully made his first and most critical mistake. He danced around, shadow punching the air, making "chicken chest," and uttering dire threats that he was going to kick the haole's ass. Then he stopped and stuck his chin out with a sneer and demanded that I throw first. By then I was just about in meltdown mode so in the grand tradition of the cornered wolf, I hauled off and socked him in the mouth. When I backed off, ready and willing—but probably not able to defend myself—it got even more confusing. He just stood there for a second, then started crying and ran off. Everyone scattered, leaving me alone under the tree.

Satisfied with a job well done, and very much hoping that was the end of my troubles, I went home. But it couldn't end there. Oh no, that would be too easy.

When I went to school the next day, to my amazement, instead of being admired for standing up for myself, I was told that I had cheated and that I had "false cracked" my opponent. This tidbit was relayed to me by the same good Samaritan who had helped me out earlier. He had to explain to me that the goal of the exercise was not to fight, but to posture until the attendees broke us apart, then we would go our separate ways satisfied that honor had been served. But I explained that he had told me to throw first. What was the problem? That's what I had done. But apparently it wasn't supposed to go that way. I just gave it up and ignored the snide comments and whispers, and eventually they all got tired of not getting a rise out of me and stopped. I guess nobody wanted to fight "the cheater" because they might have gotten hurt. At least they knew I would throw a punch and I wasn't going to back down. Maybe that's the only good that came out that whole episode.

My advisor was right, many a confrontation that I witnessed later started with the opponents squaring off, uttering dire threats of doom and damage. Then one of them would tell his supporters to "Hold me back!" and when they did, he'd tell them to "Let me go, let me go!" But don't think the other guy was being left behind either—he'd be doing a variation on the same theme with his own supporters, until calmer heads eventually prevailed and everyone cooled down and left, usually without shedding any blood.

One other tradition was the circling of each other, making "chicken chest." Not to be confused with chicken skin, chicken chest was a unique martial display that resembled the attitude a fighting cock assumes prior to a bout. It's almost impossible to describe. Shoulders back, chest out, and always accompanied by a truculent sneer and much threatening verbiage. Once seen, never forgotten. If the situations weren't so fraught with danger it might look funny, but let me tell you, when you see it, things are getting a little tense. The only thing that's worse is chicken chest accompanied by a twitch in the leading leg. Thus, the saying, "notice the leg." More likely it should be interpreted as "things are getting serious."

In any case my good Samaritan must have let people know how ignorant I was and that it might be better to leave me alone since I didn't know the rules. After that, all the while I lived in town, aside from random acts of minor violence, I was pretty much left alone.

CHAPTER 11

Dolla' Tree Eighty

Etiquette back in those days was also kind of dicey. We all got along, but occasionally there were little bumps in the road. One of them happened to me one day when I innocently asked one of the plantation field hands how much money he made working on the plantation. He claimed he made "dolla' tree eighty." I then asked him how much that was, again he told me it was "dolla' tree eighty." He got mad when I told him that "dolla' tree eighty" was not a number or an amount of money. He then told me that he was trying to be polite. What he made was none of my damn business and he wasn't going to tell me. He got livid when I pointed out that he could have just said that in the beginning. It would have been more polite than what he was doing. It was just as well I was out of his reach after that last comment. He wasn't nearly as fast as a scared kid. But I stayed away from him for a while and never again asked anyone what they made.

Later on, after thinking about it, I figured out that there are other useful amounts that can be used similarly, such as "nickel five ninety and quarter four fifty," which I have used happily for many years when asked awkward questions about money.

We had other phrases: "I know these things, 'cause when I was young," "None of your beeswax," "Time for buy watch," "Half past a cat's ass, quarter to his tail and quarter more half past."

"I know these things, 'cause when I was young" trumps all. So when someone tells you a story about how he was trapped and fought his way out of the mouth of a forty-foot eel and shows you the scars on his hands, if you imply he might be embellishing the story a little, and he says he knows it happened "because when he was young"—the discussion is over and his story has to be accepted as truth.

People in town were not averse to taking advantage of a kid, at least some of them. Remember, a quarter was big money back in those days, but two quarters was a fortune. Imagine how crushed I was when I lost a quarter in the grass near the parking lot on my way to the store. I was frantically looking for it when an older kid came up and asked what I was doing. I told him and he helped me look for a while. Then he asked if I had another quarter, and when I said yes, he told me I could use the old "brother find brother" trick to get my first quarter back. So, I was in. He told me to spin three times around, then, with my back to the grass, flip the quarter over my shoulder. He promised to watch and see where the two quarters were when the second found the first. Well, surprise, surprise. I lost the other one. He said I must not have been concentrating hard enough, but I wonder. There's a sucker born every minute and that minute was mine.

Once in a while, if one of the retirees hanging out at the store was in a good mood, he would offer to buy me a soda. I didn't have any problem running an errand or helping them out if they asked, so sometimes they wanted to do something for me. I always appreciated the gift; people didn't have a lot of money in those days, so when someone shared some with me it felt good. It still does.

But what I really appreciated was the ritual that went along with the purchase. First, the slow-motion hand reaching into the back pocket, with the tantalizing reveal of the wallet a little at a time. Usually the wallet had long since given up the ghost and split into two parts, held together with a thick rubber band and whatever folding money was in it. Then the slow circling of the fingers under the rubber band moving it toward the side where it would disengage, leaving two halves of a wallet held together by a few moldy dollar bills that looked like they'd been there since the wallet was made. Then the agonizingly slow slide of the coin pocket zipper, if it worked, until the coins were unveiled, after which came the obligatory rummaging for correct change. Then the reluctant passing of the payment for the soda. And at last, the pop of the top and the ceremonial passing of the soda to the purchaser and on to a grateful and very thirsty kid. Damn, those sodas tasted good.

We had other expressions. One of my favorites has always been "hook face." That expression usually was used to describe someone who has had something put over on them, or someone who wasn't able to take advantage of someone else. For example, a guy sells you a car for more than he thinks it's worth or that he thinks is a lemon, and then you find out it's a collectible car worth far more than you paid, and you make sure to tell the guy. Or you go fishing at a spot that someone tells you is as good place, but he's not telling the truth. He gets "hook face" if you come back with a great catch and thank him for the tip.

We also had names for different types of people, such as "babooze" and "lope." A babooze, as I understand it and how we used it, is a person who really isn't a bad or mean-spirited person, they just don't get things right. They always seem to mess up, but not intentionally. But someone who is lope is probably best described as a mean-spirited babooze. That's the kind of person who picks on kids or keeps getting fired from jobs—most people just don't want anything to do with them.

There were some unique things we did for entertainment. For a while in school some of the guys made rings out of quarters for their girlfriends. Rings out of quarters, yup. If you want to make one yourself, just get an old silver quarter and a tablespoon and start tapping the edge until it widens out and looks like a ring. Then drill or punch out the center, file and sand it smooth, and presto! You have a silver ring. That's endlessly tapping the quarter, tapping for hours and hours. I never got past the shiny edge part, but some guys did and I have to admit they were nice rings.

I was not averse to throwing my hat into the prank ring either. The incident I remember most fondly involved the oracle ants. Oracle ants? You might say, "Ridiculous!" Maybe it is, but one morning, for a brief moment, Pop thought he was getting messages from the great beyond.

The night before, I had gotten up to get a drink of water and while wandering through the kitchen noticed a trail of ants. The trail wound from the door opening out to the yard, across the kitchen, to a small scrap of food on the floor that had gone unnoticed when we cleaned up the night before. I can't stand insect sprays—they choke me up in no time—but I couldn't just leave the ants. So I turned on the light and used a "scorched earth" technique of ant eradication. It went like this: Take down the floodlight Pop used when he was filming things, fire it up, and strafe ants. Worked like a charm and no fumes. But wait, there's more.

The little imp that sometimes works on me in mysterious ways found another form of amusement that included the floodlight and ants. I took some syrup from the refrigerator and wrote "Hi Curt" in syrup letters about two feet high and then went back to bed. Later I got up before Pop and, sure enough, the ants were there, in great numbers. So I fired up the floodlight and strafed them again. They all just stopped moving and lay there, still spelling "Hi Curt." So I went back to bed, only to be awakened later by Pop loudly exclaiming, "Holy cow!" "Hey, come look at this!" "What's going on?" and the like. He was pretty excited. When I got to the kitchen, I tried to keep a straight face and marvel at the strange occurrence right along with him. But I guess he figured out it had to be me. So I copped a plea and told him how I had done it. After he had a good laugh, he mentioned that that was a pretty good way to get rid of ants.

CHAPTER 12

The Hinged Board

On the plantation, the manager was like a medieval lord. Somehow, he seemed nice but distant and unapproachable. He lived in a huge mansion, surrounded by trees, flowers, and a vegetable garden with pineapples that was guarded by a gardener by day and by his two Dalmatians by night, who weren't very friendly and had the run of the grounds. It seemed like an impregnable fortress, but there was something that the manager didn't know about.

At one point someone must have figured out that this garden produced way too many vegetables and pineapples for the manager and his wife to eat. So that enterprising person had cleverly installed a secret entrance in the fence surrounding the house. It was a hinged board, invisible if you didn't know it was there, but a ticket to the garden if you did. It was located in the back of the property, near a dirt road and out of the way behind some shrubs. It provided entrance into the garden near the tastiest fruits and vegetables. I'm not sure how Ron had found out about it; he never said. In any case, the board had become a well-kept secret reserved for those moonlit nights when the children were restless and the pineapples and other fruit were ripe.

Those in the harvesting party were sworn to utter secrecy, and had to give an oath, sworn on their blood, they would never reveal the secret of the board. The only way I found out about it was by sneaking out after Ron one night and watching as he and his friends liberated a pineapple. (That's how I learned how effective it was to walk quietly and wait patiently for the right moment to reveal myself.) As usual, they spotted me, but not until I had seen that there was something special about that section of fence. Well, what could they do? I too was sworn to secrecy and pressed into service as a fruit bearer. Somehow it seems like I've spent half my life swearing to keep secrets that weren't really secrets and carrying and dragging heavy awkward stuff that nobody else wanted to drag around. But it was great fun.

It was quite a thrill to lie awake in the hot, still night, waiting until everybody had gone to sleep. Then when Ron tugged at me, I'd quietly slip out of bed, dress, and follow him out the window to our rendezvous with the other members of our raiding party. I could never figure out why Ron always wanted to climb out the window when he snuck out. We had a perfectly good door that was across the house from our parents' room, so they were unlikely to hear us leave. When I asked him, he just said I wouldn't understand. I guess it was some kind of secret, ritualistic thing he thought he had to do, or maybe it added to the thrill.

Somehow, the town, which seemed so familiar during the day, took on a different and more ominous character during the night. Especially when there was a moon shining. It created dark and scary patterns of light and dark as we slunk down the quiet streets, hiding in the hedges whenever the rare car drove past.

Our path led through a short section of forest along the wooden fence until we reached the hinged gate. Then, a whispered conference to decide who would be the sacrifice to the dogs. That always took a while. Nobody wanted to get bitten or caught. Luckily, they usually didn't want to take a chance on a portly, uncoordinated and nearly blind kid, which was fine with me. Waiting was thrill enough. But a couple of times I did get picked. I didn't dare decline. I wanted to keep going, so it was gut up, stay quiet, and be quick.

After the potential sacrifices had been selected, the lucky one or two would carefully open the well-oiled and silent board and look around inside, listening carefully to be sure there were no dogs waiting on the other side. A couple of times there were, but we could hear them panting so we aborted before they started barking. Then, if the coast was clear, we would quietly sneak through the rows of pineapples and try to find a couple of the biggest, ripest ones. When we had selected our prizes, we'd twist the stalk slowly, so as not to make any noise, until the pineapple was loose and could be silently broken off and carried away. Then a quick scurry through the garden to the hinged gate and our waiting friends, and we'd be off to a shadowed hiding spot where we would cut up the pineapple with our pocketknives and argue over who should get the largest piece. Sometimes the arguing got quite creative. Ron would say, "I thought there would be a ripe one tonight, so I should get the biggest piece." Then I'd say, "But I went into the garden and got it, so I should." Someone else would say, "I was the lookout, so I should get it." On and on until we each finally just grabbed some and ate it.

Of course, it didn't always go smoothly. There *were* dogs in the yard, and sometimes they'd spot someone and chase them to the fence. Fortunately, nobody got caught or hurt, just scared a lot.

Once, when Ron was sneaking up to the board, we noticed he was standing very still, with one foot in the air, and had been for quite a while. Those of us following him couldn't figure out what was happening, but there was no way we wanted to know bad enough to move forward and find out. The unwritten rule and part of the blood oath was if you got caught, you climbed the fence and were working alone. Well, when a large shape exploded out of the tall grass and started after a very scared Ron, we saw that it was a steer that had been sleeping soundly until Ron stepped on its head. The steer was extremely angry at Ron and chased him to the end of its short and, luckily, very strong tether.

Pineapples weren't the only game in town; there were mangoes too. We never plundered too much or got caught, but there were some close calls and exciting moments during our nighttime forays.

CHAPTER 13

Obake

Pāhala also had its share of chicken skin places and events.
Just to be clear, there are things out there that defy explanation. That's not a problem for me. I've always felt it prudent not to scoff at things I can't explain or understand and to accept things at face value, unless something changes my mind. But back then there wasn't a lot that changed my mind about some of the events I witnessed or heard about.

One of them was the haunted tree in the forest. As legend had it, someone had hanged himself on the tree sometime before we moved to Pāhala. The tree was a short walk into the forest on the lower side of one of the streets in the town. We visited the tree quite often as we passed on our way to someplace else. The forest was full of trails; lots of them led past places of significance or interest, and this tree was interesting.

It really did seem that it should be haunted. I think it was a plum tree, but nobody I knew ever ate any of its fruit. Carved into its trunk were Japanese ideographs, just barely visible, that covered the whole tree as far as a man could reach. Mostly the tree had grown around the writing, but we could still see them clearly. According to the older folk in town who were familiar with the tree's story, this writing explained why a man had hanged himself there. However, nobody knew his name or, more likely, would tell us anything more about him.

What was "chicken skin" was that nothing—I mean nothing, not even a weed—grew under the tree in an almost perfect circle. It was spooky. The forest was normally blanketed in foliage, even under the trees, but not that tree. It was said that the man's spirit was tied to the tree and he was doomed to circle it forever, and that's why nothing could grow in that circle.

The old folks also said that his spirit was visible on Halloween if you were brave enough to visit the tree at midnight. They were a little sketchy about some things, such as why the spirit of a Japanese man would be visible on a pagan holiday, but that was the story.

Ron—yup, this was all Ron—he just had to go and see the spirit. One restless spirit looking for another, I guess. But he had one problem—there was no way he was going alone, and nobody would go with him. Back then we generally didn't mess with things we didn't understand.

I don't remember if I was bribed, threatened, cajoled, promised great favors, or all of the above, but I did agree to go with him one Halloween. Truth be told, I kind of wanted to go but couldn't see why I should waste the leverage and, of course, there was no way I was going alone. This was serious, so we swore an oath to see the adventure through to the end, sealed with blood from a couple of cuts in our thumbs, then saddled up for another adventure.

After trick-or-treating we snuck out of the house about 11:15, giving ourselves plenty of time to sneak undetected to the tree. We made our way down to the low stone wall at the border of the forest and started stealthily and quietly down the path to the tree with one flashlight, which we'd taped up to allow only a small beam of light to illuminate the trail.

But we never made it to the tree.

There was something very ominous about that night and that place. I don't know about Ron, but I just knew something was in there, something scary, and I just knew something terrible would happen if we kept going. Neither one of us wanted to pull the plug, but without saying anything we both knew it was time to go, so we backed out of the forest and ran home as quickly as we could and never went back at night again. Funny, after that night I gave the story a lot more credibility.

Another time, shortly before I was drummed out of the Boy Scouts under a cloud, our troop was camping on the grounds of the Catholic church, near the Quonset hut that served as the church hall.

It was a beautiful moonlit night and after dinner someone suggested a game of hide-and-seek. We all thought that was a great idea, so we agreed on rules (only one: no hiding in the forest) and started our game.

I had found a perfect spot behind a stone wall bordering the forest, not technically in the forest, but hard to spot if I hunkered down. The guy doing the hunting had the only flashlight so we could track and evade him if we had time. One of the other Scouts had hidden behind a gravestone on a fresh grave, thinking no one would ever look for him there, probably because nobody would ever consider a fresh grave a wise choice, or safe hiding place, because of the spirits. As it turned out, it wasn't a great hiding place, or a great idea.

Sometime during the game, the Scout next to me nudged me and whispered, "Look at that," and pointed to the grave site. Talk about scared, I mean really scared! A little ball of blue white light was coming out of the grave and rising up behind the guy hiding on the grave. He knew nothing and we were too scared to speak. I couldn't even make a sound I was so scared. I wanted to, but I just couldn't. Not even close.

Then it got worse—the light moved up his back and hung in the air near his neck. I guess he felt something then, because he brushed his hand behind him without looking, but the light just bobbled a little and moved even closer. Then he turned to see what was tickling his neck, and all of the Scouts who were watching panicked and ran back to the safety of the church hall, shivering and still very scared, trying to explain what had happened to a skeptical and unbelieving audience.

I never found out what that ball of light was or what became of it that night, but when the pundits in town heard what happened there were dire predictions of doom and consequences to come. Unhappily, they may have been right. Years later, the guy who'd been hiding by the grave killed his brother in a hunting accident. Very sad. They were both really nice people. But guess what? The town still remembered. I guess in a small town nobody ever forgets anything.

There were other *obake* stories. We always called them obake, not ghost stories. But there were too many of them—often from people who weren't given to making things up—not to believe.

We were also raised on stories of the night marchers, the spirits of Hawaiian warriors who marched along the king's road or other paths. We were always told not to look at them, otherwise we too would have to march. I did know one older Hawaiian man who said he had looked at them one night, but just as he was going to follow, a warrior came over and turned him around and pushed him away. He told me his grandfather said it was one of his relatives who'd saved him, and that he should make an offering to thank him. I'm sure he did.

Ron and I did a lot of hiking as kids, but one thing Ron taught me that we did without fail was to take a couple of *ti* leaves with us, and if we came across a house foundation or heiau we would exhale from our diaphragm making a deep "ho" sound, then we would wrap stones in the ti leaves and leave them in a corner or a higher area. While we were doing that, I always tried to send thoughts out that I wasn't going to bother anything, just look and move on through. It seemed to work. I guess respect is never out of place.

In our adventures we went into places I won't ever share, places that belong to and were meaningful to others. We were always respectful and never took or destroyed anything, and I always felt what I was doing was okay with whatever spirits were watching.

CHAPTER 14

The Gulches

In the countryside around Pāhala, there were lots of areas of interest to a kid. It might be a gulch, or a place named for a prominent feature of its location, like Cow Pie—named after the decorations dotting the landscape, courtesy of passing herds of cattle.

As an aside, it was at Cow Pie where I learned the difference between a fresh cow pie and one that had aged. It was important thing to know, because the pasture was full of thorny bushes and stepping on them hurt quite a bit. Remember, we never wore shoes, so knowing where to set foot out of harm's way was a critical life skill.

For example, if you can tell the difference, you can step on a hard cow pie, and avoid stepping on the thorns. If you can't tell the difference and step unwisely, you end up dirty to the ankle, with no place to clean up.

I've had lots of fun with visitors from the city; I wasn't always a good kid.

Okay, okay, I'll tell. The secret is to look at the cow pie before you step on it. If it's shiny and there are flies, avoid it like a pile of cow droppings. If it's dry, gray, and wrinkled on top, it's okay to step on, even if it isn't completely dry. But if it isn't dry, watch out for the wet parts that get squeezed out of the sides. Good luck. Remember, practice make perfect.

Gulches in Ka'ū always seemed to be named after someone who died in them. We had two main gulches near the town. Scotty White Gulch was named after a daredevil driver who fell victim to the combined influences of hubris and alcohol. In a lapse of judgement and despite the warnings of the people he was drinking with, he drove down the old road one rainy night into a flooding gulch and from there into oblivion. With extreme relish, Pāhala old-timers who'd seen the aftermath regaled us with stories of the twisted wreckage and Scotty White's various body parts, brains, and blood on the rocks in the gulch after the crash, to help illustrate their lectures on vehicular safety. That was pretty ironic because most of them drove like maniacs themselves.

The other major gulch was named after a girl who'd plummeted to her death while trying to pick plums from a tree that overhung the gulch. No wonder there was always lots of fruit on that tree. Yup, more lectures on the dangers of climbing trees on the edge of the gulch.

But there was water in gulches, even in the summer. Looking back, it was kind of silly, but great fun. We'd pack up our gear and hike miles under the blazing sun, following a gulch to a tiny, smelly, and stagnant pool full of dirt and mud and thousands of mosquitoes, in which to swim or more likely wallow during the summer. Of course, after our dip, we'd have to hike all the way back in the blistering heat, with dried mud we couldn't wash off in every crevasse of our bodies, itching and uncomfortable.

But some places were special. There was a pool in Scotty White that never dried out or emptied, even at the hottest times of the year. During the summer it got a little thick, what with the dead insects, dirt—and we kids playing in it whenever we could. But during the winter it changed into a little slice of heaven, a sparkling pond so clear you imagined you could almost see the bottom if you looked closely. We'd gather and see who could dive the deepest and longest, watching the divers vanish into the cold water. It was pretty scary in water we couldn't see into, but we never jumped or dove into water we hadn't first reconnoitered to see if it was safe. If it was okay, we'd move down the gulch to a high ledge above a small pool and jump from there.

It probably wasn't more than a twenty- or thirty-foot drop, but it was plenty high enough for me, and pretty scary. Still, the ledge we jumped from hung over the deep part of that pond and nobody ever missed or got hurt there. Ron used to tell me tales of some kind of initiation he claimed happened only at midnight with boys standing around the chosen one with lit torches and chanting something or other until he jumped into the dark water. Right!

Regardless, it was a pretty far drop that took some guts for a kid to jump. I never got to the top myself; always afraid I'd hit the rocks instead of the pool since I was always jumping blind without my glasses, and placement was critical. It didn't help that the farther up we went, the smaller the target seemed.

One trick I learned was to hold a leaf (large and nontoxic) in my mouth, so that when I jumped it would cover my nose and keep water from rushing into my sinuses. That hurts. I learned the hard way.

When someone else jumped from the top of the cliff, it rivaled the cliff divers of Acapulco for purity of form and expertise. First, the jumper would climb up and out to the small ledge perched above the pool. Then, waiting until everyone was watching and silence had fallen over the crowd, a quick leap and down they went until there was a splash and they disappeared into the bubbles, only to bob back up. Then it was back up the cliff to do it again for hours.

Kids, don't try this anywhere, ever: We would also take dynamite blasting caps down to the pools in the gulch. I'm not going to say how we got them, but the dynamite shack that used to stand below and away from the town had a window that was usually open. I guess the powers-that-be were worried that someone who didn't have the key would need to blow something up. We would light the waterproof fuses, then throw them into the pond, empty of kids of course. Then there'd be a brilliant flash below the surface, and a huge column of water would blow twenty or thirty feet out of the water and shower us with whatever was in the pond. We didn't do that very often. It was kind of scary.

Gulches held other dangers as well. Once, a couple of us were amusing ourselves in a gulch, mindlessly prodding tadpoles with sticks in a shallow pond (small town, small amusements). Suddenly we noticed a strong wind coming down the gulch. We didn't wait around to see what it was. We had learned early on that it's way better to get some distance between ourselves and an unusual occurrence. So, we didn't wait to see what was happening, just climbed quickly out of the low wall of the gulch until we got away and clear. Only then did we look back to see a wall of water rushing down the gulch and on to the ocean. The gulch ran with high water for quite a while until the level went down and we could cross it to go home. We learned later that when it rained high up in the hills, runoff could cause a flash flood that nobody could see coming. We never forgot that bit of info and always checked the clouds up the slope just in case.

There was another special spot up in one of the gulches. Sometimes, when the snow is melting on Mauna Loa, the gulches run with cold but clear water. When that happened, usually in spring, we'd hike way up in the hills to a distant part of the gulch, taking some lunch. Then we'd follow the clear, clean water down the gulch, swimming where we could and climbing or walking around impassible parts of the gulch.

It was on one of those expeditions that Ron found a spot he called Kapu-C. He never explained the name but he sure found a beautiful spot. The pool was shallow and clean, fed by two or three small waterfalls, and surrounded by low cliffs and trees that lined the pool but didn't keep the sunlight out at midday. After Ron found Kapu-C, we hardly ever looked anywhere else, it was so great.

Near the pond on the cane road was a high dirt bank rising about twenty feet above the loose dirt on the slope below. We'd spend hours pretending to be paratroopers, yelling, "Geronimo!" and leaping out to land on the soft dirt below. Great fun until someone jumped and knocked a chunk of the dirt bank loose and it bounced off Ron's head, leaving a huge cut behind. We wrapped his head in a dirty T-shirt and hiked back for the six or seven stiches it took to close it up. Ron was bummed; no swimming, no active stuff, no nothing for a week.

We eventually explored every gulch in the area from as far up as we could hike each gulch down to its end or below the town. By the time we were done, we knew every water hole and swimming hole for miles.

CHAPTER 15

Killer Bees

There's one episode in one gulch that I'll remember the rest of my life. It was summer and early in the morning, just before sunrise. It was one of those mornings where I just knew something was going to happen, it had that kind of feel to it when I'd gotten up earlier than usual. The air was clear and the daytime heat had yet to bake the small town of Pāhala. Ron had already left the house.

Something Ron had in his knapsack was the reason I feigned sleep while he was leaving. For the last couple of days, he'd been assembling and constructing some kind of mysterious outfit. He wasn't talking, but from what we could see and guess, it was made of mosquito netting, an old army helmet, a glove, and various bits and pieces of heavy clothing and other household oddities.

My accomplice and I had planned our strategy carefully. We knew that whenever Ron took that much trouble and spent that much time planning, something was up, something he didn't want us to know about, something that could get us in trouble. So of course, we had to be involved. What else could we do? When Ron got up and crawled silently out of the loose window, we weren't far behind. But we used the door. We followed just far enough back that by the time we were discovered it would be too late to send us back. We did have plan B to use if necessary: the words that send fear into every plotting child's heart, the ultimate threat, "I'm going to tell Mom," or "It's dangerous." Worked every time.

As we watched from behind a hedge, Ron met Phillip, who also had an outfit and some long poles, and we then snuck after them down to Bobby's house, where they met the other two members of their expedition. They showed each other the outfits they had patched together from whatever they could beg, borrow, or steal. There were old pots and pans, military equipment, gloves, mosquito netting, and various items of clothing. They grabbed long bamboo poles with baskets lashed to their ends, loaded a couple of big tin washtubs with everything, and hiked off towards the old road. We were following, hot on their heels. We had no gear so we were able to stay close and quiet until we reached the gulch, just *makai*, or oceanside, of the old road. That's when we were spotted. The guys were pretty upset, especially Ron, but they knew we weren't going to leave without finding out what was going on. They did the only sensible thing they could do under the circumstances: They made us accomplices and, of course, porters. So, I ended up sworn to secrecy and drafted as an equipment bearer. Still, all in all, it was way better than a punch on the arm and being sent back.

We followed Ron and his friends, dragging and carrying the washtubs and gear with great difficulty (and no help, of course) down a faint trail leading to the edge of a gulch about a half a mile from the old road. When we got to the bank of the gulch, we saw what all the fuss was about, and I have to admit, it was worth the effort.

Picture a deep gulch cut into the rock about forty to fifty feet across and about sixty to seventy feet deep, with a rock overhang and niche on the far side. Under the niche, and overflowing from it, was the biggest beehive I'd ever seen. It had to be three feet across and six to seven, or maybe ten feet long. It was alive with bees and dripping with honey. This was the mission of the honey raiders.

Ron and his crew set up their headquarters on the far side of the gulch and suited up. That's when the reason for the mysterious outfits was finally revealed. The guys had made protective gear so they wouldn't be stung by the bees while they looted the hive. Ron was a vision of honey hunting splendor, in his army helmet with the mosquito netting draped over his face, covering the large black plastic raincoat that covered the rest of his body. (Just coincidentally, this was the raincoat that Ron swore he'd never seen when Pop asked where it was during the next heavy rain.) He even had twine to tie around strategic points of his body for a better seal. Phillip and Bobby had gone all out with the kitchen look, with red kerchiefs that they could barely see through, jackets, gloves, and rubber boots. The other lad had an old gas mask, a straw hat, gloves, and a poncho. They made quite a picture, especially since by then the sun had come up, and it was quite hot in those outfits. They huddled to plan their attack, sweat running down their faces and staining their outfits. My accomplice and I had no protective gear and were forced to stand back, out of danger. After seeing that hive and all those bees, I had no problem with moving back twenty yards or so to watch.

There was of course a reason this hive was so big, with so much honey: Nobody had figured out how to get the honey away from the bees. Their defensive position was perfect; they were across the gulch, protected from above and below and out of reach of the poles we had laboriously dragged through the brush. This was determined when all of the poles were tied together, with a basket at the end, and pushed out toward the hive, and they fell short—way short. They made it to about ten feet from the hive before falling into the gulch when their weight broke the string that tied them together. Too bad they were fishing poles; worse luck they broke. Phillip's father was quite upset later when he couldn't find them. Naturally, nobody knew what happened to them.

The rock overhang protected the hive from an assault from above, as it was too steep and dangerous to go close to the edge. Even when Ron and one of his friends made their way to a precarious perch on the far slope above the hive and pushed a huge boulder over the side, nothing happened except for a huge splash down in the gulch. The bees weren't even upset. In fact, there weren't many bees that even seemed interested. I imagine they'd been through this sort of trouble before and had seen legions of honey snatchers come and go, but they were still there.

Someone had heard that bees could be put to sleep if the hive was smothered in smoke, so two of the boys reached a spot just upwind of the hive and started a fire. It was quite a sight: two sweating, cursing beesters throwing wood, both dead and green, on the blazing fire in the sweltering heat, dodging the occasional scraps of wood that their helpful, if less active, friends threw down from above to help feed the fire. It looked even more interesting when the smoke wafted down the gulch and disappeared without reaching anywhere near the hive.

You may wonder what the bees were doing while all this fuss was going on around their hive. Well, nothing; they seemed merely to be interested observers, making an occasional overhead flight to see what was coming next. It was then, as our troops were divided—three on the top, two in the gulch on the bottom—that someone finally got their attention. I don't know why nobody had thought of the direct approach before, but in a flash of brilliance, or more likely an incredible act of frustrated lunacy, one of the guys threw a huge rock at the hive.

We watched it sail slowly toward the hive, and when it hit, that hive exploded into millions of very angry bees, all coming our way. I was exposed, with nowhere to go, so I ran as fast as I could in the opposite direction. Ron and his friends foolishly trusted in the integrity of their armor.

When I got far enough away that I thought I was safe, I turned to see the protective gear at work. I have to say I was impressed. I've never before or since that day seen more bees trapped in one place or more active people than I did when the bees slipped through the chinks in the armor and started to sting the troopers. They were staggering around blindly screaming at the top of their lungs trying to shed themselves of their portable bee traps. It seems a pity now that we tied them in so tightly. But they had insisted.

I guess I shouldn't have spent so much time laughing at the others, because some of the bees must have spotted me staggering and holding my stomach and came over and stung me a couple of times, just to show they could. I couldn't help it; I was so sore from laughing I couldn't run. Anyway, the damage was slight, and it was well worth a few stings to be there watching the madness and chaos.

After the bees had had their fun and the dust settled on the battleground, most of the bees returned to their hive and settled down again. A few squadrons flew overhead to keep our heads down and to remind us it still wasn't safe. One of the participants made a break and made it up to my location un-stung. The other troops picked themselves up and hobbled up the hill out of danger. They were so swollen they looked like mushrooms. We helped them out of their bee suits and picked the stingers out of their skin.

Later the other guys who had been in the gulch joined us. They had survived by jumping into a pool of filthy, stagnant water, hiding under their hats. They only had a few stings on their heads and hands from the bees inside their hats and their hands where they were exposed. One of them had managed to carry a five-to-six-pound block of honey that fell off the hive with them, so we didn't leave empty handed. A victory, but a Pyrrhic victory of epic and legendary proportions.

Oddly enough, the bees didn't bother us anymore as we left, even when one of the guys defiantly waved the honey at the hive while limping away. Maybe they knew that though they had lost some honey, they had won the war. We ate that honey later, late at night when we snuck out of our houses to a secret rendezvous up near the school. Never was there sweeter, better tasting honey. Naturally, the gulch water it soaked in added some favor.

We never bothered the beehive again. We'd go back every now and then to sit and look at it, trying to devise a better or safer way to get the honey. But we never did, and after a while the story of the killer bees was a secret shared over a campfire on a dark night with good friends or family.

CHAPTER 16

The Pool and Other Assorted Swimming Opportunities

We didn't restrict our swimming to the beach or gulches. Sometimes opportunities presented themselves to kids who were adventurous, or foolish enough to take advantage of those opportunities, and we were never slow to take them up.

During the hot summer months we were not averse to hiking three or four miles up a dry gulch to find a pond we could wallow in, like a bunch of hippos in the African dry season. Dirty, filthy, muddy, mosquito larva–infested water. But it was wet and cooler than the air. Too bad about the hike back in the heat with the drying mud-encrusted clothing. Still, for a while it was the only game in town. So what could we do? We went.

Then there was a change, a big change. When we lived in Pāhala, some of the men in the American Legion and Lions Club decided it was a shame the town had no swimming pool.

Quite often large projects got done in Pāhala with lots of cooperation, very little fuss, and copious amounts of beer. The swimming pool was no exception. The plantation donated the materials and machines, the school chipped in with the location and a promise to maintain the pool, the men donated the time and work, and we kids helped however we could. Back then, the men in the town were mostly veterans of World War II. They were smart, skilled, and knew how to work together to get things done. So going from a hole in the ground to a brand-new swimming pool didn't take very long, even though the men worked mostly on the weekends and after work.

Of course, there had to be a catch, and there was: It was never open. For some reason, once the pool was completed, they put a ten-foot chain-link fence around it, locked the gate, and never let anyone swim after the grand opening.

Maybe it was the diving board.

Pop had been quite the diver as a lad and could still throw his body off a board with some style, if not grace. When the pool was completed, he insisted on taking the inaugural dive off the board in front of an admiring crowd to officially open the pool. He was magnificent. Dressed only in a pair of red shorts and sporting a generous and well-filled beer belly, he pranced lightly to the end of the laminated wood board, leaped into the air, and landed on the end of the board. The board gracefully bent until his ankles were awash in the pool, then flung him through the air like a portly superman into the shallow end of the pool, half the pool away. I can still see him flying off into the shallows with a grimace on his face. Luckily, he dove shallow, no injuries. He graciously accepted the acclaim of the crowd at the incredible length of his dive and the size of his splash. I think they thought he did it on purpose.

Seemed the men, in their hurry to finish, had cemented the supports for the board a little too close, making it a tad more supple and whippy than safety would allow.

Much later in life I got a lesson in diving that kind of reflected Pop's experience with the Pāhala diving board. I had become a rather large and portly chap, kind of like my father. But like him I have always liked swimming. It doesn't matter whether it's in a pool or the ocean. I just like water and being in it. So some of my friends and I went to the Mānoa community pool in Honolulu one very hot summer's day. The pool was great, and we were cool at last. There was a diving board elevated about ten feet above the water. It had a funny looking wheel on the side, but other than that it really looked inviting. My specialty in those days was the cannonball; no finesse, just moving large quantities of water. Just so you know, when it's done right the cannonballer can hear a *ka-thumb* under the water upon entry. I never got to see any of my splashes, but they were the marvel and envy of my friends who couldn't find the sweet spot. So I climbed up the ladder, lightly danced to the end of the board, and jumped up. But just like Pop, I noticed I went down a lot further than I thought I would, then the board flung me into the shallow end of the pool. As I was traveling toward disaster I flashed back to Pop, and like him I dove shallow, scraping the lip between the deep water and shallow with my stomach and coasted to a halt about ten feet from the end of the pool, near a lifeguard who was not amused. She did tell me that the wheel adjusted the spring of the board and that someone of my girth should never roll it all the way back, which is where it was when I lifted off. Lesson learned—although she did kind of ask me to leave when I got a little off course on one of my cannonballs and washed a kid out of the pool when I got too close. The kid was ecstatic, and he and his friends were lining up for the same ride, but she'd had enough and asked me to behave or leave. She was really nice about it, so I took my show on the road.

Whatever the reason, they took their time opening the damn pool in Pāhala. There it sat closed, in winter, spring, and, worst of all, summer and fall, the hottest months of the year. Taunting us day after day, its crystal-clear water sparkled in the incredible heat of a Pāhala summer.

Well, what could we do? Day swimming was out, but some enterprising kids decided to try night swimming instead. Of course, Ron was involved, but this time he just asked me if I wanted to go without a song and dance first. He didn't even ask me to be a lookout or watch the clothes or anything. Just asked me if I wanted to go swimming. Heck yeah, I did!

On my first foray, we snuck out of the house and joined the others when the moon had nearly set, but there was still light enough to see things. When we got near the pool, we all took off our clothes and hid them in the bushes nearby. Then one by one, we climbed silently to the top of the chain-link fence, then over and down to the deck of the swimming pool. There was no room for error on the fence. We had no protection, and one mistake and the jagged fence top could do some major damage to some very sensitive body parts, which only added to the danger and thrill. Once we were all assembled on the deck of the pool, one by one we slipped silently into the freezing water and swam around in the dark, diving and whispering to each other until we got too cold. (Even summer nights got a little cool in Pāhala, and we were skinny).

After the first time it seemed pretty easy, so from time to time we'd organize an expedition, trek up to the pool, and get in a midnight swim. I can't remember all the swims, but one sure stands out in my mind.

It seems like we'd gotten so cavalier about getting caught we made a little too much noise and someone heard us. As luck would have it, we had already gotten out when the keeper of the pool arrived with a flashlight, and there was nothing to be seen. But as Pāhala was a somewhat sleepy and boring town at night, it appeared that, just as we were amusing ourselves by breaking into the pool, someone else was amusing himself by trying to catch us in the act. It got to be quite the game. We'd spread out and scout the area, and if nobody was spotted we'd go for it and climb over and jump in. Well, one night we got it wrong, way wrong. Same routine, different ending.

That night, after our check, we climbed over the wire and onto the deck. But before we could get into the water, the flashlight hit us and someone started yelling from up by the band building. Then five naked and very scared kids scrambled madly and recklessly over the wire to disappear into the bushes that lined the school, where we huddled scratched and bleeding while the hunt was on.

He never found us, but he scared us half to death, searching for about a half hour, shouting out an occasional threat, while we watched the flashlight scan the bushes before he gave up for the night.

That didn't stop us from going. In fact, the thrill was now even bigger. But we tapered off as we got older, until one night in an act of defiance some other kids pushed a section of bleachers into the pool. It took a crane to get it out and there were dire threats of doom for anyone caught near the pool at night. But oddly enough they got the message and started to let people swim there sometimes. No, it wasn't me that committed the dastardly deed. Luckily, I hadn't gone that night. But as much of a rascal as I was, I wouldn't have helped. Vandalism just didn't make sense to me, then or now.

There were also other venues for swimming.

The school's water came from a large redwood tank that also provided watery diversion on occasion. Usually, on a really hot school day we could make ourselves scarce, stash our clothes, and climb up the retaining rings that encircled the tank until we reached the top. If the water was high enough that we could get back out once we got in, we'd go for it. It was cool and wet, which were the main attractions. But sometimes someone who may have been mad at a teacher would add a little extra fluid to the water level. Normally, we'd just wipe off with leaves, get dressed, and slip back into the next class. But the last time we jumped in we must have been making a bit too much noise. When we climbed out, our clothing was gone. School was still on, and to get home we would have had to walk through town or wait till dark and sneak back to our houses. Luckily, after we had festooned ourselves with banana leaves and other foliage, one of the other kids snuck up to the ag building and saw our clothing on the ag teacher's desk. Well, he gave them back, but we had to promise to leave the water supply alone. Fair trade.

Well, they finally did open the pool, but we could only use it during our PE classes. But that didn't go well for everyone either.

There was a kid who lived up in Ocean View Estates who had moved to Ka'ū from the Mainland. Not the best fit.

In my experience there are two kinds of people who move in from outside the Islands—the kind that try to transplant their lives intact, and those that leave those lives behind and try to make a new life. That may not seem an obvious or simple thing to understand, but it's pretty easy to tell which type a person is when you're dealing with them. That kid lived here, but never left the Mainland behind and never really fit in with the rest of us. Not that I was a great example; I didn't fit in seamlessly, but I did okay. He seemed to be living just on the other side of everyone else, always looking in, but never getting through the door. I felt for him, but it seemed like he expected me to be like the kids he knew on the Mainland, which wasn't going to happen, so I didn't have too much to do with him.

Well, he had his moment in the spotlight one day when we were doing swimming tests in the pool one sunny afternoon. Swimming tests were pretty much a formality for most of us. The drill was easy: Jump into the deep end of the pool and swim as far as you could underwater. For most of us, that meant from one end of the pool to the other and back on one breath of air. Easy money. Most of us weren't even breathing hard when we finished. After all, we spent a lot of our spare time at the beach.

Everyone had finished, but there was still one pale, skinny, and very nervous kid to go. So the teacher told him to get to the end of the pool and get going. Nobody expected what happened next. I'd really like to tell you he dove in and swam like Johnny Weissmuller and aced the test no sweat, but that's not the way it went.

He jumped in, then sunk to the bottom of the pool still standing. We were all standing around the pool speechless, just watching to see what would happen next. At first, he didn't look very uncomfortable, but after a bubble or two escaped from his nose he suddenly burst into action and started clawing his way up the side of the pool. I thought that was kind of odd since he was standing in front of the pool's ladder and could have just climbed out. All too quickly, he arrived at the surface blowing and gasping and we grabbed him and pulled him out and on to the edge of the pool. That's when the PE teacher who had watched this all unfold without a word asked the kid the magic question, "Do you know how to swim?" Guess what? The answer was no. Then the next question, "Why didn't you tell me?" And the answer, "I didn't want you to think I'm chicken." I'll never forget what the teacher said then: "Well, if it's any comfort, I don't think you're chicken, but you sure are stupid."

CHAPTER 17

Caves

Not only were there gulches around Pāhala, there were also caves, lots of them. I'm not fond of caves. Maybe because of that day when Ron and I were in a cave and he turned off our only light.

The cave we were exploring was called Turtleback Cave, named after a hump in the floor that looked like the shell of a green turtle. I never could tell if it was natural or had been carved, but it was covered with petroglyphs, as were the lava ledges that lined the cave's entrance. We could only reach the cave by hiking up through town on the cane haul road, past the Japanese cemetery and the little airfield from where the plantation's small biplane dusted the crops. We always stopped at the airfield for a drink of water.

The biplane's pilot was a short Filipino man who supposedly learned to fly in the Philippines before the war—I'm not sure which war, he was kind of old. He was quite dashing in the leather coat, helmet, and goggles he wore whenever he flew. He looked like a World War I flying ace, especially since he also smoked a pipe and wore a scarf wrapped around his neck and high-topped boots, really. At least I never saw him with a swagger stick and bulldog.

In any case, it seemed he didn't learn very well; he kept crashing. At least once every couple of years he'd pancake the plane into one of the fields and walk away. They'd pick up the plane, fix it up, and he'd be back at work in no time. We liked him because if he was at the airfield when we got there and nobody else was around, he'd let one of us climb into the fertilizer hopper, which he wouldn't top off for that run, and take that guy up with him.

For a kid, it was really exciting. The pilot had made this run so many times he could probably do it in his sleep. He'd taxi down the short runway, turn the plane around, push down on the throttle, wait until the engine was running fast enough, and finally let it go down the runway and lift gently into the air. Then he would wheel around until he saw the waving flag that marked the field and make his approach. He'd put the plane into a shallow dive, yell "Look out!" and spread the fertilizer in a long run down the field. Then after a few more passes he'd take the plane back to refill and drop us off. He always seemed a little more careful when he had someone with him, and nobody ever got hurt. I didn't get to go more than once or twice, but it really was a thrill, especially looking over the side and seeing the town and countryside from up there. No wonder he liked his job.

But back to the cave—from the heights to the depths. To enter the cave we had to scoot on our butts down a short trough in the rocks at the side, then swing down into the mouth of the cave over a deep pit that discouraged mistakes. At the entrance, hard mud covered part of the floor, while petroglyphs lined the lava on both sides of the tunnel that led further into the cave. There were pictures of men, canoes and turtles, plus other images that we couldn't identify.

The tunnel from the entrance grew smaller toward the back, and there was also a small passage that ran alongside but separate from the main tunnel. We'd find *kukui* nuts, used by the Hawaiians in years past as candles, which were partly burned and strung on sticks, sometimes on the floor or in niches in the sides of the cave. There was more debris on the floor that must have been carried in by earlier visitors. Farther along we'd reach the turtleback the cave had been named after, then beyond that a drop in the continuation of the tunnel.

When Ron turned off the light, he and I were trying to find the end of the cave, which we'd never reached nor had heard of anyone else reaching. Probably with good reason, but of course Ron had to be the one to do it. We had one light and no spare batteries. That wasn't too bad because there was only one tunnel, so we really couldn't get lost. That day we hiked for what seemed like an hour or two but never found anything that looked like the end. We finally had to stop when we reached a very small, tight opening mostly blocked by mud. Ron wanted to dig it out and go on, but I'd had enough. That opening looked way too small and scary to even try to push through, just on the off chance there was something on the other side. It was so small we would have had to crawl, and there was no space to turn back or around if something went wrong. No dice for me, but Ron wanted to go on. I wouldn't. That's when he turned off the light, saying he wouldn't turn it on unless I agreed to go on. That's when I started to feel closed in and started to hyperventilate. Until then I hadn't thought about where we were, way underground, just the two of us, in the dark. We were alone, and panic closed in on me really quickly. Even worse, we hadn't told anyone where we were going, so we were completely on our own. Talk about the heebie-jeebies! It didn't bother Ron. He kept taunting me and threatening to leave me, which didn't really help. But at least it got more real for Ron when I picked up some rocks and started throwing them in a panic toward where I last heard his voice. I dimly remember saying something to the effect I would kill him and take the flashlight off his body to get back. Something must have made him believe me. He switched on the light and we went back. We never said too much about it, and I pretty much avoided caves after that trip. But ever since then small, dark places have always given me the willies. I never told my parents about our foray, but years later Ron saw me break into a cold sweat in a secret short tunnel that led to a hidden freshwater spring at the beach. When he saw what was happening, he asked me why I was having so much trouble. It was a short tunnel and I could see the end, but it still wasn't anywhere I would have chosen to enter. When I explained, he realized what he had done all those years ago and apologized. He said he never would have turned off the light had he known how scared I would be. I believed him. I never really blamed him anyway; the fear belonged to me and I've always been the one who had to deal with it, and Ron, while not a saint, was not a cruel person.

There were other caves. One I remember very well. It had a name I never could remember, but the entrance was guarded by two *pueo* (owls) that used to fly away when we approached its low entrance. Just inside the cave, the floor dropped off and there were boulders that had fallen from the roof littering the cave floor. The light from the entrance only extended a short distance into the cave, which grew smaller in size the farther back we went. In the middle of the cave skeletons lay scattered about, without coffins or any other objects around. Most of these skeletons were intact but some of them had holes in their skulls. On a ledge further back were three skeletons that looked like a family—one large, the second smaller, the last a child—lined up together in a neat row. They all had large holes in their skulls. I only went there once or twice. It was a sad place; all those people had died there and everything they had taken from them, even the dignity of a grave. There were no local legends about the remains that I ever heard, but inside the cave, off to the side, I found a place where someone had carved some Chinese writing into the lava. Later on in school I recognized one of the characters; it meant "prisoner." We do know that Chinese workers were sometimes smuggled in illegally. Maybe they were being held there and someone got scared and killed and looted them. We'll never know.

One thing, though, I never took anything out of any cave I ever visited, except some rubbings of the petroglyphs and some memories. I never felt it was foolish to honor and respect the people who came before me, so I always tried to treat their remains and memories as I would my own. Maybe that's why I never felt threatened or uncomfortable in most of the places I've visited. That's also why I won't tell anyone how to find those caves and others I've visited containing artifacts or remains.

CHAPTER 18

Trees

Somehow it's different for me now. I guess all things change. I see lots of trees, but they don't seem the same as the ones that were my playmates when I was a child. Maybe it's because I'll probably never climb a tree again. That's okay, I had my turn and it was great fun.

The first tree I really remember was the banyan tree in Hilo just outside of the fence surrounding the manager's house, overhanging a small, normally dry streambed. There were other trees in Hilo that we played on when we could get into them, but that tree was special.

I wasn't the only one who thought so. Someone had climbed up the tree and, at great risk, installed a wire cable to the largest branch that spanned the streambed. At the end of the cable was a seat with a long rope that could be used to pull the swing up to the fence. Someone would climb into the saddle and off they'd go, up through the leaves and back again a couple of times until someone caught the rope and the next guy would take a swing.

Naturally, Ron found out about the swing. I think he had some kind of radar that singled in on fun, and mostly dangerous fun. In any case, he and I would watch and when we saw lots of older kids sneaking into the forest we would tag along. Usually it wasn't a problem for the bigger kids since we were careful not to tell anyone what we knew, and they trusted us to keep the secret of the swing. After all, if we got busted there would be no more swinging. But they had a way to seal the deal; they sometimes let Ron or me swing.

As I write this, it all comes back: the hushed voices, the promise never to tell, the other disclaimer that if I fell or got hurt it would be my fault. Then the instructions, mostly to hang on for dear life, since a fall would have probably been fatal. Then up into the swing, sitting on the plank seat, holding on to the two ropes that leaned in from the swing to attach to the loop of the cable. Then it was one, two, three, and away, down into the streambed then up through the leaves into the sunlight. Then back through the leaves and up to the slope where someone would grab the rope and slow us down until we could be pulled up to get off the swing. Great fun.

When we lived in Pāhala, there were many different varieties of trees—eucalyptus, *koa*, mango, avocado—all kinds of them scattered throughout our yards and the forest across the street. There were also fruit trees in the yards and planted in rows along the older roads and surrounding the town.

Back then trees weren't merely decoration or part of the landscape. They were an essential ingredient in our lives and our play. We climbed in them, made swings, treehouses, nests, and secret hideouts—and fell out of them. Trees were airplanes, ships, castles, and whatever our imaginations desired or our games required.

Some trees had special significance, like the kukui tree behind our first house. I discovered that kukui nuts, when eaten in an irresponsible quantity, are guaranteed to keep a young lad as close to a toilet as he can be for two days. A truly enlightening experience. Or the ʻōhiʻa tree we all climbed to take pictures of the volcano. That same tree and branch are still there and every time I pass by, I stop and remember our picnics in the park.

The second house we lived in had a cluster of different kinds of trees growing in the yard. Along the back were banana trees, a pear tree, guava along the border, an avocado tree in the middle, and a huge mango tree right behind the house. Those trees and lengths of rope, boards, and nails provided us with hours of fun, as well as some times that weren't so much fun.

We mostly climbed the pear tree in the back, as it was the easiest. I still remember the way up to the top. First a short jump to a low branch, on up to the main trunk, along a narrow rising branch to the short thick cross branch, up the trunk on limbs that circled upward around the main trunk, then a swing out around the last fork, up, and bingo—there you are, sixty feet above the ground. When we reached the top, we'd sit in the highest crotch of the tree swaying with the wind with a magnificent view of the house, part of the town, and the school field. There was fierce competition among us kids after school to be the first to get home and up the tree to get to the highest spot.

That's the tree from which I fell from the top. Maybe I got what was coming to me, since on that day I had left everyone behind and was climbing faster than normal to get to the highest point. I was going to drop firecrackers on the others as they climbed, to make their climb more interesting, no doubt.

I climbed rapidly and surely until I reached the top fork in the tree. All I really remember at the end was swinging by one hand, firecrackers and matches in a paper bag held in my mouth. I felt my hand slip off some moss. I was paralyzed. I could only watch as my hand, usually my trusted friend with a grip like a little gorilla's, slowly and agonizingly slip off and cast me adrift. It was one of the clearest and most horrible moments of my life. As I fell backwards, all I could see was a blur of green. My body tensed and waited for impact. Then I hit, and hit hard. Lucky for me, what I hit was someone else. Unlucky for him, when he broke my fall, I broke his collarbone. After I bounced off him, I fell the rest of the way to the ground and landed flat on my back, knocking the wind out of my lungs. That's where I lay gasping for breath when Ron ran out of the house in his Scout uniform to take charge. What pandemonium there was! I was wheezing, and everyone was running out of the house to see what happened. Over the din, Ron kept proclaiming, "Don't move! Don't touch him! I know first aid!" as he did a cursory check for injuries. Nobody was paying any attention to the real injured party who was hanging on to the tree with one hand, teeth clenched in pain. Ron helped him down, and didn't do first aid, luckily. We figured out later that he had saved my life; if I hadn't hit him and slid off, I would have hit squarely on the branch he was sitting on and broken my back.

We finally got that mess sorted out, but it took a while before I worked up the courage to climb that high again.

We also had banana trees, which weren't much use. Spiders lived in them, they were too weak to climb, and they made our knives black. We usually ignored them unless we were forced to clean up the rotting bananas that we hadn't picked and eaten.

But one day, a day that will live forever in our family's history, Ron discovered another use for the bananas and some overripe mangoes we had in the yard. Ron had read a comic book that contained the seed of the idea. Someone in the comic had slipped on a banana peel and had fallen. Ron deduced that if someone's foot could slip on a single banana peel, a whole body could slide on lots of peels. He took that deduction one step further and figured out that if the proper amount of banana/mango mixture were applied to the slide on the swing set in our yard, then not only would someone slide further, they would go faster.

Well, I can tell you it didn't take long for Ron to convince the rest of us kids that it would be fun to squish rotting fruit into an unsightly, putrid mess and smear it all over our slide. By then, it looked like so much fun we'd have paid him to help, even if he hadn't promised we could all have a turn if we wanted. Once we had a sufficient amount of Ron's marvelous, putrid, and ecologically sound slide lube, we smeared it onto the slide and in a line up to the low stone wall at the edge of the yard.

When we had assembled the grand banana slide, we had only to find out if it worked. I don't remember who went first or second, but I sure remember who went last. It wasn't Ron or me; it was our volunteer test pilot. During the first runs we had discovered that the drop from the top of the slide to the bottom and out onto the grass was okay, but it wasn't far enough to get a good run. Ron, after pondering the problem (I'm sure it was him), suggested he and I give our brave pilot a little assist by pulling him down the slide by his feet and arms, one on each side, letting go at the bottom when he had a good head of steam built up. The good news was that the idea worked. The bad news was that it worked too well. None of us had anticipated that he would scoot down the slide, onto the trail of slime on the lawn, travel its length and much further than anyone else had gone. Too bad about the stone wall, it kind of got in his way and stopped him when he hit it.

When Mom heard the noise and came outside, she hosed our pilot off and took him inside. But before she left, she let us know in no uncertain terms that she was not happy, not at all impressed, and she expected the yard to be clean before we came back into the house. The rest of us kids hosed, scraped, raked, and cleaned up the mess. Before we finished, four kids and especially Ron and I were wondering who the lucky one actually was.

After we had scraped for a couple of hours Ron suggested that we hose the yard down to conceal the scraps under the grass, since we weren't going to get them anyway. Sounded good at the time. We were all tired and there were still lots of bits clinging to the centipede grass. Bad idea. We discovered the worst adverse side effect the next day around midmorning, when the smell of the ingredients started to envelop the yard, getting worse as the day trudged on. That damn smell lingered in the yard, baking in the summer sun for days. It sure kept our experiment fresh in our minds every time we went out there. Lucky my parents rarely went out into that part of the yard. I haven't eaten bananas since. I can't even smell them without getting nauseous.

We also made swings, many swings. Any stray bit of rope was fair game, and usually ended up dangling in one of the trees with something to sit on tied on to the end.

There were other objects we pressed into service from time to time, but none was more memorable than the donkey pack saddle. One of us had *found* an old one somewhere; its ownership was sort of vague. I never knew where it came from and Ron never said, but we figured that at last we had found the ultimate swing seat. Ron rigged it and it looked great; well padded, it even had stirrups and it was secured with the latest in Boy Scout knots Ron had learned that week. All we lacked was a test pilot. Test piloting usually fell to someone other than Ron or myself. As I remember, someone usually volunteered when we pointed out that the test pilot had to be small, light, and brave. It probably didn't hurt when we also pointed out that whoever it was wouldn't have to wait for a turn later if our projects worked. Whatever the reason, someone, usually our younger brother, always volunteered, and Ron and I didn't have the heart to say no. Our brave pilot climbed aboard the saddle, got firmly seated, hung on to the cross piece in the front, put his feet in the stirrups we had installed, and hung on for dear life. Ron and I pulled on the accelerator straps hanging from both sides of the saddle and off he went. The swing worked perfectly. Our brave volunteer was having the ride of his life, shouting, "Giddy up! Higher, higher! Faster, faster!" Ron and I obliged him by pulling harder and harder on the straps. It looked like we had a winner. In fact, Ron said later he was about to take a turn himself, but then the knots he tied stopped working. Our volunteer, who was at the top of a swing, was screaming in delight until he realized he was all alone up there, just him and the pack saddle swing, sailing toward the clump of banana trees at the edge of the yard. Under the circumstances, it must have been a softer than usual landing; he was willing to try again later, after Ron had retied the knots and tested them himself.

The pear tree was fun, but it couldn't compare with the mango tree. I still don't know how tall it was. It was cut down long ago, but it looked about a hundred feet high, much taller than the pear tree. It was so big we five kids couldn't hold hands and surround it at the base. We constantly climbed that tree and found places special to each of us where we could be alone, or together, and feel that bonding you only get with trees you climb into and play with for hours. We also constantly challenged each other to climb higher and farther out on the tallest branches. I have great respect for the strength of mango branches. We also discovered, when we had mastered the entire tree, that we could jump out of a higher part of the tree and move like little apes from level to level on the numerous and closely packed branches until we reached the ground. What excitement to look below for a strong branch with bushy ends and jump with your heart pounding and arms outstretched, falling until your hands hit something, then hanging on while the branch bends lower, then whips back up into the branches above. Then, quickly before the fear sets in, off again until the lowest branch drops you softly onto the ground.

Mostly we didn't fall off the mango tree. Probably because it was so big and tall, we were extra careful. But there was one incident when someone did take a dive.

It happened when we discovered that one branch of the tree almost touched the roof of the house. Since the opportunity for another forbidden place to play had presented itself, what could we do? One by one, we kids got on the branch and pushed it up and down until it bounced a little higher than roof level and we could step off onto the roof. We all got on successfully, but after sneaking up to the peak of our hot tin roof at the front of the house and spying on everyone who drove past the house, there wasn't much else to do and we got bored. One by one we jumped on the branch, rode it down to the ground, and let go. All but one of us. As you may have gathered by now, our three siblings had no real reason to trust their two older brothers. After all, I had fallen on one, Ron had sent another into space, and there was that unfortunate accident with the stone wall. But there was no other way down.

We had no ladder. I think Mom and Dad didn't want us climbing on one and getting hurt. We couldn't use a rope and it was too high to jump down. We went back up and demonstrated; we walked him through it; we threatened, bribed, cajoled, and finally begged, but still he wouldn't jump. Even our two sisters had made it off the roof and it was getting dark. In desperation, Ron and I said we would leave him there until Mom saw him and all of us kids would say it was his idea and blame him for his predicament. He very reluctantly decided to go for it. We had a plan, of course. The plan was that Ron and I would pull the branch down with our combined weight then jump off, and when it sprang back up he could just reach out, grab it, and ride it down to where Ron and I would be waiting to make sure he was safely on the ground. It should have worked, but of course it didn't. Bad jump, wrong moment, belly flop on the ground. Ron and I raked up a lot of mangoes and leaves to work off that little miscalculation.

There were also trees above the pigpens below the town. Guava trees were planted to give shade as well as feed the pigs that people raised below the camp. On occasion, we would quietly climb one till we were over a pen and wait until a likely looking porker idled below, then we would spring onto the pig's back, and hang on to the enraged and panicked pig for as long as we could until we were thrown off, then run for the rails as fast as we could with the pig chasing behind. Simple pleasures and what a rush!

One more notable tree that I recall was the big mango over the corral that the plantation's donkeys were stabled under in the hills above town. When I was a kid, the plantation used donkeys to pack fertilizer up from the town and into the fields, where it would be spread by the fertilizer crew by hand. Once or twice a day there'd be a pack train moving from the stable into the fields to deliver bags of fertilizer to the gang.

Sometimes if we were out of school we'd go down to the stable and talk the donkey skinners into letting us ride up on top of the bags, into the fields with the pack train. It was kind of quiet fun. The donkeys knew the routine, and once they were loaded with bags of fertilizer and a couple of kids they would slowly start up the road into the crisp morning, on their way to the field where the fertilizer would be spread. We'd sit quietly on the slowly rocking bags, smelling the donkeys and fresh dirt and not talking much or making any sound at all. Up and up into the hills, looking around as we went. When we got to the field we'd help the men unload and then pack the donkeys with empty bags for their return trip into town, where they would load up and head out again. These donkey trains ran all day, but most often we'd leave them up in the hills and hike down the road or explore gulches and forested areas as we made our own way back to town.

There was something else a lot more fun about the donkeys, and that was their corral under that huge mango tree in the hills. It was quite a hike from town, but there was something in the corral we kids desperately desired: big golden swordtail fish. The plantation put them in the water troughs to eat mosquito larva that could infect the donkeys and make them sick. We wanted those fish.

The problem was that the trough was situated near the trunk of a tree and a fence surrounded the tree as far as the leaves provided shade. Pretty neat when you think about it; shade, water, and food, all in one compact package. It didn't help that the donkeys were not friendly; in fact, they were downright mean if the men weren't around to keep us safe. But the men were never there when we went to get the fish.

There was a way to catch them. Not easy and not something anyone could do alone, but it could be done and if it was done correctly we could usually get some of those golden swordtails without getting hurt.

One day three or four of us went fishing. After a long, sweaty trek we reached the tree in the corral. What we'd do is rope a long, low branch that dipped near the fence and pull it down within reach. Then a couple of kids would wait while the others went to the opposite side of the corral and made a ruckus. When the donkeys rushed toward the noise, the waiting kids climbed up onto the limb and inched their way as quietly as possible along the branch to the trunk of the tree and then to a branch just over the water trough.

From that perch, we'd lower tin cans with pukas punched in them so they would sink into the trough. Then we would wait patiently until a fish swam over the can, pull it up quickly, and hopefully see a golden swordtail in the can. We did catch swordtails that way. I guess they were rarely bothered, so seeing the tin can didn't seem to faze them—that is, until one of their pals vanished into space.

When, and if, we caught one, we'd put it into a jar of water we brought with us with small holes in the lid, wait until the donkeys were distracted again, then inch back along the branch and down onto the ground. There was one low spot on the branch, which just about within donkey reach if they reared up on their hind legs. You had to trust your friends.

Then the real fun started. Do the math: four or five kids, one fish. That meant that none of us had a whole fish, just parts. Once we got the fish back to town safely and alive, the negotiations started. It always went like this: "I caught the fish." "Yeah, but I kept the donkeys busy." Then it would move to: "I roped the branch and held it down so you could climb on to it." "I showed you the tree!" On and on endlessly.

I usually traded my share away for a cheap candy bar or something else of little value. I never wanted to end up with the fish for part of a month and deal with everyone else if it died when I was taking care of it.

I guess, at least with swordtails, the journey is way more fun than the finish.

There have been other trees in other places that I have climbed in and played on, but they can't compare to the trees that I considered my friends when I was a child. I hope there's a tree heaven for trees that have passed on, and I hope that our trees will grow happily there forever, with lots of children to climb and play in their branches.

CHAPTER 19

The Forest

Looking back, I'm not sure it was a real forest, but it was our forest. It didn't take much to get there; just a dash across the street, through the yard with the Portuguese oven that was always painted a brilliant white, through the gap in the tree covered with lilikoʻi vines, and there it was. That's where all the paths we children had made in the forest converged. From there we could venture up into the territory of the kids who lived in the upper part of town or to any of our friends' homes with backyards bordered by the brush.

We used the smaller trees to climb into when we played "bang, *make!*" (bang, you're dead!), and sometimes we'd use them to build log cabins (with small logs) that never quite got finished. Many of them had fruit; we'd climb those to get what was hiding in the leaves. There were also lots of tall trees; ones we couldn't climb since the lowest branches were way out of reach, even though we tried to tie rocks to ropes and attached them to arrows to get them over the lowest branches. No doubt it was a good thing we never got that high. But sometimes, during a storm or if a tree just got old, they would fall. These windfalls hardly ever reached the ground, the other trees were so thick, but they made a great place to play when we could climb up the sloping trunks to the branches that were on top. We'd make forts and secret places for as long as we could before the leaves dropped off and all that was left was the skeleton of a tree, which was more depressing than fun.

CHAPTER 20

Learning the Hard Way

Growing up on the Big Island in a small community really taught me the value of other people and the need to try to get along, especially since I was always a member of a minority. It never really bothered me, but there were some reefs I ran aground on while I was growing up. Mostly I look back and think that what I learned helped me get along. But I have to say there were other lessons that weren't so nice. I mentioned earlier that I'm not much of a joiner. I'm not. Ever since I was a kid, I've avoided joining or belonging to clubs or groups.

I always try to remember that not everyone is nice or fair or respectful. It doesn't mean that I am constantly mad at, or untrusting of, other people and their motives. But it does make me a lot more careful. (Remember my first day and all those unwritten rules that stalked me for years?)

It started like this. Ron was a Cub Scout, so when he moved on to the Boy Scouts I tried to follow in his footsteps—mostly because of the glowing reports he gave me of the fun I couldn't have because I wasn't a Scout, like camping, meetings, Scout knives, and other Scouting activities. I already had his old uniform so I joined as soon as I could. I never really connected with the other Scouts—maybe it's because I was the only haole in the troop, or maybe it was just my attitude. But to be fair, it wasn't all me. It didn't take me long to get tired of being the Cinderella of the troop, with no fairy godmother in sight. The Scouts operated out of an old clubhouse in the middle of town, so it needed ongoing cleaning and upkeep. I understood that, but I got really tired of cleaning toilets and scrubbing and cleaning and pulling weeds alone while the other guys did fun Scouting stuff. What made it worse were the benign smiles of the Scoutmaster when he kept assigning me to latrine duty or some other distasteful chore, without trying to even things out.

When I asked why I was always getting the dirty jobs, he unfailingly acted surprised that I would even ask and replied that we all had to pull our weight in the Scouts. But he didn't seem to think I could pull my weight in a different and more Scouting way. So, I kept cleaning and weeding and wasn't able to get any of the badges that the others earned for things like tying knots, building fires, and other things I really wanted to do.

I'd had enough and was getting ready to bail. But at one meeting we were told that the annual Makahiki event ticket sales were coming up and we should prepare by preselling tickets. Best of all, there were prizes for the number of tickets sold. Hokey, cheap, easily broken prizes. Prizes like crystals that never really grew in water, sponge animals that grew when they were soaked, plastic divers with cavities in their fins for baking soda, and other useless stuff. But they were prizes!

I took the Scoutmaster at his word and the next day after school I started preselling tickets. To be fair, I didn't even try to sell tickets to the families, friends, and neighbors of the other Scouts. But everyone else was fair game and I took my composition book and started canvasing the town.

Eventually I had tickets preordered from just about everyone I approached. I never knew what the other Scouts were doing, but later the people who'd ordered tickets from me told me that about one week before the deadline, the other Scouts had started coming around, only to find that I had already been there.

I collected my tickets, delivered them, and gave the money I collected to the Scoutmaster, who seemed kind of surprised at the amount of my sales, but just took the money and never said anything.

Then came the big event, the cookout and the awarding of prizes. I thought it was going to be great—a bonfire on the beach, hot dogs and fellowship, and best of all, no latrines to clean. I just knew this time I was going to be rewarded for my efforts, and I was proud of what I had accomplished. I thought maybe, just maybe, there was a future in Scouting for me.

It didn't take long for that balloon to burst. It was quite a shock when my Scoutmaster, without any advance warning or even talking to me beforehand, proceeded to tell everyone there that he had to award the prizes—but that he really didn't want to, because the boy who had won all of them had not sold his tickets in the "spirit of Scouting," and it hurt him to award the prizes.

I looked around, trying to figure out who had committed this dastardly deed. That "spirit of Scouting" thing sounded really ominous, especially since an adult said it and none us knew what he meant. I sure didn't. But I found out, of course, that it was me. I guess nobody else had taken him seriously when he told us to go out and presell, and I had won all the prizes. What was even worse was that all of the parents were there and didn't know the truth about what was going on; they thought I was a cheat. But he wasn't going to tell them the truth, and I knew they wouldn't believe me even if I got the chance to tell my side of the story.

I learned then that sometimes life wasn't even in the neighborhood of fair and people remember things the way they want, even if it isn't true or just. When I went up to get my prizes, I reminded the Scoutmaster that I had only done what he told us to and asked him what was wrong with that. He replied that wasn't what he said, but we both knew he was lying.

I took the prizes, retired the shirt, and quit the Cub Scouts. The saddest thing was that if he had just talked to me instead of blindsiding me, I would have been glad to share the prizes.

I guess I didn't learn very fast. Three or four years later, one of my friends asked me to join the Boy Scouts with him. I did. Maybe I was delusional and thought that this time it would be different. It was, but not the parts where I dug latrines, covered the latrines, and did most of the dirty work and menial chores at our annual camp while the other Scouts again did Scout activities like tying knots, hacking at wood with real axes and making fires, shooting bows and arrows and BB guns, and other fun Scouting stuff.

When I questioned the division of labor, again the Scoutmaster—a different Scoutmaster—told me we all had to contribute where we were best suited or some BS like that. He must have gotten the CliffsNotes from the Cub Scout leader. But I soldiered on. Camp lasted a while and I was still hoping to have some fun. Besides, all the other Scouts kept telling me what a good time they were having.

At camp, the Scoutmaster's son was in my tent with two other Scouts. One night, with lots of giggling and snickering, he produced a small hip bottle of cheap whiskey he had lifted from his father's liquor stash. He opened it and passed it around for us to smell, and we all agreed to have a capful. It tasted terrible, but we all took one for the brotherhood. That was okay. We each felt real grown up, and I could almost feel the hair starting to grow on my chest.

What wasn't okay was that someone heard what was going on and ratted us out to the Scoutmaster. I shouldn't have been surprised when he ripped open the tent flap and started in on us, railing against the demon rum and questioning our characters. After the tirade, he asked who'd brought the bottle. To my chagrin, my tentmates, all three of them, pointed my way and proclaimed it was me and that I had forced them to drink with me. Silly me. In the combined glow of fellowship and whiskey, I felt like we were brothers in arms and would all take the hit together. I was prepared to suffer torture or extra duty or punishment before I would rat out a fellow Scout and the real culprit. But I guess they weren't, or maybe their brotherhood didn't include me. The Scoutmaster grabbed my arm to march me out of the tent in disgrace to be taken home. When I was getting my stuff, I told the Scoutmaster they were lying, his son was the one who brought the whiskey and we all had taken a hit. I also pointed out it would have been hard for one of me to force the three of them to take a drink.

I'm sure he recognized the bottle and inside really knew who was responsible, but true to form he went to the dark side and blamed me for the whole mess. I walked out with my head high, despite the snickering and taunting of my "fellow" Scouts.

When my mother came to bail me out, I left with my Scouting career in tatters and, according to the Scoutmaster, as a disgrace and a delinquent without the moral or ethical standards required of a Scout. I told her what happened. She heard me out and believed me, but we both agreed there was no point in continuing my Scouting career.

I did feel better when I confronted the guys in my tent in front of some other Scouts at school and called them gutless, lying cowards who would sell someone out to save their own asses. They slunk off and I felt a little better. At least everyone knew there were two sides to that story.

I kept having similar experiences, like with school sports and even in the Civil Air Patrol, but eventually I figured it out. Suffice it to say, I learned I'm not a joiner. I wasn't a loner, I had friends, but as I grew up I have always been reluctant to be part of a team or organization because I learned there are bad eggs in every batch, and rotten eggs that, against all that is right and good in this world, more often than not float to the top.

Funny thing about growing up like I did: There weren't many adults in positions of authority—like teachers, Scoutmasters, and others—who treated me and other kids with respect.

Oh, they demanded respect, but it sure didn't go both ways. I've always been the kind of kid, and adult, that would try to do anything reasonable, if asked. But I never appreciated people telling me what to do and expecting me to just do what they told me. As an example, when I was attending Catholic school in Hilo, not one of the nuns who had a problem with the way I was behaving ever sat me down and explained why my behavior was a problem and simply asked me to help them out. Being me, I would have had no choice, I would have tried to help. Instead they demanded, bullied, never explained, and tried to punish me by shaming me and using me as an example of a bad kid. Like that was going to work. Kind of sad really.

There were some other nails in that coffin and more good times to come. Looking back, I can understand why I am an optimist; I foolishly have always believed I have the power to make things better and fairer if I stay true to my values. That's a belief I've never regretted.

On another wonderful day at school in Pāhala, one of my teachers called me up in front of the class. I didn't know what he wanted, but I went and stood where he indicated, facing everyone. I wasn't sure why I was up there; I hadn't done anything really bad, like missing my homework or getting into any fights. But I soon found out when, without any warning, he proceeded to tell the other kids that I was an example of what they never wanted to be—sloppy, for instance, and other bad stuff.

Listening to him, you'd have thought I was the son of the devil, and messy too. Now I knew I wasn't the messiest or sloppiest kid in that class. The truth was that I was not neat, but I sure wasn't the worst in the class.

He droned on for a while, but while he was speaking all I could think of was what an ass he was. After that, nothing he said had any credibility with me. I just ignored him. I never even bothered to tell my mother. She didn't need another battle to fight for me. I just ignored him for the rest of the year and made a special effort not to be neat or organized, and to live down to his expectations.

And it just kept coming. My next teacher, in a futile and twisted attempt at discipline, organized student firing squads complete with plastic Luger water pistols and blindfolds for offending students, those of us who weren't punished for slight transgressions by holding rubbish cans full of basketballs over our heads till we dropped them, or made to hold pencils with our arms extended till our arms gave out.

I guess it could have been worse. He seemed to relish threatening us with the punishments he got as a child, like kneeling on uncooked rice for hours. I guess he was no saint either as a child. But he didn't have to take it out on us. We really weren't that bad.

His firing squads were reserved for the real hardened criminals, like students who couldn't do three months of math homework in a single night, or those that he felt questioned his authority. Worse, those firing squads were made up of "good children" that he deputized and instructed to drench the offending students with the water pistols. All this and we even had to face them with blindfolds on our faces after a reading of our crimes. Of course, as one of the offenders in the grand tradition of Beau Geste and the like, I refused the blindfold and went to my doom like a man with a sneer on my face and a light heart. All I needed was a candy cigarette to complete the tableau.

But it's not all bad. Most people are good and the things that happened to me made me determined to treat people the way I would have liked them to treat me. I like to think that's something I've done for most of my life and is a big part of the code I live by.

I do have to be honest, at least with myself. I really did cause a lot of my own problems. I've always known there is more than one path to take and more than one way to get from point A to point B, at least when I was a kid. I made my own choices knowing I would have to take the consequences. And I always knew that if I just kept quiet, did what they wanted, and said what they expected, everything would be just fine.

But that just didn't feel right. I couldn't be that kind of kid, the kind they wanted. Maybe it's because I read so many books where the heroes overcame impossible odds, or maybe because deep down inside I always knew who I was and wasn't going to sell myself out for an easier time. Maybe I'll never know, but I know this: I wouldn't change anything, the good, the bad, and sometimes the ugly.

CHAPTER 21

Television and the Beginning of the End

I guess this is where I break ranks with myself and get on the old soapbox. Hang with me, there's a good reason why I'm going down this road.

Sometimes, in my memories, it seems like Ka'ū is a mist-shrouded mythical region, with Pāhala kind of like Shangri-La; only the people were testy and it got really hot in summer, really cold in winter, and much of the time the mosquitoes wouldn't let you sleep unmolested. But I just can't tell you how great it was to grow up there, in that place and in that time, with those people.

When we moved into our first house in Pāhala, I still remember Pop asking for the key. He was taken aback when the guy showing us the plantation house said, "No key, no need. Nobody's going to mess with your house." But he was right, for a long time.

There wasn't much to do in Pāhala at night. Those of us who liked to read had it great; it was quiet, except for the occasional car passing by or the sound of the wind or rain on our tin roof. Very soothing. We had record players and sometimes would listen to 45 or 33 1/3 records (you youngsters are going to have to look those up) on our record players. The sound of those scratchy songs that we played over and over until we knew the words by heart and could sing along. I still remember the first record I ever got, *G.T.O.* by Ronny and the Daytonas. Ron got *Ride The Wild Surf* by Jan and Dean.

But you get the idea. We amused ourselves. There was another nightly ritual we all did most every night that it wasn't raining. Pāhala could get hot and, with nothing much going on when the town buttoned up for the night, most of the neighbors would leave houses that were still hot from the day and stroll up and down the streets in front of our homes, usually in our pajamas. I guess it could sound pretty creepy, a bunch of people milling about aimlessly in their PJs and talking about nothing.

Nothing could be further from the truth. That was one of the ties that bound us together as a community. We talked to each other and no matter what, we valued one another and looked forward to checking in at the end of the day. That's when we let go of all of the heat, troubles, and problems and just hung out with people who cared about us and whom we cared about as well.

Looking back, I think those were the golden years. Sometimes in my mind, if I try really hard, I can still see a golden glow over the town when I remember those days.

People got along with each other. I can't remember any fights, angry voices, or problems between neighbors back then. But a sea change was coming.

We had some radio reception, but not much since Mauna Loa was between Pāhala and any station within range. Sometimes we could get a little static-filled music if we kept fiddling with the radio dial. I always figured the wind was blowing the radio waves just beyond the spot where we could actually get reception. Trips to town weren't much better. Pop liked to listen to KUMU from Honolulu; we called it elevator music. He didn't demonize rock and roll; he just wouldn't listen to it.

That's where everything stood until word spread through the town via the coconut wireless: Someone had bought a television set. We knew about and had seen them prominently displayed in stores in Hilo, but not in our town. But I guess every dam breaks some time.

The rumor was true, and after they got their television that family stopped taking their evening walks. Then they invited us over to watch. Honestly, it looked and sounded like a polar bear in a snowstorm. Nothing but shadowy figures in the snow and static, with an occasional almost word uttered by the polar bear. The guy who owned it was constantly running out to adjust the forty-foot antenna it took to get any reception at all. But he was convinced he was having a great time. I guess a lot of other folk thought so too and scrimped and saved to get their own little slice of televisionland.

That was the beginning of the end. It started slowly, but family by family was picked off and the number of families that stopped walking and visiting and instead stayed inside grew larger and larger. Then Pop got his own television—a brand-new top-of-the-line console. Then we stayed inside too. After dinner when the TV was turned on, I just took a book and read in my room unless there was something interesting, which wasn'tt very often. Personally, I got really tired of Pop telling us that he had met Myron Floren, Lawrence Welk's accordion player, every damn time he appeared on *The Lawrence Welk Show*, year after year. Ed Sullivan wasn't bad; at least he had the Beatles and Elvis on his show.

But fate, cruel fate stepped in. Pop was pretty discouraged when one of my sisters spilled water on his brand-new console, complete with radio, record player, and TV. That would have been okay except she got worried that she had ruined it and turned it on. I wasn't there, but I heard about the *snap*, *crackle*, and *pop*, then the blank screen. Pop wasn't happy, but he got another TV somehow, and we kids were happy to use whatever worked on the console for years. He got better reception with the other TV anyway.

So it went. I always thought the town took a long downhill slide into a TV wasteland, but there was no going back. Pandora's box without the hope just about covers it.

That's progress for you.

Like cell phones and computers. Someone much wiser than I am figured out that cost isn't what you pay for something, it's what you give up to get it. Kind of puts it into perspective, at least for me.

CHAPTER 22

Kids, Don't Try This at Home*

Playing was serious business. There were games we'd play with others, team sports like "bang, make!" and games we'd play with one or two others. Looking back, I do feel the passage of time and see the changes in our culture. Honestly, I do think those changes have taken something out of being a kid and learning how to take risks and deal with the consequences, something very precious and valuable and unfortunately something all too rare in these days of televisions, computers, and cell phones.

Now this is the part where you should pay attention. I'm sure I'm not the first person—or the last—who will tell you this, but if you get anything out of this vignette, this should be it: Fun is better if it's shared, and even more important, it's not right to try to have fun for yourself by taking it away from someone else. For what it's worth, I've had a lot of fun and I'm still having it. I guess you can tell that from what's in these pages, but I always tried to include other people in my fun and never tried to hog it all to myself.

Some of the "toys" we used would definitely be in the "don't try this at all" category, or the all-inclusive threat of my childhood, "You'll put someone's eye out." Even though I never saw a one-eyed kid, there must have been legions of them lurking out there, just out of sight. Or at least there should have been from the way adults kept bringing them up as cautionary tales to scare the fun out of us.

I'll freely admit that lots of what we did for fun was risky and not advisable. I'll never know how much of what we were getting into my parents knew about. But if they knew, they still let us have our adventures

---

*That's my disclaimer. If you try to do what we did, you're on your own.

and our victories and inevitably let us deal with and learn from our failures. I guess that's what growing up is all about. But that being said, it was fun, lots of fun. Danger adds a little spice to an otherwise ordinary life. Nobody I knew got badly hurt, or turned out badly, because of the things we did as kids. That's how we learned the things we could but shouldn't do, the things we needed to do, the consequences of our actions, and what we could accomplish if we tried and didn't give up.

Our heroes, taken from books, comics, movies and our games, reflected our belief that those were the kind of people we should be: honest, brave, skillful, and not afraid to take risks.

A side note on our heroes: It seems to be fashionable for some of us to periodically debunk and strip the luster from past heroes. Fair enough. Usually there is some justification. The reality of those guys wasn't always pretty and they did some real nasty things to other people.

But that part of them wasn't the reason we looked up to them as our heroes. We looked up to them because of the way we learned about them and saw them portrayed in books and on the silver screen. We learned they were brave, we believed they were honest and kept their word, and we knew they tried and did great things in spite of almost insurmountable obstacles. I'm not convinced those are bad lessons for a kid to learn. But in the end, they were people and, just like you and me, there was a mix of good and bad in each of them. I always try to remember they lived in another era, in different times when people lived by different codes. Not all of them passed the test of time or lived the way they should have. I'd like to think we've evolved and changed for the better along the way, but I'm not sure that's what happened.

Somehow, it doesn't seem fair to take away a hero unless you can replace him or her with another one. At least not to me. But as my life unfolded, it turned out that I never lacked for heroes. My heroes included people that I could see and talk with and learn the same kind of lessons from. And they were right next door and lived in the same town! They watched over me and helped me grow into the person I am today. Because of them, I still try to be brave, honest, and keep my word—and maybe someday I'll do something great.

From my earliest days in Hilo until we moved to Pāhala, as soon as we were old enough Ron and I would be dropped off on Saturday morning at the Palace Theatre to amuse ourselves with the *Mickey Mouse Club* and whatever movie Disney chose to grace us with that Saturday.

My personal favorite was Davy Crockett. But sometimes it would be Robin Hood, Daniel Boone, or any other larger-than-life hero that made us feel bigger, braver, and stronger than we really were.

We made swords out of any scraps of wood that could be peeled and made to look even remotely like a sword, such as branches from our hedge, bamboo, or any wood laying around. We'd spend hours with our dull Scout knives whittling the perfect sword, wearing our dashing Robin Hood hats with pheasant feathers, no less. But wait, Merry Men! What's a sword without an accompanying bow and some arrows? (I can feel you cringing. Projectile throwing implement—not the eyes, not the eyes! Kids with sharp things?! Next thing you know they'll be running with scissors, or maybe cats and dogs will live together in peace, or pigs will fly or something else will happen that is against the laws of nature and good sense. Bah humbug!)

Relax, we knew better. We wanted to have fun, not hurt each other. We made our bows from supple wood or bamboo, strung with fishing line. We made arrows from fairly straight branches tipped with bits of tin or just sharpened. We never fletched our arrows and they never went where we aimed them, and we knew better than to aim them at each other. We hit each other's swords but rarely each other and we had tons of fun. Fun that we created and acted out, from our imaginations and our collective belief that having fun together was way more fun than playing alone.

We had toy guns, including some we made ourselves from wood. Rifles and pistols and, for the lucky or creative, machine guns. We'd research the profiles of the various guns and saw or carve until we got close. We supplied the sound effects too. With all of that, we'd slip off into the forest, form into teams, and play army, cowboys and (well, you know, but I'm not going to say it), or any other game that pitted two groups of children in not-so-mortal combat.

The forest provided a network of trails, hiding places, and lots of places to ambush our foes or fort up and wait them out.

Sometimes we would get toy guns for Christmas. They never worked for very long but their usefulness far outlived their ability to function. If

I close my eyes and lean back in my creaking, 1950s vintage oak office chair, I can still see in my memory my brace of toy cap pistols, my trusted companions on many a foray into the forest to engage in desperate battles against impossible odds to defend the right and punish the evildoer.

Right about now is probably a good time to describe the stores in Pāhala, since that's where we procured most of the things we used for play. Early on, there were stores spread out through the town—two stores and a barbershop near the post office, a row of stores down the mill road, and a couple down in the camps below the mill.

Mostly they sold the bare essentials—milk, bread, meat, and the like. But they also sold other things, like toy slingshots, pocketknives, pocket watches, corncob pipes, soda, ice cream, comics, and candy. The prices, by today's standards, were incredible and the things we bought were way more durable than what we can buy today. For a dollar, one single dollar, I could get twenty Hershey bars, or ten sodas, or ten comics, or a Scout knife (Kamp King with four blades), or one corncob pipe but no tobacco, or a pocket watch guaranteed to run till you passed the door on your way out. (There was a saying: busier than a one-armed man with a dollar watch and a seven-year itch. You can believe that one). The proprietors always asked us if our parents knew we were buying knives and the like. We always said yes. But when we were asked by an adult where we got the knives and such, we always

Saddle up, pardner!

said from "a friend." But we never got busted for hurting each other. As I said, they were tools, not weapons, and we knew the difference.

One other thing the shops sold every year was firecrackers, lots of firecrackers. I guess the original thought was that we would pop them at New Year's to scare away the demons, but really it was just a lot of fun.

There were four kinds I remember best. The smallest was called Camel Brand. This came in little packets that held about two hundred or more firecrackers. They were the cheapest so we mostly bought them, with our parents' approval of course, at least that's what we told the owner of the store. The next size up was Duck Brand. Those were a bit more powerful and we were way more careful using them; they could do a lot of damage to an unwary hand. There were what we called "cracker balls," small teardrop shaped tissue wrapped bits that we threw against a hard surface to pop. We often used them with our slingshots when we played "bang, make!" They didn't do much damage, but they could smart when one hit. The last kind, and my favorite, was the penny rockets. That's what they were; little rockets that cost a penny each. Think of it, all that potential for mayhem and chaos for a single penny, and in the hands of a kid. The trick with the rockets was to light them and hang on as long as possible, then fling them at whatever the target was, quite often another kid. But we all survived and nobody ever got really hurt, just some smarting fingers and injured pride. We heard about the legendary cherry bombs, and I once saw one, but those weren't very accessible to us kids. Maybe because of the urban legend of the kid who flushed one down the toilet at the school and blew things to hell in a hand basket.

In Hilo, it got better, way better. There was a surplus store that sold used military gear that made up the major components of our play equipment. We got helmets, holsters, belts, knapsacks, bayonets, machetes, canteens, hats, and lots of other stuff, and it was all affordable.

There was also a Kress Store in Hilo, with a real toy department carrying all of the toys that we lusted after in the Sears catalog. If we were lucky, once in a while our parents would spring for a toy that they approved of that we really wanted. The store even had a talking mynah bird, but when he started to respond to customers' hellos with one of several totally inappropriate and obscene replies, store management made him disappear. Seemed that some of the kids in town were spending time teaching the mynah the wrong kind of phrases. I guess it's a little bit of a surprise to say, "Hello, bird!" and get a "Kiss my ass!" in reply. We thought it was kind of funny. I often wondered if they have a home for retired mynahs who learned to swear, where they sit around in their cages prompting each other to belt out utterances that would make a sailor blush.

The girls got things like dolls that talked or, my personal nemesis, the Seasick Sea Serpent. That one came equipped with a plastic ring that could be pulled, at which the doll or Seasick Sea Serpent would say in a weird, scratchy voice, "I'm coming, Beany Boy!" or some other inane phrase. I got so tired of hearing the same old "I'm coming, Beany Boy!" over and over, but of course everyone had to pull it time and time again. That damn thing wouldn't break. Even after the green velour sea serpent skin had taken on a shine it was never intended to have, with a hue that I still can't describe, it still responded to every pull with the same old "I'm coming, Beany Boy!" Thankfully it disappeared one day, but I'd be willing to bet that if someone ages from now found it in a landfill or floating at sea, if the cord was pulled, they would hear a hearty, "I'm coming, Beany Boy!"

While I'm on this diversion I might as well describe the fortune-telling eight ball, which looked like a small bowling ball with a triangular panel that, when shook, revealed a fortune. I can't remember what the fortunes were, but I don't think any of them ever came true.

Typically, at Christmas, Ron and I would ask for pocketknives or bowie knives from the P & S December catalog. We got them, along with essential things like *mukluks* (moccasins, for us woods runners and Scouts), holsters, aluminum copies of World War II pistols, and other stuff we used in our war games. I sometimes think Pop let us have the knives for three very credible reasons: they were cheap, we never hurt anyone, and to keep his kitchen knives from vanishing into the forest. Poor guy, he never could keep a full set of knives. So, the gear was not very safe, but just what we needed.

It gets better.

Pop had guns. But to be fair, just about everyone had one or two for hunting or target shooting. Nobody thought much of it, and I never knew anyone who said they felt threatened by having them around.

Remember, just about every grown man in Pāhala had served in one of the branches of the military during World War II or the Korean conflict. They rarely, if ever, talked about their experiences, but sometimes we'd see a medal they earned or something they'd brought back with them from the war.

One of my father's best friends spent four years as a tail gunner in a B-29 bombing Germany; another served in the Pacific as a marine. I knew a couple who were paratroopers who had jumped or glided into France on D-Day. Many of the men on the plantation served in the 442nd. But wherever they served and whatever they did, they always seemed to have a quiet confidence in their abilities and what they could accomplish together, like our swimming pool. They valued their families and friends, and they were kind to kids. They drank a lot of beer, but none of them ever hurt a kid or even got into a fight that I knew of. And those men who had used guns to defend themselves and their country were the ones that taught us how to use guns and to respect the threat they posed to the careless. The adage that sticks in my mind is what they always said: "The gun is always loaded." I've never forgotten.

Those were the grown-ups we looked up to and, for me, the kind of person I've tried to be as I get older. I haven't always hit the mark—I guess these stories will prove that—but I've never given up trying.

I realize in these trying times that lots of things that were normal back then have been demonized and somehow have morphed from tools to implements of death and destruction, and there are people who think they should all be taken away and destroyed. Suffice it to say, I disagree. Nobody was ever made safe by taking things away from people who haven't misused them. The bad guys just find ways to get them, or switch to another way of harming people with what's available.

If this doesn't sit well with you, I suggest taking a page from Mark Twain and other writers who we consider great chroniclers of their lives and times. They wrote some very controversial stuff and used some very racist language. They would probably know better now, but they didn't live now; they lived then and that was their culture and reality.

Ditto for me.

CHAPTER 23

Games

Well, back to the story. We also played other games. Sometimes we would play hide and seek. It got quite interesting, especially when we would get together before the game and try to agree on rules. The rules always ended up getting very flexible, with lots of gray areas that we each tried to use to our advantage.

One particular game stands out in my mind. We were playing in the backyard of one of my friends and had just chosen the seeker. The rest of us hiders had scattered and were running for cover as fast as we could. One of us didn't make it; he found an old cesspool that nobody knew was there. That wasn't so bad, but what was bad, very bad, was that he found it by breaking through the top and falling in up to his chest. We found out something had happened when an army of huge roaches exploded out of the ground like a swarm of locusts, like they had been lurking under the ground for years waiting for their moment to attack any small child who was nearby.

We all panicked, but it was worse for my friend. He was stuck in the middle of the cesspool. Worse, since the roof was weak and crumbling, he couldn't put any weight on it to climb out. Every time he tried it just got worse. It was bad, really bad. He was calling for help, but the rest of us kids were too afraid of joining him or getting eaten by the hordes of roaches to do anything besides scream loudly, especially the girls. He told me later that he would have just climbed out, but since he was in the middle and it was round there was nothing that he could use for a purchase for his legs. There he cowered, covering his face with his hands as the roaches crawled all over and engulfed him, until the swarm finally slowed to a drizzle of smaller roaches and we were able to find an adult to help.

It didn't get better any time soon. The kids were screaming, my friend was hysterical, and when the adults came on the scene there was a spirited and technical discussion about the lack of strength of the top of the pool and the urgent need to get him out as quickly as possible without anyone else falling in with him. Finally, someone came up with a plan after about thirty endless seconds of shouting at him not to panic. Way too late; we were all panicked. I can't even imagine how that felt—gives me the willies just writing about it even after all these years. They got a couple of long boards that spanned the weak ground and two brave souls eased him out and lifted him up, one on each side. He was covered with what looked and smelled like twenty-year-old—well you can figure it out. Shaken but unbowed and otherwise unharmed, he was hosed off in the yard and marched off to a bath. The rest of us left. The fun was over but the memory lingers.

The next day they brought in a bulldozer and plowed the cesspool under and covered it up with a grand pile of dirt we played in until the next big rain. Pop told us later that the cesspool was made from a section of culvert blocked up on both ends and it just got old, tired, and weak. But we all wondered what those roaches were living on. They were huge! Way bigger than anything I've seen since. I'm not even going to say how big they were—nobody would believe me anyway. But I wonder where they went after they were set free?

Since we had a huge field at the school, there were other things to play on, like swing sets that rose some fifteen feet into the air, with chains and seats made from old conveyor belts that were indestructible. A kid could really swing on those things. Once, in a delusional moment, one of my schoolmates decided he was going to make history by being the only kid ever to swing completely over the top of a swing set, all the way around. He got two or three of us to stand next to the swing and boost him every time he came by, ever higher and higher. It really looked like he could make it, but fate intervened. On his last swing, he got almost straight up, but then, with no more momentum, he just fell, straight down, until he hit the end of the chain and bounced off. They said he was lucky he didn't hit the bar or break his neck. No more of that for us.

We also played hopscotch, endless games of hopscotch, on the painted game boards on the school walkway. There was one every fifteen feet or so and we played every day. The rules were simple. First, throw your *kini*. (The best was a chain, 'cause no bounce. Next best was two of the stems from the trees near the school. We used our pocketknives—no expulsion, believe it or not—to split one of the stems and thread the other through the slit to make a cross. Not the greatest, but these were easy to throw and pretty much stayed where they hit.) Then, starting at one, go around the board until someone finishes. That's about all I remember, but it was great fun.

We also played tetherball. The best part I remember is learning how to serve so the ball flies low at the serve and over my opponent's head, leaving me to finish the game pretty quickly.

Along with the other gear, someone had welded up several pipe jungle gyms and a large wheel with spokes and bars along the sides that we could use to move the wheel around the schoolyard. Kind of like the famous and ill-fated British Great Panjandrum of World War II. The wheel was really fun when it rained heavily and a low spot in the schoolyard flooded. Then, it was two or three of us running along the spokes until we had a good head of steam and steering the wheel into the water at great speed. What fun!

We also rode bikes, those of us who had them. We'd take turns so everyone got some riding time in. We'd jump ramps, play chicken (not a great thing if nobody chickens), and, my personal favorite, riding pell-mell down the main street that fronted our house as fast as we could go, braking at the last minute with those awesome coaster brakes. We'd take clothespins and cards (plastic was best, but Pop got real mad) and let the cards run over the spokes to make a sound like a weird motorcycle.

But as often happens with the plans of children, it didn't always go well. One day, bike-less, I was enviously watching the fun when one of my older friends suggested he could make a run down the hill with me sitting on his handlebars. I was a little leery, but this was a kid who could do things like throw a knife between a kid's toes and never miss and other useful stuff, so I foolishly put my safety in his hands.

Oh, it began like many of my other adventures, with an incredible rush when we started down the hill, me perched on the handlebars with nothing between me and the road but trust. We proceeded down the hill with screams of delight until the front of the bike started weaving from side to side. It shifted to fear when my friend yelled that the front wheel was letting go and he couldn't steer. It ended in disaster when all the spokes gave up at once, throwing me onto the road hands first. Luckily, all I got was road rash on my hands. But he never stopped blaming me for the damage to his bike. Totally unjustified. I really wasn't that heavy, and it was his idea.

We were always on the lookout for things we could use to play with. I guess my mother was too. One day we came home from school and there was a brand spanking new wooden shipping container in our back yard. I mean a huge container; six feet high, six feet wide, and about twelve to fourteen feet long. I know what you're thinking, but give it up, that was one of the best toys we ever had been given, even if it was a little on the big side. It became the Alamo, Fort Apache, a bunker, and, when stood up on end, even a castle and climbing wall. We played with that thing for months until it finally gave up the ghost, then we took it apart and used the boards for other stuff.

Mom had a unique gift for gifts. Somehow, she always seemed to give us things that we had to make work. Like fifty feet of manila rope, which we used to make swings, to rappel down tree trunks, and even to make a tightrope between the clothesline poles that we used for a very short and wobbly time.

Once she even gave me a real bow and several arrows that someone in South Dakota sent her (I'll never know the backstory to that one). I used to practice with it in the backyard. Sadly, I didn't have it for very long. One day while I was Robin Hooding the pear tree, my younger brother said he wanted a turn. He'd had one turn before, in fact several befores, and was never able to pull the bowstring back far enough to shoot anything. So I told him no. He proceeded to run over to my target and jump back and forth from behind the trees on both sides of the target, taunting me. I told him to stop. I didn't want to hurt him, but I didn't stop either—my bad. Then came the disharmonic juxtaposition of my arrow in flight and my younger brother jumping out from behind the tree, right in the way. I had let go already and all I could do was watch in cringing disbelief, hoping against hope that it would miss. There was some hope; mostly I did miss, as I wasn't very good with that thing. But go figure, cruel fate, with a meaty *thunk*, the arrow hit him and stuck in his right shoulder. I looked at it, he looked at it, then he looked at me and said, "You shot me." Yup, I had. Then he said, "I'm telling Mom," in a calm, threatening tone and walked into the house with the arrow still sticking out of his shoulder. Shortly thereafter, Mom marched him out, arrow still in his shoulder and yelled, "Did you do this?" When I tried to explain, she yanked the arrow out and proceeded to hit me with it until it broke, all in complete silence. Then she took the bow and broke that over her knee, then the rest of the arrows and broke them over her knee, all in threatening silence. But I could hear was the unsaid "Wait till I get back." Then without saying anything more, she marched him back to the car and off to the hospital to get fixed up. He came back with a smug look and a bandage. I just waited for the other shoe to drop. Somehow it never did, and I guess she told Pop, but he never said a word about it, I guess they thought it was handled. I certainly did. When things calmed down, I got a chance to explain what happened, but she knew where the elephant in the room was and she asked me why I didn't just stop shooting. I had to admit, she was right and I knew it. All I could say was I was sorry.

Sometimes our play took a turn for the worse. I found that out one day when I spotted Ron running with two larger boys behind him, close behind; they looked like they had mayhem on their minds.

Ron dashed across from the school field to our yard with his pursuers hot on his heels. A scared Ron could outrun a cheetah any day, even if the cheetah got a head start.

I'll never really know why I did it, but when the first boy started to come into our yard I yelled, "You can't come in here. That's trespassing and it's against the law. I'll have you arrested." To my surprise, he and his friend stopped. I guess it was the big word linked with law and arrest. Ron wisely kept going. But I stood my ground and moved over near the edge of the yard. When I got there, the big kid, a bully I knew well, started yelling at me. Then I told him he couldn't come in the yard without being invited. He yelled at me to invite him in, but there was no chance of that happening. Then he said he was going to punch my face. I walked up to him and stood well outside of punching range and told him I would not be visiting him in jail. He stopped and asked me what I was talking about. He looked a little confused when I told him it was against the law to hit a kid with glasses because splinters could blind them. He told me to take my glasses off so he could hit me. Guess what? No fool, I told him I wasn't going to do that because if I took them off he would hit me. It seemed to be too much for him, probably an information overload, so he and his chum left. When I went into the house, Ron asked what had happened, but all I would tell him was that we talked and they went away, hoping he would attribute godlike powers to me and treat me less like a little brother.

Luckily, it blew over by the time we went back to school and nothing else ever happened. Later, much later, while Ron and I were sitting together watching a Kona sunset, he asked me what had really happened. Then he told me the kids all knew I read a lot and probably that kid believed I knew stuff he didn't or wasn't going to take the chance I was right.

We also played other games like "crack bat." Crack bat is a game any number of kids from two to a bunch could play. I guess it was a substitute for baseball; we never had enough kids to make one team, let alone two. To play crack bat, we would *jan ken po* (rock paper scissors) to determine who would bat first. (No, I'm not going to explain jan ken po in detail, but here's a hint: Paper covers rock, rock breaks scissors, scissors cuts paper and you can take it from there.) Once we had a batter, whoever it was would take the ball (any ball that could be hit) and a bat (or stick or whatever) and belly up to the figurative plate. Then, they would hit the ball as hard as they could. If it went up and someone caught it, they were out and would be replaced as the batter by whoever caught the ball. If it landed on the ground, whoever got the ball rolled the ball toward the bat, laying on the ground, and if they hit it, they replaced the batter. It's a great game for kids; no teams, no fighting, just good clean fun.

We also played marbles. I was never good at marbles and lost every game I ever played, along with my marbles because when we lost, we lost the marbles. We made walkie-talkies out of tin cans and string. We tied string to tin cans and used them to walk on and we made stilts out of boards that we could use to run around on. Years later I made a pair for my daughter, inspired by a child's book. When I finished them, my wife dared me to use them. Total victory. Though much portlier now, I still had it. I could stay up, walk forward, backward, in circles, and, I think, look damn good doing it. Kids back then had lots of fun with those stilts.

But it wasn't all play; we did science stuff, too. Here's one trick that still makes me wonder who figured it out. Kind of like, how did they get all those little fish lined up so neatly in the *bagoong* jar, all lined up head to tail facing the same way? I always pictured little ladies with chopsticks, licking each one and pasting them on the side of the bottle, round and round until they got them all. You get the idea.

But this is what I am really talking about. One day Ron came to me and said, "You gotta see this." By then I was a little gun shy, I guess by now you can figure out why. But this time all he was holding was a medicine bottle with a black cap and a box of matches. So, what the heck, I said, "Okay, what is it?" Then he showed me. First he carefully peeled the striking paper off one side of the matchbox. Then he lay it on the black plastic medicine bottle cover and set it on fire. It smoldered for a while and went out. After that he said it was ready and led me into a dark closet. I could hardly wait; I wanted to see where this was going. After we closed the door, it got dark and he started rubbing his finger on the medicine bottle cap and, lo and behold, it started to glow. It glowed an evil yellow green until he stopped rubbing, then slowly faded back to nothing. I thought that was pretty neat. But somewhere along the way I had to ask myself, who the heck figured that out? And more importantly, why? I'll never know.

But what I do know and remember is how much fun we had. I wish everyone could have that much fun in their lives. But I figure I used up a whole lot of other people's quotas in my life. Maybe that's where grumpy people come from. If that is so, I'm sorry. If I could give it back I would. I've had plenty.

CHAPTER 24

Gravity Has Its Way

No doubt I've said it way too much, but I like to read. There's something about the feel of a good book in the hand and fodder for the mind, whether it's real or not.

I read everything I could in Pāhala. Eventually I read every book in the library I thought was even remotely interesting, and some, out of desperation, that I didn't. To be fair, it wasn't a big library, but it was all we had.

We had a librarian I will always remember. She's probably not with us anymore, but if I could I would have nominated her for sainthood. She was an adult I looked up to and respected, not for what she said, but for the way she treated and cared for people. After I had read everything, I spent my hours in the library endlessly searching the library shelves in the vain hope I had missed something interesting. I guess she was watching, or maybe she got tired of my asking what books were new that week. One day she called me over to the counter and set seven books down on the counter, seven books I had never seen but would have wanted to read if I knew they existed. It started when I was about thirteen or fourteen and lasted until I graduated from high school. It was always seven books; one a day. I read all those books; some that are still my favorites, like Robert Ruark's *The Old Man and the Boy*, which became the inspiration and model for my writing about my time in Pāhala. She did a good thing, and life was a lot better for me because of her. Thanks, Mrs. R. I'll always remember you. Sorry about that overdue book I found five years after the due date. I uncovered it behind some papers in my school locker when I cleaned it out after graduation—thanks for not making me pay the fine.

But it wasn't always sweetness and light with libraries, and it was all my fault.

When I was in elementary school, the only library we had was a one-room canec building that stood in a corner of the school field. Canec is a byproduct of sugar; a weak, structurally unsound but cheap type of particle board.

One Sunday some of my friends and I organized a game of "bang, make!" The game had a simple goal: hide, and when you see someone who hasn't seen you, yell "bang, make!" and their name, until there's only one kid left. I had found the perfect sniper's lair. I had scoped it out for about a week and had the perfect plan. If I was careful, I could climb up the small tree alongside the library until I could just reach the eaves, then clamber up to the peak of the roof. A perfect vantage point, I could only be seen from one small angle because of the tree and the roof line. I lay down on the roof and got ready to snipe everyone who came near. I had already spotted two or three kids and had them in my sights. They would only be the start. Chortling with glee, I just knew they wouldn't even know what hit them. That's because, being overweight and nearly blind I normally got picked off first—plus nobody would believe I could have gotten to the roof without help. But not that time. Or so I thought.

The plan worked perfectly. From my eagle's lair I could see some kids positioning themselves near the library. I was ready and just about to bring the hammer down on them, when the hammer came down on me instead. Just then, the roof collapsed under me, dropping me about ten feet to the floor of the library, leaving what looked like a kid sized hole and me, unhurt but shaken, laying on a bed of what had been the roof. Canec gets really weak if it gets soaked, and I guess the rain the night before had seeped under the roof covering into the canec, right under my ample weight.

When I caught my breath, I realized that nobody knew where I was or what happened. So, I slunk out a window and ran home. But I was too scared to tell anyone about it. I kept silent. Looking back, I guess I was hoping for divine intervention. But that's not what I got.

Monday morning, I trotted off to school, me and my guilty conscience. I'd like to say I took the high road and told an adult, but I didn't. Not my finest moment.

The school day unfolded normally until after lunch when a very large policeman appeared and rapped on the door of our classroom. Then in his cop voice, he said very loudly, "I'd like to speak to John Walters." When I got to the door, he told me we were going to take a walk. Total surprise. We started walking across the school field toward the library. From that angle we could see there was something not quite right about the roof, but I played ignorant and stayed silent.

When we got to the library, he produced a key, opened the door, and we went inside. Then he walked around the floor under the hole in the ceiling. The floor had been swept and I did my best to ignore the huge hole in the ceiling. Then he said, "I understand you like to read." When I nodded, still ignoring the sunlight from the hole, he pulled a book off the shelf and asked if I had read it. I told him I had. Then he pulled a couple more I had read off the shelves and I started to relax a little. Then he pulled another one and asked if I had read it. I told him I had not read that book. Then he gazed skyward and said, acting more than a little surprised, "Look, John, there's a hole in the roof," after which he looked at me and lowered the boom. He asked me, "How do you think it got there?" No fool, I said I didn't know. Then he lowered another boom: "What do you think would have happened to these books if it rained last night? All of these books would have been soaked and spoiled and nobody could read any of them."

That got me thinking about all those books ruined because I was a coward. I cracked, started crying and confessed. I told him I was sorry and ashamed but too afraid to tell anyone. Then he lifted one of the booms off me. He said, "Anybody can make a mistake. We know you didn't mean to fall through. That's not the problem. The problem is you didn't let anyone know so something could be done." Then he said something I'll never forget: "John, it takes a real man to admit when he makes a mistake and try to fix it."

So, we walked back together and I never forgot what he said and tried to live up to that standard. It's not always easy, or comfortable, and sometimes it doesn't work out in my favor, but that's okay, I still feel better doing what I think is right.

That last book, the book that lowered the boom, *Galloping Broncos* by Max Brand—I borrowed and read it, and he was right. It's a rousing tale of adventure and redemption and has always been one of my favorite westerns. I still have a copy.

CHAPTER 25

Kau Kau

If it's true that an army marches on its stomach, then one of the ties that binds a community together is the food we share.

Like most places in Hawai'i, we blended our cultures together in Pāhala in one way or another at dances and parties, in school, and on the playground. But one of the most significant ways we shared with each other was our food.

For me, sharing food was an adventure, but an adventure that I always approached cautiously. After all, many is the party I've been at where someone asks after I finished a serving of very tasty meat, "How was the dog?" usually with a roguish grin on their face, like they were waiting for me to get sick or something. After a while I started saying, "It was okay, but I've had better. It was a little tough. Couldn't you get a black dog?" After a while teasing the haole wasn't fun anymore so it stopped. To this day I don't know whether I did eat dog, but if I did, it was okay.

Sometimes it was difficult. Pop was from South Dakota and, with the exception of some things like sashimi and snails, he thrived on a diet of meat, more meat, lettuce with vinegar and oil dressing, corn, and some kind of starch (either potatoes or rice). That's what I ate at home and what was most familiar to me growing up. Pop considered things like broccoli, cauliflower, and especially garlic contaminants. He wouldn't even get near Spam or Vienna sausage (foods of the gods to me) because he ate so much of them during the war. As a result, they never got served at home. But shopping was easy.

That meant that all of my food adventures happened outside of the home. I tried a little of just about everything put in front of me. But I had limits, like tomatoes, peas, and mushrooms. Still can't get past them today.

But there was lots of other stuff I did like that might be considered a little out there today, things like smoked donkey. I generally like any smoked meat, but donkey was something special. It had a really unique taste and color that set it apart from regular smoked meat.

We had lots of kālua pig, which I loved, but the best were the pigs that had been eating blackberries up in the hills. When they were cooked, they had purple meat and this meat was sweeter.

We also ate turtles.

Yes, turtles. We could hunt them back then and let me tell you, prepared correctly, they did not taste like chicken. They tasted like turtle. Delicate, firm fleshed, and very tasty. Don't get me wrong, I don't eat turtle anymore. It's not legal and they did take a huge hit in the '50s before the authorities decided to protect them. I've even paid money for small turtles so I could turn them loose.

The worst thing about turtle is getting it ready to eat. I used to call them "meat in a drawer" because they were pretty easy to process. First, we would turn them over. (If you are squeamish, better skip down to the cooking part now.) Then we would cut their heads off, which was always hard for me because they seemed to be looking at me and crying when I did. Once we got past that part, it was a simple matter to cut around the inside of the shell, following the natural border. Then we'd lift the bottom up and there you'd have it: the muscles, which is what we were after, one for each flipper. Dark red meat with little strings of yellowish green fat. We had to work fast because the fat would get rancid quickly. What was disturbing was the tendency of the meat to jerk every time it was touched by a knife. I heard that is what happens with reptiles, but I wouldn't know. Once the meat was cut into the right size portions, we cooked it by dipping them in an egg wash and bread crumbs and frying it. But we couldn't fry it in any oil that had cooked something else, like bacon fat, or the turtle would taste like bacon.

We had lots of eating opportunities provided by nature. Like guavas, which came in sweet and sour versions. We used to say we could eat the sweet ones till we got the runs, then eat the sour ones to get things back to normal. There were also mountain apples and a small guava-like fruit we called "vi vee." There weren't a lot of them around but they really were good. There were lychees, bananas, rough and wrinkled oranges, and breadfruit, or ʻulu.

To cook the ʻulu, we normally just wrapped it up in tin foil and tossed it into a fire for a while, then when it was softish we'd break it in half, toss in a cube of butter with some salt and pepper, and away we'd go.

We had lots of Hawaiian food that we ate at people's houses and at the many lūʻau held in people's backyards and down at the community hall for more formal affairs.

There can't be anything more fun than going to a lūʻau in someone's backyard with a bunch of your friends and gorging on kālua pig, chicken long rice, sashimi, sushi, and all the other good things people brought when they came. But sadly, I never got a taste for poi and some of the other foods like *balut* and *ʻopihi*. But I did try them. I always figured life is too short to eat food I don't like; someone else will and I don't need to eat everything.

We also foraged for food at the beach. There were always coconuts, and we could pick and eat *wana* from the ocean. I liked them way better than the *pipipi* shells that we sometimes we picked at the shoreline, cooked, and ate, which were good but way too much work for me.

Pipipi are little black or sometimes gray snails that cluster on the rocks in the shallows. There are lots of them and they aren't real big, so we had to gather a huge bunch to have enough to make it worth our time. We'd spend about an hour putting the ones that looked big enough to eat into a can or bucket. When we had enough, we normally parboiled them for a couple of minutes. Then we'd all sit in a circle around the pipipi, and each of us with our own pin or needle would dig them out one by one, popping them into our mouths and chewing, then on to the next one. They were okay, but I've had way more fun. It took about a dozen of them to make one mouthful, and I'm not sure I ever even tasted them. So after a while, I would help pick them but hardly ever ate them.

We also ate ʻopihi. We'd pick them on the rocks until we had a pile, then eat them by sliding our thumbnails under one edge and popping them into our mouths. I hate to admit it, but I never liked them and hardly ate them unless I wanted to gross out a tourist at the beach. They would call them limpets and pay us a dollar to eat one while they took a picture. I never had any problem helping pick them even though they weren't my favorite. Everyone else liked them so much and I didn't mind helping out.

There were lots of different kinds of wana. There were the sea urchins with the really long spines and some with short, very sharp spines. Those were the ones we worried about; they hurt and often stuck in our feet. We did walk around everywhere barefoot, even in the water, so it wasn't unusual to pick up a spine or two. The thing is that the spines couldn't be pulled from the foot in one piece; they always broke off at the surface. They couldn't be dug out; they broke into pieces in the wound and seemed to work their way further in the longer they were untended. They didn't even pop out when they festered and got infected. The only remedy I knew of was for someone to pee on the wound as soon as possible after the injury, or somebody told me to soak the spine in vinegar or lime juice to dissolve it, since it was made of calcium and those liquids would dissolve calcium. So we were really careful. The wana would start out small in the coral bed and some of them would eventually be locked in a small cave not much bigger than the sea urchin itself. They just kept wearing away the coral as they grew, and as they got bigger the hole got bigger to accommodate them. We saw lots of them that were too big to ever get out of their holes, but their spines still stuck out a little, so we avoided them if we could.

There were wana we used for chalk. Those were the ones with the long dull spines. We pretty much left these alone. They weren't food and were kind of nice to look at, so unless we found some spines from one that had died, we let them be. We also used the spines for wind chimes and mobiles.

We also had wana we used for food. They were the ones with the very short spines, the ones that wouldn't hurt us if we picked them up carefully. They were all around so we didn't pick any up unless we were going to eat them. They were easy to eat; you just bashed them with a rock or broke them in half and dug the little yellow bits out of the shell. I kind of liked them, but if we had something else to eat I left them alone.

There was another wana, the purple one with the short purple spines, that lived in the surf zone where the water washed up with the surge. I never ate them, but I heard they were edible. They hung onto those rocks and were hard to get off, so we liked to leave them alone. They weren't slippery like the rocks and were someplace solid to hang on to and use as stepping stones on the way up out of the water where they grew.

What I liked way better than wana or ʻopihi was coconuts. We had lots of coconuts. But just like wana, there were several different kinds, mostly described by their growth stage. The first ones were the ones that only had coconut water, the youngest and easiest to get into. Then there was "spoon coconut," the ones that just barely had meat in them. We called them spoon coconut because that's how we ate them, with a little spoon we made out of a slice of the husk. There was the "just past spoon," my favorite because it was soft and could be taken out by running a thumb under the lip of one side and between the shell and the meat until you had a big, almost intact chunk of coconut meat. The last kind we ate was the fully developed coconut with hard meat that we really had to work to get out. Mostly we just used our pocketknives to dig out whatever we could get.

Getting into a coconut could be an adventure. On the green ones, we just bashed the end on a rock until we saw splits in the husk. Then we peeled everything away from the shell leaving it intact so we could poke out the three little holes on the top and get the juice out before we moved on to break the shell and get the meat. Most of the time we tried to get a clean break when we broke the shell. We used the shell halves for water cups and other stuff.

The hardest coconuts to get into were the older, drier, and almost brown ones. Those were work. We broke into them a lot like their easier cousins, but everything was harder. They took more to break. The husks had to be torn off the shell and the shells were harder. Not our first choice, but if they were on the ground and the tree was too high, we just picked them up and went to town, if we could get to them before the rats did.

We normally got our coconuts by climbing up into whatever tree seemed to have the most nuts. We'd use the natural steps in the tree until it got too steep, then it was legs and then arms around the tree until we got to the section of the tree that was under the fronds where the coconut cluster hung from a thick stalk. To get them off we'd hold on with one hand and twist the coconut with the other until it twisted off and fell. Then after we got enough, we'd slide back down the tree and *kau kau*!

We also used the tree for other things. We used the fronds to make hats. The husks we got off the shells were dried and used to make fires to cook over, used as mosquito punks, or just light up and watch at night on the beach.

We didn't only get food at the beach. We could go up into the forest and up into the hills surrounding the town. Mostly we went for *maile* that we used for leis, but sometimes we would get fern shoots and blackberries that grew on shrubs with lots of thorns. I can't even describe how good a kālua pig tasted after it had been feeding on those berries. The meat was purple and the taste was just amazing. Berry season—one of my favorite times of year.

We also ate fish. I know this is going to sound kind of bad, especially since I like fishing so much, so I'll get it off my chest. I'm just not that fond of fish. Mostly at home we ate *mahimahi, ono, aku,* or *'ahi.* I guess we had so much of it I got tired of fish dipped in egg, covered with breadcrumbs, and fried. Back then I'd take a bologna and cheese sandwich any time. We never paid for the fish; it was always the fish Pop caught in Kona. Maybe that's why we had so much of it around.

My mother spent a lot of time cooking. She was probably the best pie maker in town, at least I thought so. Her lemon meringue pie was terrific. But what I liked the most was when she would make doughnuts. She only made them two or three times a year, but when she did, she made a whole bunch. She got up early and mixed the dough, then heated up the Wesson oil while we rolled out the dough. Then we cut out the doughnuts with special cutters that made a ring and a doughnut hole. Then into the hot oil until they floated and were turned over and taken out when they were golden brown. Then the best part was dusting them with sugar and packing them into jars to be shared with our neighbors. One for them, one for me, one for them, one for me. No matter how many she made, they never got stale.

We made liliko'i and guava jams and jellies. She made banana bread and just about anything she could make with whatever was in season or around at the time.

She would also go down into the camp and make Portuguese sausage. She and a couple of her friends would grind the meat in an old hand-crank meat grinder she had, stuff them into intestines (cleaned, of course), then tie them into rings that she took down to the camp for her friend to smoke for her. I guess the deal was her friend got some of the sausage for helping out. It was definitely worth the work.

CHAPTER 26

"Come eat, boys!"

While I was growing up, wherever we were around lunchtime, whichever adult saw us would call out, "Come eat, boys!" Their doors were always open and we were always welcome. They shared what they had and when we ate, we all ate the same food. Sometimes it was nothing more than ketchup, *shoyu*, and hot rice; sometimes it was more. Sometimes it was more than we bargained for.

Ron came to me one day and asked me to go with him on one of his adventures. He wasn't too specific, but he said it was going to be fun. I was in, as usual. As we hiked, I kept asking him where we were going, but he evaded the issue until we were about an hour out of town and further than I'd want to walk back alone. Then he told me we were tracking down the rumor of a hermit who was supposed to live out near where we were hiking. He kind of knew where we were going, or at least that's what he said.

After two or three hours of hiking, I wasn't so sure he knew what he was doing, but I really didn't want to go back alone. At least we weren't lost. I knew all I had to do was walk downhill and I'd get somewhere. Luckily, that wasn't necessary. Just when we were getting ready to go back, Ron noticed a small trail leading off to an area just off a gulch we hadn't seen earlier.

Just a little bit about paths and trails. The neat thing about them is that they are always going from one place to another. They never just stop. As kids we spent a lot of time finding and hiking down paths and trails. It never got boring and it was amazing the places people and animals were going and what was at the end, like the old sugar mill, places to camp or hang out, pools of water to swim in, and other destinations. Kind of like growing up; I guess we all are presented with paths and we have to choose which ones to follow. Hopefully we find one with something good at the end of the trail. Pāhala was a small town, but it had a lot of paths and trails, and not only the ones we could see.

So we followed the small trail that Ron had found. Sure enough, after following it for a short distance we could see a small, one-room wood shack with an outhouse off to the side.

A little old man sat on a bench outside the shack smoking a hand-rolled cigarette that we could smell as we approached. The first thing he said was, "Come, boys. Come eat!" We went inside and he pulled down all the dishes he had, three forks, and three jars full of water and we sat around a small table on the one chair, a wooden box, and an upside-down five-gallon bucket. He fussed around on his kerosene stove and a pan for a couple of minutes, then he dished out three portions of rice and some kind of meat. I hit mine with ketchup and was having a grand old time. I was really hungry and it tasted pretty good.

Then Ron asked the question I usually avoided and hardly ever wanted to know: "This is good. What kind of meat is this?" Spam and Vienna sausage were easy to figure out, but this wasn't either of them. The meat was stringy and shredded, and it was hard to tell what kind of meat it was. I never ask; it's usually a surprise. It could be beef, chicken, donkey, horse, dog, turtle, or most often pork. But this time I was a tad surprised when he replied, "Mongoose." But it was good and I was really hungry, so I finished my portion, as did Ron.

When Ron asked him how he got the mongoose he said he would show us. We had eaten his dinner and he needed to get a couple more. (We always ate some of what was offered. It really would have offended anyone who asked us to eat with them. We never said no, even if they didn't have much. Just not done.)

We went outside to the side of the outhouse where a slingshot made from the crotch of a guava tree was hanging. He asked Ron to take the few scraps that were left over from lunch to a small mound of garbage near the border of his yard. Then we took up our positions and waited. The old man had the slingshot and a ball bearing he shook out of a tin can on the bench. Then we waited silently, but not for long. Sure enough, after a short wait a mongoose head stuck out of the grass near the mound. Then after looking around when it thought it was safe, it scurried to the food and started in on it. Then the old man drew the sling back to his ear and let out a low whistle. Damn if the mongoose didn't stop eating and look up to see what the noise was. Bam! One ball bearing, right in the head. Ron was getting ready to retrieve the mongoose when the old man whispered, "Wait, I need one for breakfast," so again we waited. Then right on schedule another mongoose moved up alongside the first one, until there was another whistle. Then there were two dead mongooses. Then Ron ran out to get them. The old man asked him to find the ball bearings as well; he liked to use them and they weren't easy to come by where he lived, and he didn't like to go to town much.

We sat and talked with him for a while about being a hermit. He explained he wasn't a real hermit, just a guy who likes being alone and he mostly didn't mind visitors even though he didn't get many. He didn't have a car, but he just walked to town if he needed something. He said mostly he bought rice, coffee, and tobacco. Then he told us the best way to get back to town and we left. I guess he liked us; he told us we could come back anytime.

On the way back Ron and I decided we wouldn't tell anyone where we had been. It just didn't seem right taking away his solitude; he seemed so happy. I never went back, but I know Ron did. Once or twice he asked me to help him rustle up some ball bearings the same size as the old man used or a bag of rice or maybe a couple cans of Spam or Vienna sausage. Always something useful or good to eat. Then he would put them in a sack and disappear for a while. But when he came back the bag would be gone.

We never talked about it, but I guess he liked the old man and wanted to help him any way he could, in a way the old man could accept.

That's the kind of guy Ron was.

CHAPTER 27

Animals

There were always animals and pets around when we lived in Pāhala. Just in the time we lived there we had three dogs, four cats, three white mice, some birds, a Rhode Island Red hen, and a psycho bantam rooster.

Our first dog was named Pal, a black and gray poi dog. He had to have been some kind of hunting dog. By and large, he was a very tolerant and docile dog, especially with kids. He was not given to rushing around in the heat of the day and never chased a car or a kid the whole time he lived with us. But he hated cats. That's not so bad. I've never been fond of cats myself, but I never killed them. That's what Pal did, but he was really good at it and that was the problem.

Pal wasn't only a hater, he was a hunting hater, and apparently was way smarter than the cats he hated so much. In Pāhala we never chained up dogs that didn't bite. We just let them have the run of the town. We never seemed to have a problem and we knew all of the dogs in town, which ones weren't safe and the ones that we liked to have tag along on our adventures. But soon after Pal was given to Pop, we started to get calls about him from irate neighbors. The ones where someone said, "Your dog killed my cat. Come get the body and get rid of it." Then Ron and I would be instructed to march over to the scene of the crime and pick up and dispose of the body that was once a beloved pet. It started slowly, then it seemed like Ron and I were making a burial run every week. We'd get the call, pick up a paper bag and a couple of shovels, and off we'd go to the cat graveyard.

I should explain that after the first couple of cats we had to bury, Ron and I picked out a nice plot of forest, in a small open glade with grass and chirping, or maybe gloating, birds. We started over on one side and lined them up back and forth, planting rows of cats side by side until the space got smaller and smaller. We even made chopstick crosses for all of the tenants. I know it sounds kind of sick and macabre, but really, it had to be better than a paper bag that got thrown out with the trash. And in Ron's and my defense, we never thought it would get that bad. I can only wonder what anyone who ran across the cemetery thought was going on, but we never heard anyone ask. We sure never mentioned it to anyone.

But it got worse, much worse. Word must have gotten out in the feline community about Pal's predations because for two or three weeks we got no calls. Then Pal figured out a way to up his game. It seemed that a kindly soul who worked in the hospital kitchen had taken to feeding a large group of stray cats living under the hospital where they were safe. They were loud and flea bitten, and the pride kept growing year after year. They seemed to multiply in front of our eyes. I had sometimes heard an adult who noticed what was going on saying something had to be done. I've noticed it a lot; whenever someone says something needs to be done, they want someone else to do the heavy lifting. Well, something was done, and Pal and a hunting partner did the doing.

Those cats had it pretty good. The hospital was situated on a small hill that commanded a fine view of the surrounding area. There was no cover near the hospital and there were lots of small holes to run into under the hospital if things got too risky outside, like when a dog was sighted. Pal had been trying to get those cats from his first sighting. To Pal it must have looked like dog heaven: twenty or thirty plump cats ripe for the kill. He tried many times to grab one and had picked off one or two of the less alert cats. But they appeared to reach a standoff, with the cats staying close to the hospital and safety and Pal making one or two futile attempts a day just to keep his paw in, since other people were keeping their cats close and safe.

That was the status quo, that is, until Pal made friends with another dog and they became a pack. Then the situation changed, and changed big time. It didn't take long for Ron and I to get the call and we walked over to pick up what we thought was one cat. But it wasn't, it was five cats and the lady at the hospital was livid. Nobody had seen what happened. They just heard the barking of the dogs and the screaming of the cats and the results. We took them away, but by then the glade was full and we had to move to another area, and by then we were getting really tired of burying cats.

Ron and I had to know what was going on, so we staked out Pal and the hospital. It was quiet for a couple of days, and then there was another raid, and that time we saw the whole thing unfold. It seems that Pal and another dog had outsmarted the cats. Pal's partner went out in plain sight and started barking at the cats, who must have thought they could get to cover if danger threatened. They were all lined up, just out of reach, taunting the stupid dog. But while they were focused on the barking dog, the quiet dog, Pal, had crept up silently in from the other side until he was within reach. A quick spring and he was among them, biting and snapping. The cats panicked and ran away from the hospital, right into the jaws of the other dog, and round again. When the lady came out with the broom and the dogs ran off, the body count was an incredible eight or nine cats. Ron and I had our last burial and Pal had to go away; I guess enough was enough. But it all ended well. Ron and I didn't have to bury any more cats, the population of cats at the hospital was somewhat under control, and Pop gave Pal to one of the cowboys at Kapāpala Ranch. His new owner claimed he was the best hunting dog he ever had and treasured him until he died.

We had another dog named Lady, but she couldn't figure out quickly enough that cars were dangerous. She didn't last long.

CHAPTER 28

Tina

One Christmas Tina became a member of our family. Tina, or Katrina of Ka'ū, her registered name, was a full-blooded basset hound with a bloodline better than mine. She was undoubtedly the finest, bravest dog I've ever known. One of my younger sisters picked her out of a litter from one of Pop's fishing partners who raised them in Hilo. She was the runt of the litter, but her heart was way bigger than her body. (In case you can't guess, I really loved that dog.)

She was definitely a character. She slept in the house and taught us things, like you can't teach a dog to pee outside when the carpet in the house is green. When they brought her home, the only place they could put her was in my room, off the kitchen. They bedded her down in a box with old towels and a clock to keep her company, but she was small and lonely and whimpered so long that I just couldn't take it anymore, so I put her in my bed next to me, asthma and all, and she slept quietly. After that, every night she would be put to bed in the box with many comments about what a good little dog she was and how well she was adjusting, but when everyone was gone I'd pick her up and let her sleep with me. Just the thing for an asthmatic kid, but she never seemed to make my asthma act up. I spent most of the night sitting up in the living room anyway. Of course, eventually we got busted, but by then it was too late and everyone just bowed to the inevitable.

The first month we had her she got run over by the Catholic priest, who blessed her and offered prayers for her to heal well. He was a good guy for a priest and maybe the prayer helped. She got a cast on the broken leg and hobbled around until the vet said the leg was healed. But when he took the cast off, she wouldn't walk on it, she just kept hobbling along until Pop called the vet. No problem, the vet said, just bandage the other leg. Sure enough, after we bandaged the other leg, she stood there thinking for a while, then started walking as though the bandaged leg was broken. We left the bandage on until it fell off and Tina had no more problems.

She chased cars but never caught them, chased cows who ignored her, and wasn't real interested in cats. But there was one trick she had that I've never seen another dog accomplish. She could catch mynah birds. We discovered her talent when she proudly started coming home engulfed in the heady odor of something dead. After watching her for a while, she led us to the hedge and a dead mynah bird that she rolled back and forth over on her back, picking up its smell.

We buried the bird, washed her off, and she didn't smell bad for a while, but then she came home again stinking. So off we went and she proudly showed us her latest toy. Guess what? Another dead mynah. After we buried that one, I started watching her and one day I found out what was happening.

Our yard was large and full of things that mynahs liked to eat. We were so used to them we hardly noticed them or paid attention to them. But Tina must have been watching them very carefully. Mynahs are smart and really skittish creatures and mostly didn't let anything bigger than them get very close. But Tina had figured out a way to get close. It was quite funny. She would walk up toward the mynah birds until they started edging away without flying off. Then she would pretend not to pay attention to them, biting grass and rolling around and generally acting like they weren't there, but she kept rolling closer and closer. I could almost hear the mynahs talking about that crazy dog. *Look at those short stubby legs and floppy ears. She'll never get us.* But she did. When she got near enough, that rolling, playing, and seemingly harmless dog pounced on the nearest bird and ripped it to shreds. Then she took it into the hedge to let it season in her special place and left it to rot. Well, there wasn't much we could or wanted to do about the mynahs, so until the birds realized she was a threat she would come home stinking and we'd have to hunt down the bird, bury it, and give her a bath.

She also had an established route in the town. As I said, nobody tied their dogs up unless they bit and she didn't. Like the other dogs, she roamed wherever she wanted. Nobody bothered with any of the dogs in the town much unless there was a problem, which was rarely. People with the mean dogs mostly made sure they couldn't hurt anyone. I was in school so I didn't find out till much later that she had a routine and a route she followed every weekday that started from our house when the kids went to school, with stops at neighbors' houses and a morning snack at the hospital, and ended up in the plantation manager's chair where she would snooze until she came home to meet us after school. Funny thing, even the manager liked having her around. Once my father came home and told us about a meeting with some Honolulu honchos. The meeting was held in the same room where Tina snoozed in the afternoon. When the managers gathered for the meeting and one of the Honolulu guys moved to chase her out, Mr. Tate, the manager, told them to hold off, that's her seat in the afternoon and she isn't bothering anything. He took another seat and they held the meeting while she slept. He was a cool guy.

Yup, she wasn't a mean or angry dog. She was brave and loyal, and one day she stepped up and really saved my skin.

Not all the dogs in town were safe. One of the families in town had a dog, not just any dog, but one of those dogs we stayed away from. It was a mean German shepherd. That dog could and would bite, and there was many a kid who suffered at his fangs. The problem was that the owner was related to a policeman, the sergeant in Nāʻālehu who investigated *every* biting incident involving that dog. Guess what? It was always the kid at fault and the dog was free to bite again. He was supposed to be tied up, and mostly he was, but sometimes he got loose. When he did, he would remember kids who had baited him while he was chained. Sometimes he would catch them and bite them. I never teased him. I never baited him. He was just too big and too mean, and I stayed as far away from him as I could.

The family lived near the school and we had to walk by their house on the way home. Every day before I left the safety of the schoolyard, I would check out the house and see if the dog was chained. If he was close to the house, that usually meant it was safe to proceed. He never really bothered me and I left him alone.

That is, until one day, after I had checked and thought he was chained up. Thinking it was safe, I proceeded across the football field toward home. I could see him in the yard looking at me like I was his next meal. Then he started edging out from the house, way beyond the length of his chain. That's when I *thought* there might be a problem. I *knew* I had a problem when he started running toward me. I knew I couldn't make it back to the school so I ran as fast as I could for the safety of the tennis court. My plan was to climb the chicken wire wall and wait him out until he left or an adult rescued me. But it was too far, way too far. He was too fast and I knew I wouldn't make it. I ran, and ran, and kept running as fast as I could, but inevitably I could hear him growling and panting behind me and knew it wasn't even going to be close. I was dog meat. No fence, no cover, no hope. All I could do was run and cringe while waiting for the bite.

But I had a friend. As I was running, out of the corner of my eye I saw a little black blur fly past me going the other way, then the sounds of battle. When I turned around, there was my pal Tina attached to one of the back legs of the way bigger dog. She still had the element of surprise and the upper hand, and the other dog looked like he was in shock, but I knew it wouldn't last long. I also knew that if he got his jaws on her he would eat her, so I started whopping on him with my books. (In those days, we just ran an old belt around them to keep them together and it made a great flail.) Confused, he ignored Tina and turned toward me. Tina hit him again and when he turned back toward her, I banged on him some more until his owner ran over yelling about *us* attacking his dog. I was still so pumped up I started swearing at him and yelled that I was going to tell my mom, so he backed off, grabbed the dog, and left. After that the dog got loose a lot less. But Tina, my pal, she saved me. She strutted alongside me all the way home. She sure deserved it.

Funny thing about that German shepherd, a couple of months later he got loose again and was chasing a kid across the main street when he got clipped by a car and thrown into the hedge in front of my house. As in any small town, a crowd immediately appeared out of nowhere, talking, pointing, and speculating on the condition of the dog. That is until one of the local gendarmes happened by. From the general babble, he figured out the kid-biting dog was chasing another kid and had been hit, was in the bushes, and nobody wanted to get near him to see how he was because he was so mean. That brave man peered into the bushes, then waved us all back after he proclaimed, "He can't be saved." He pulled his pistol, leaned in, and pulled the trigger. *Bang*, right through the head. After the mercy killing, he put the dog in his trunk and took it back to the owner. But controversy reared its ugly head and there were questions about how badly the dog had been injured, even though everyone who'd been there had agreed it was the right thing to do after it was done.

But as the officer, who knew about the dog and could do nothing about the biting, said later, with a roguish smile, "At least he won't be biting any more kids." He must have been tired of the complaints, the bitten kids, and the knowledge that it would never stop as long as that dog was alive. He was the one people complained to, but he couldn't overrule his sergeant.

Tina had one more trick. When I was in eighth grade, I used to go home for lunch every day. In those days we could get a lunch pass and, after being stopped, show it to a campus police officer, the grown-up junior police officers. Tina would usually be at home in the morning there but stayed when I left after I petted her and said goodbye. My seat in the classroom just before lunch was near the door and I could see the back entrance to our yard. One day, while waiting for the bell that announced lunch, I saw Tina walk out of our backyard and amble toward the school field until she disappeared from sight. When I walked out into the hall after the bell, there she was, patiently sitting alongside the door. I petted her and we walked back to the house together. After that, she waited at the door every day that year. It was really nice to see her and walk home together, and the best part was that nobody had a problem with her coming to get me. Like I said, we all knew the dogs in the town and everyone liked Tina, even the teachers.

We lost Tina when I was attending school in Hilo in 1964. I'd see her every weekend when I came home but once she didn't come to greet me. When I asked where she was my father said she was sick, she had gotten into some kind of chemical. He didn't know where she was, but I did. When she didn't feel well, she had a spot under the house she would go to, so I crawled under the house and found her in her spot whimpering and shaking. I brought her out and Pop took her to the vet in Hilo, who tried to give her meds to help her stomach while he kept her at his office. It didn't work. Pop called me a couple of days later to tell me he had let her go. She was in too much pain and nothing could be done for her, so they made her comfortable and turned her loose. It was the right thing to do and it bothered me that I couldn't say goodbye, but I sure didn't want to see her suffer or die. When I got back from school on Friday, Pop and I talked about it and he told me he had buried her in a special place he would take me to in the morning.

It sure was a special place. Pop and I got into the car in the morning and he drove down to a spot on the highway in the middle of nowhere, then he got out and walked about a mile over a cattle trail toward the ocean. When he stopped, I couldn't believe it. He had found a small green clearing that looked out over the Ka'ū coast as far as the eye could see, up toward the volcano and down toward Nā'ālehu. It was a very peaceful and beautiful place. I wouldn't mind being buried someplace like that when I die. Toward the edge was a small mound of fresh dirt with some flowers on it. When we walked over, he told me she was there, buried in her favorite blanket from my bed, looking out over the coast. He had hiked in alone and laid her to rest. Chicken skin moment, I can hardly write about it. What a guy—I guess he loved her too in his own way.

We also had cats. Kitty was a black and white cat who never did much of anything except have more cats.

We also, for a very short time, had three white mice. White, hairy, red-eyed rodents that didn't do much besides perch and crap on our shoulders and hands. They didn't last long, just until their owner, my sister, decided to clean their cage and put them into the same cage as her Rhode Island Red hen, who stood about two feet high and had a temper. I guess she thought because they were all her pets they would get along. I guess Henny also had an appetite because when my sister went back to retrieve them, all she found was a little blood. Henny had eaten them, and for the next couple of weeks she laid eggs we almost had to chisel to crack.

Later on, Henny got a mate, a psycho bantam rooster. We moved them into our old sandbox that had been converted into a chicken coop and they lived together somewhat peacefully. Henny never got out, but the psycho did, and it wasn't pretty. The problem was, when they converted the sandbox to a chicken coop, there were some design flaws and the rooster being smaller than the hen could sometimes squeeze out and run amok. I mean really run amok; he would attack anything that came into sight, biting and kicking with his spurs.

When that happened, the rooster would lurk in the yard waiting for a victim until some unwary kid came near, then run out and try to hit whoever had offended him with his beak and spurs. Luckily the spurs had been trimmed, but nobody was safe. When that happened, about once a week, we children would gather up wicker baskets and towels and chase him around the yard screaming and waving whatever we were carrying until he short circuited. It was the funniest damn thing. He'd last about ten minutes fighting a desperate battle against overwhelming odds, until suddenly he would stop, stand still, then run over to the edge of the yard and stick his head in the bushes, freezing into that position. Then either Ron or I would quietly sneak up behind him and, after quickly grabbing both feet between the fingers of one hand, swing him around and around, screaming to the others to open the coop door. Then with a last swing, we would fling him into the coop and slam the door. He would slink away and sulk until he could break out again.

Both birds vanished one night, and we couldn't figure out what had happened to them. There was much speculation, and it became one of the family's unsolved mysteries. But later, much later, Ron confessed to me that he knew where they had gone. One night he and a couple of friends were out getting into trouble and decided to experiment with chicken *à la* clay cooking. It went pretty much like this: First, steal two chickens (Henny and rooster); kill them; clean; pack with clay with feathers on; throw onto coals for a while, then crack open clay; and eat half-cooked chicken. Ron claimed he never really liked the chickens and we all slept a lot better without that punchy rooster waking us up every morning.

CHAPTER 29

The Pugnacious Porker

The high school in Pāhala featured an agricultural program that included the raising, caring for, and harvesting of different kinds of animals. Behind the school there were pigpens, chicken coops, and a pasture with cattle.

It was there at school that I had a run-in with a very pugnacious porker. As I've mentioned, there wasn't a whole lot going on in Pāhala, so once in a while we would gather up the younger siblings and make a run to the school to look at the animals. Mostly we just looked and didn't bother them. But one day I was carrying a brand-new slingshot I'd made from a guava branch and was just itching to try out.

You have to understand that the selection of the proper fork from a guava tree, and the crafting of a slingshot along with the selection of just the right size ball bearing (preferred) or marble, was an essential skill and almost a rite of passage for any young lad of my years in Pāhala. We carried them a lot and hunted for bird scalps with varying degrees of success. I wasn't much of a threat to the birds, but I sure enjoyed pulling back and letting one go.

That day I was armed with my slingshot but not much judgment. I was Davy Crockett, Daniel Boone, or another of my childhood heroes, scanning for threats and ready to respond accordingly. At least that's what I thought.

But somewhere between being armed and knowing when to use the arm, I lost my way. Not my finest moment.

When we got to the school pigpen, I spotted one of the boars and a sow in a very compromising position, facing away from me. In a moment of temporary insanity, I sent a marble downrange. But instead of my usual abysmal performance, the marble struck the pig in a most sensitive part of his anatomy with a distinct *thud*. He left the sow, looked around, and somehow figured out I was the cause of his discomfort and pain. Squealing madly, he tried to climb the bars of the pen to get to me. Scared the crap out of me, and I very quickly ran away and never told anyone.

To be truthful, I was kind of ashamed of myself and felt bad. But there was no way to communicate that to the boar and from that day forward, any time I got near the pigpen he started gnashing his teeth and lunging at the bars until I left. For years I had dreams about him breaking out of the pen and tracking me down at night to exact his revenge.

What made it worse was that I knew I was wrong. It didn't help that he just kept getting bigger and bigger. It was so bad that three or four years later, when my seventh grade class went to talk to the ag teacher about joining Future Farmers of America and we got to the part where we visited the pigpen, he again attacked the bars and tried to eat me alive. He hadn't forgotten and had kept on growing. He was a very large and still angry porker. The teacher was astounded; he said he was normally a very placid pig and he couldn't figure out why he was going off. I said nothing, figuring it was best not to clarify. Needless to say, no FFA for me. I moved on to other academic endeavors.

But everything comes to an end. I can tell you it was a great relief when that pig became the guest of honor at a school lūʻau. I must have eaten ten pounds of meat that day to make sure he was really gone. But in the end, he was a very tasty porker, and I could sleep at night.

But that was the first and last time I ever did anything like that to an animal. I have no problem dispatching a fish or other living thing that I'm going to eat, but otherwise I just leave them alone.

There were lots of other critters around. One of my friends caught a hoary bat and brought it to school. It was tiny and really neat—a real bat, wings and all. Too bad they didn't just let it go, but it was such a rare sight they killed it and preserved it in formaldehyde. Just like they did with Hawaiʻi's only native snake, a tiny thing that looked like a worm except for its little forked tongue.

Sometimes we'd hear the honking of *nēnē* geese in the hills, or we'd see *ʻio* (Hawaiian hawks) in the sky above the newly harvested fields, riding the updrafts to gain altitude, then circling until they peeled off to hunt.

There were lots of *pueo* living in caves near town, Hawaiian owls that would wing off when we got too close. Once in a while as we ran around at night, a pueo would fly silently past a streetlight, and all we could see was a shadow that moved quickly over the road then vanished, or sometimes just a glimpse of its wings as it glided on its way to the next meal.

CHAPTER 30

Stalking the Wild

Hunting has never been as much fun for me as diving. It always seemed like lots of work, hard work. I'd much rather be swimming or surfing or diving. But in Ka'ū, hunting was something we all did often. We hunted near and in the ocean, but that's another story. What follows is about what we hunted on dry land.

I guess the earliest hunting we did was with slingshots and, if we were lucky, BB guns. We hunted small birds for their scalps and to eat. Like most of the gear we used that could cause bodily harm, we made our slingshots ourselves, without adult supervision. We never asked or told them what we were doing. After all, there were those legions of children with missing eyes due to their misdeeds or the mistakes of others.

First, we would look for the right forked branch, and not just any tree or branch either. It had to be a guava tree and the fork had to be just the right size, not too big to hold and not so small that it would twist when we shot it. Once we found the perfect fork, we had to use our dull Scout knives, which was all we were allowed, to extract only the part we needed from the tree. Not an easy chore; guava is a tough wood and we had to carve carefully. We also needed to whittle all the way through the branch because bending and breaking it prematurely just about always resulted in the fork or the branch splitting, rendering the entire thing unusable. I did that a couple of times before I learned. You may be wondering why we didn't just use a saw—a hacksaw, for instance. I can't tell you, but they never seemed to be around when we needed them and going back home for one wasn't a good plan. Saws were awkward to carry through the forest, and if an adult saw us he or she probably could figure out what we were doing.

Once we had the rough slingshot shape, we spent hours stripping off the bark and carving and sanding the fork until it was just right. Then it was time to attach the *sugi*, or rubber tubing. Not just any sugi, but the yellow one; it was more flexible and stretched out further than the black. We'd lash it to the top two forks by slipping it over and tying it off so it wouldn't let go when the sling was pulled back. Not good to get it wrong; the backlash could be quite painful. Then we attached a short strip of leather—well used and pliable was best—by cutting two slots and weaving the sugi through them and tying it off.

Then we would sneak down to the yard with the derelict farm machinery and procure ball bearings from the stuff that was lying around. Mostly they were rusty, so we had to shine them up before using them. Then it was off to the woods, hunting the elusive and very quick-moving birds through the trees. Funny, I can't remember anyone ever shooting anyone else, either on purpose or by accident. I guess slingshots were one of those things we never really considered a toy, but a tool we had to use responsibly.

I was a terrible shot. Aside from that unlucky boar, I don't think I ever shot anything, just rained ball bearings down throughout the forest. I hate to think what will happen if someone ever takes a metal detector into the forest after all those years and legions of boys.

If we were lucky enough to hit and kill a bird, we hardly ever wasted them. First, the lucky marksman would take the scalp, a tuft of feathers near the throat of the bird. Then we would carefully clean the bird and cook it over an open fire until it was singed, then eat it. Great hunters, but I can tell you there isn't much to eat on a cardinal or rice bird. Once cleaned, they looked like miniature game hens with less meat.

We also stalked the wild and wily boar. (As with squid, even though we knew there were boars and sows, we called them all boars.) In Kaʻū lots of times we hunted them with dogs and knives. Not for the faint of heart.

CHAPTER 31

Glasses

I've never had the strongest eyes. I'm really nearsighted. It's never been too much of a problem, except in lining up large waves, but until I got a prescription dive mask nobody would dive with me if I had a speargun.

I didn't even know I was nearsighted until I reached the fourth grade. Up till then, I spent a lot of time in the back of the class because of my behavior. Luckily, I could hold books close enough to see the words.

One day in fourth grade, a public health nurse came to our school to administer eye tests. I had been exposed to eye tests before, but I had no idea what they looked like; I couldn't see that far. That day, just like every other eye test day, I was called and walked up to the little feet on the floor. When I was asked which way the letters on the test poster were pointing, I did the same thing I always did: just randomly pointed until the test was over. After all, what did I know? I'd never actually seen the test.

I'll never forget what happened next. First, the teacher told the nurse that it was only John the class clown acting up again. She suggested the nurse move on and pay no more attention to me. But instead of moving on like all the others before her, this nurse came close to me and looked into my eyes. Then she asked what nobody else had ever thought to ask—she asked me if I could see the chart. When I asked, "What chart?" you could have heard a pin drop. She told me to move forward until I could see the top of the chart and show her which way the letter was pointing. It was a long, quiet walk that seemed to take me forever. But I got about three feet from the chart and at last there was something I could see.

The nurse asked my teacher where she had me sitting. Naturally, it was in the back of the room with all the other disruptive elements in the class.

Then she dropped the bomb on my teacher. She said, "No wonder he clowns around! With his vision, he wouldn't be able to see anything on the blackboard, let alone any writing." The next day I was in the front row, reading the words on the blackboard that had previously been only a blur. I was tested and got a pair of glasses, and I could see details that had only been vague shadows before. It was one of the greatest moments of my life.

Sadly, the teacher asked me why I hadn't told her I couldn't see. She didn't get any happier when I told her there was nothing to tell; I thought everyone saw things like I did. I'll never know who that nurse was, but I'll always be grateful she took the time to ask the right question and listen to the answer.

CHAPTER 32

Kindergarten

When I was five, we lived outside of Hilo in Pāpaʻikou. Ron and I both attended Catholic Elementary School in Hilo; me in kindergarten and Ron in first grade. Not the greatest academic beginning. I could never figure out why the nuns who taught us were so committed to being in charge. Respect didn't matter. It was all obedience, enforced by ruler or shame.

Every weekday morning, Ron and I would get dressed in our little Catholic school uniforms—white shirts, khaki pants, Buster Brown shoes. Our school bags looked like miniature briefcases and our lunches were in brown paper bags. We looked like little office workers. I figure they did it that way so there could be no escape from school, since kids at no other school dressed that way. It also made us easy targets to pick out of a herd, just in case any bigger kid wanted to pick on us.

Ron and I would walk down to the main highway and wait for the sampan bus to take us into Hilo. From there it was a short walk to school.

My memory of Catholic elementary school in Hilo is kind of a blur. All I remember is rules, raps on my knuckles, bigger kids picking on little kids—as the nuns looked on benevolently without intervening—and marching everywhere. Seemed like they punished us for everything. But their special bone to pick was nap time. We all had denim sleeping bags that we had to unroll and lay on the tiled floor after lunch for our "naps." More like being put on a rack; nothing between the kid and the hard, cold floor but a thin layer of denim. If we fidgeted, we were warned. If we continued, we would have to cross-dress for the rest of the day.

Yup, that's right. Boys had to wear dresses and girls had to wear pants and shirts, provided by the nuns. I'm not even going any further with this. Sick and twisted. Wonder who thought that up. They must have been on drugs or delusional. But it worked, mostly. Most of us were so afraid of being shamed we pretended to sleep just to keep safe.

Our desks were old-school (pun intended) wood and iron in rows. They even had holes for the ink bottles we used to fill the fountain pens we used at school. We filled the pens by sticking the pen tip in the ink and working a lever on the side. What were they thinking? Remember the white shirts? It didn't take long for the ink to spill, drop, or squirt onto those once white shirts.

In first grade, I sat behind a girl with long pigtails. I don't know why, but she kept flicking her pigtails into my eyes. Back then they didn't know I was nearsighted, and my eyes were focused on my book to try to see the pages, so I couldn't avoid her whips. Finally, I'd had enough. I got angry and told her that if she kept doing that I would cut one of her pigtails off. Not an idle threat; we all had real scissors. I had the equipment and the will. She dared me to. Bad move. I guess she didn't believe me, but the next time she hit me in the face I grabbed her pigtail and snipped it off. The girl started crying; the nun was unhappy. My mother was unhappy too, and the girl's mother was very unhappy. But I was okay, no more hair in the eyes. Inevitably there was a big fuss after school that day. All the fingers were pointed at me, the little juvenile delinquent and son of the devil. Nobody could believe that this little angel had been pestering me. Nobody bought my story, and I was headed for deep trouble.

But for one of the only times in my life, someone stepped up and told the truth. When the girl whose pigtail I had severed saw what they were doing to me, she told everyone that I was telling the truth—that she had purposely been flicking her pigtails at me and wouldn't stop, and that she dared me to cut one off.

Bless her, even though I got a lecture and we had to move seats, I still respected her and liked her for standing up for me. And I knew I really shouldn't have cut that pigtail off.

In due time we moved from the Hilo area to Pāhala and I started in second grade there.

Pāhala Elementary was almost the opposite of Catholic school. Someone very kid-friendly had helped design that campus. Instead of an empty, dusty or muddy field, there was a magnificent playground with swing sets, tetherball stations, jungle gyms, and other wonderful things to play and swing on. Unlike the generic, pop-up playgrounds currently in vogue, everything in that field was made right there, of industrial grade, kid-proof materials. Every day at recess there was a mad dash to the playground to *kapu* (reserve) our favorite activity. The swing set was about twenty feet high and linked to chains and seats. There were huge, long slides, and also wheels made of pipe to climb on. What we really liked was that the wheels and jungle gym were not bolted down, so we could work together and push and pull them around the playground into different configurations, depending on what we were doing.

Just about every section of the sidewalks in front of the school had been painted with different hopscotch patterns. Those usually were the first to be grabbed at recess. We all played hopscotch, endlessly, and we had our favorite kinis that we would use to toss into the squares. The best kini was a small chain because it wouldn't bounce and would stay put. Next best was two of the stems from the trees near the school. We would use our pocketknives (yup, no expulsion) to split one of the stems and thread the other through the slit to make a cross. Not the greatest, but they were easy to throw and pretty much stayed where they hit.

Recess was monitored by what were called junior police officers (JPO in those days. That meant that selected students were given a tenuous authority over the other students. Of course that really depended on who was exerting authority and who the offender was. The JPOs pretty much knew which kids to leave alone. After all, there was plenty of opportunity for revenge after school if a JPO abused his authority. Consequently, they pretty much restricted themselves to what I always thought was unique to my school. We had two or three staircases, a couple of small ones and one real tall one. Depending on our class we'd use whatever stair was nearest. But the thing was, we couldn't run up the stairs. That was a problem because we wanted to squeeze every bit of fun out of our recesses. So when the last buzzer sounded, there was a mad rush to get to class without being late. But the problem was that JPOs stationed at the bottom of the big stairs decided which kids were going up too fast. In that case they would yell, "Walk back!" which meant trudging back to the bottom and going up again, only slower. The teachers were usually watching, so there was no flouting the JPOs authority. So typically there'd be two or three kids walking up and down and back up again before they got to go to class.

CHAPTER 33

That Wasn't So Bad

In elementary school in Pāhala we ate in the cafeteria. People said our head cook-and-cafeteria manager was a gossiper, was bossy, didn't like my mother, and loved to exert her authority. But she sure could cook, and despite the occasional faux pas like brown gravy with hot dogs she was an excellent cook and made the best curry stew I've ever tasted.

Mostly I was okay with her food and looked forward to lunch—except those days when the menu featured dishes with tomatoes. I don't eat tomatoes. I never did, never will. They make me sick and I've always made sure to eat around them if a dish has been "contaminated." If I don't have to eat tomatoes I have no problem with them—I just avoid them. Everyone else is welcome to relish them and have my share. I don't know why that became a problem for the cafeteria manager. After all, I had happily not eaten tomatoes in her cafeteria for at least three years before she decided it was a crisis.

But you never know. One day she made beef tomato. As usual I just ate around the tomatoes and was just getting up to dump the rest when she happened to be strolling by, scanning the crowd. Of course, she had to spot the leftovers on my plate. Naturally, she had to take offense that I had not eaten the tomatoes. Silly me, why would I expect to be left alone, even though there were lots of kids with food (including tomatoes) left on their plates that she somehow seemed not to notice. Somehow it was okay for them to not eat everything on their plates. But not me. Just my luck to be the one she decided to make an example of to scare the other children.

Predictably, leaving the tomatoes just wouldn't do. Probably because of all the poor children starving in China. (Back then we heard plenty about them every time anyone wanted us to eat something we didn't like, or just didn't want to eat. From the way adults talked about it, nobody in

China ever got a meal. But we knew better than to suggest they send the food there instead of making us eat it. That would not have ended well for us.) She stopped, looked down, and asked in a loud, demanding voice why I had not eaten the tomatoes. By then everyone was looking at me and grinning. They knew something was going to happen to me, and it wasn't going to be good.

I truthfully told her tomatoes made my stomach hurt and I didn't eat them. But she ignored my explanation and pronounced that since tomatoes were good for me, I would just have to sit in the cafeteria until I ate them. The snickers of the other students sitting on my table didn't help. I didn't see what her problem was, but I knew one thing: I was not going to eat those damn tomatoes, no matter what happened.

An hour passed, then two, then three. Everyone else had long since left the cafeteria, but she kept trolling by, getting madder and madder each time she saw the tomatoes still uneaten on my plate. Believe me, after all the time that passed, those tomatoes weren't looking any better or more edible. By the third hour, the grease from the beef had coagulated and the flies had started to swarm. I did nothing to discourage them in the vain hope that she would say the flies had contaminated the food and it wasn't fit to eat. No such luck.

Finally, toward the end of her day she'd had enough. I could see her coming down the aisle in her white cafeteria uniform flanked by her backup—her two very large henchwomen. We stayed away from them if we could; they were not the nicest or most patient of people. They stood on either side of me beaming as she told me I was going to eat those damn tomatoes or else. Ah, the infamous, ominous, and vague "or else."

When I refused, in a well-rehearsed and planned maneuver, both of the very large and well-fed henchwomen grabbed me, one on each side, while the manager grabbed my head and pinched my nose. Even though I tried to keep my mouth clamped shut, inevitably I had to open my mouth to take a breath. That's when she took a large wooden spoon, filled it from my plate, and shoved a spoonful of tomatoes down my throat, holding my nose till I had to swallow.

Then she glared down at me and said, "Well now, that wasn't so bad, was it?" Right, I'm sure *she* didn't feel a thing. Not bad for her, not yet. But little did she know that things were about to go horribly bad.

She was beaming smugly down at me, happy with a job well done. Her assistants had let me go, thinking the show was over and they had won. But while that was going on, I could feel things percolating and rumbling. My stomach was way unhappy, and something had to blow. So, while she was smirking at me, I just let it go. I'm not going to say I aimed at her, but she was in the way and I puked on her. Red chunky tomato puke all over the front of her white uniform. I felt a lot better, but she didn't. She stood there in disbelief. Then she got mad, then madder, then livid with rage. I guess I moved up a notch from resistant to an insolent pup that need to be put in his place. At least she didn't hit me with the spoon.

Then she made her worse mistake. She dragged me into her office by the ear and called my mom and told her what happened. I could hear my mom yelling over the phone. I couldn't make out all she said but some of the highlights were phrases like "stupid cow," "bitch," "idiot," and "I'll sue your ass!" after she asked if I had told her tomatoes made me sick, and she had to admit that was the case. (There was no love lost between her and my mom.) I didn't hear the rest, but it was clear that I wouldn't be force-fed any more tomatoes. But I wasn't going to be on the A list either.

I went home, somewhat victorious, but I avoided her for as long as I could when I had to eat lunch at school. As soon as I could, I got a home lunch pass.

I guess it didn't help that there was some prior history between her and my mom. One day I was dragged along while my mother accomplished the impossible. It was a herculean feat, and I was lucky enough to watch it all unfold.

Ron and a couple of his chums were playing mumblety-peg. It's a game played with pocketknives where the players take turns throwing the knives different ways, with the goal of making them stick in the ground by the point. Some of them were really good. One of his friends could throw his knife between the toes of an unsuspecting victim, every time. I can't remember that he ever missed but I always watched him real closely and never left my toes unwatched.

Anyway, I was there so I saw what happened. It was Ron's turn. He misjudged the throw, and the knife bounced up and scratched another kid's leg. Just a small red line, and he didn't even bleed. No problem, we just kept on playing until we were done with the game. After a while some of the other kids got bored and left, as did I.

Imagine my surprise when I got home and my mom grabbed me by the ear and yelled, "Where is Ron?" I told her and asked what was going on, and she said that one of the other mothers had called her and reported—with some spite, I guess, since Mom was so mad—that Ron had stabbed a kid. I told her that wasn't true and explained what had really happened. Once she decided I was a credible witness she took me in tow and started looking for the rumormonger. Our first stop was the mother who called her who claimed she didn't remember where she had heard the story. Sure she didn't. A juicy bit of gossip like that in a town as small as Pāhala!

But Mom had an unbeatable strategy. She worked her way down the coconut wireless and confronted each mother in turn, asking who had called, and saying that if they didn't want to tell her, she would hold them personally responsible. I didn't know what that meant, but it sounded pretty ominous. Maybe that's why each of the mothers ratted out their sources.

One by one, we worked our way through about five mothers—with me explaining the true story at my mother's insistence each time—until we finally hit the mother lode. It was the other kid's mother who had told the mother who had then created the chain of gossip. It turned out that my mother's nemesis had seen the scratch and asked the kid what happened and, with great glee, started that chain.

Later Ron and I talked to the kid who was scratched, and he said he told her it was nothing. The knife bounced, no big deal. He was as surprised as we were to learn he'd been the victim of Ron running amok and stabbing other kids. That's how far it had gone.

Well, Mom collected Ron and we went to have it out with Mrs. B. It was not pretty and did not go smoothly, but there was no violence—even though this was thrown into the ring of possibilities. The end result was that she never said another word about our family, that we heard anyway. (And Pāhala was a small town, so we would have heard.) Needless to say, Ron's knife was confiscated and he had to do without until he could scrape up the dollar it took to get another one from the store that sold them.

All of us kids had pocketknives, very dull and not very good. We took them to school and carried them everywhere. We used them to sharpen pencils, make toys, peel fruit, cut up fish, take thorns out of our feet, and anything else for which a knife might be required. They were tools, not weapons. The adults knew we had them, but as long as we were using them appropriately there was no problem with us having them in our possession. No one I ever knew as a kid threatened or used a knife on another kid. We all knew that was just wrong. We had our fights and issues, but that wasn't one of them.

I'm going to take the high road and not compare those times with what is happening today. But I can't figure out how taking something away teaches anyone how to make good decisions. I guess when that happens the real lesson they want the kid to learn is he or she can't be trusted to make good decisions. That's a game-changing learning experience for a kid, right along with the old saying, "Do as I say, not as I do," and finding out that adults aren't always right.

Most of my time in elementary school is a blur. I did like school and didn't have much trouble keeping up. It wasn't as bad as Catholic school in Hilo, but there were some low spots. I got over the tomato issue okay. After it was done, I pretty much let it go and mostly I got along with my schoolmates.

But there was one day that didn't go very well. After school, as I made my way across the football field, two kids from school accosted me. I still don't know why; I didn't play with them and we hardly even talked. But for some reason they took it upon themselves to jump me. The bigger kid grabbed me from behind and held me so I couldn't move and the smaller guy beat the crap out of me. Then they ran off, leaving me bewildered and hurting. So I ran back to the school and told the principal what had happened. Go figure, he told me there was nothing he could do, or more likely would do, to help me. His excuse was that it had happened after school, it wasn't on the elementary school grounds, and he hadn't witnessed the event. I guess the bruising and blood weren't enough of a reason for him to act. So I went home feeling like I had been ambushed twice.

When I got home my mom asked me what had happened, but I didn't tell her. I said I had fallen on the playground, so she cleaned me up. Then I found Ron and told him what had happened. All he asked me was which kid I wanted to get back at. I told him the one holding me for the beating. Not the high road, but good enough for me. After all, it didn't look like anyone else was going to keep me safe.

(Parents, just a tip: Any time, and I mean any time, a kid has trouble and tells you they can handle it themselves, pay attention, and find out what is happening. I think you'll find most often it has gone beyond anything they can do to change or fix the situation. So step in and figure out what is happening. If it's kid stuff, back off, but quite often it will be more than they can handle. After all, it's better to head off trouble than to fix it.)

So the next day after school, but not on the school grounds, Ron and I ambushed the kid who had held me; Ron held him and I beat the crap out of him. I have to say it felt very satisfying and, really, I felt no remorse or guilt. They could have left me alone, after all, and this kid didn't have to keep me from defending myself. When we finished, we told him that if it happened again we would also get him again and started walking home. We figured that would end it.

But it didn't, go figure. Guess what? The kid ran to the principal's office and complained about Ron and me. Even worse, the principal ran out and grabbed us, took us back to his office and proceeded to tell us what cowards we were, and how we should be ashamed of ourselves, and how lucky we were that he didn't report us to the police. Of course he had let the other kid go before he apprehended Ron and me, so we couldn't confront the liar.

That was a mistake, a big mistake. I'd had enough. I hadn't forgotten the response he gave me the day before, so I lost it and started yelling at him. I reminded him that we had done it after school, not on the school grounds, and he hadn't seen it, so why was it different for me? I yelled that he wouldn't help me, so why was he helping the other kid when I was just protecting myself? Ron didn't say anything, just watched me run amok with a smile on his face. Then I dropped the bomb. I asked him if he had different rules for haole kids and was it okay to beat us up? Then I dropped the bigger bomb. I grabbed his phone and started to dial. When he asked me who I was calling, I told him I was calling my mom and I was going to tell her the whole story. He knew my mother. He grabbed the phone away from me, thought for a while, and told Ron and me to report to him the next day. So we didn't tell Mom. To be truthful, I'm not sure how she would have responded, so that was probably for the best.

The next day all four of us kids involved were in attendance, and we were told in no uncertain terms that there would be no more fighting between us—none. He didn't care who started the problem, or who finished it. It was done, or else. (I still don't know what "or else" really means.) On our way out, in the hall, Ron whispered to the other kids that it would be best to end it all now, or we'd be back and it would be worse. I guess they took him seriously; I never had the problem again.

Back then it wasn't unusual for kids to fight, but there was a code. One-on-one, up-and-up, and when it was over, it was over. Not a good thing to break the code. Bad things happen. But I had a brother and we had each other's back, and that meant a lot to me.

In Ka'ū when we graduated from sixth to seventh grade, it meant big changes. We had to start wearing shoes and we moved from the elementary school to the high school. That was a big change. It meant we would be up at the campus with the higher grades and way bigger kids.

Ron had preceded me, so naturally I asked him for some tips. He only gave me one. He said the bigger kids picked on the smaller kids, so if someone accosted me I should just punch them. They would be afraid to fight at school and that way I would get respect and probably be left alone.

As usual it didn't quite go as planned. Sure enough, my first day I was walking down the hallway when someone grabbed my shoulder. With catlike reflexes, I turned and without even looking threw a punch. I hit something real big and real solid. Then the boom lowered on me. I found myself looking up into a scary face and hearing a voice ask, "Are you okay? Are you crazy, kid? Why you wen' hit me?" So I told him. He started laughing and said, "You got guts, but you not that smart." Looking at him I had to agree; he was huge. I got up and we shook hands. Then he did something that I still appreciate to this day. He looked around and said, "I like this kid. Nobody pick on him anymore." Turned out he was the toughest guy in school and I was safe, for that year anyway.

CHAPTER 34

Catholic Interlude

My parents divorced in early 1964, and Ron and I were shocked to learn that we had been enrolled in Catholic school in Hilo and were going to live with my aunt and uncle there during the school week. As usual, the kids were the last to know and it was clear our input was not needed or wanted.

I've always known that we lived a little differently than other folks. Not that we weren't clean or didn't brush our teeth and all that stuff. But we never put out tableware, ate most of our meals on a picnic table in the kitchen, and never did things like make our beds or keep our rooms neat or orderly. Just not our style, still not mine.

Of course my aunt was old school. She and Unc lived in a huge three-story house with a cook and a maid and all that other stuff. My cousins were older and had left the home by the time we arrived, which meant that my aunt had to put up with two wild Indians. Make no mistake, both Ron and I were aware of the manners and other protocols of civilization, but we firmly believed that they served no practical purpose. Regardless, we really loved and respected our aunt and even though we were never converted, we toed the line for her.

I was no stranger to St. Joseph School. Ron and I had already attended kindergarten and first grade at the school. Our past attendance did not inspire me with confidence in the patience and wisdom of the nuns. After all, most of what I remembered was khaki pants, white shirts, rock-hard floors we had to sleep on, and rules that always resulted in wooden rulers hitting little hands at the slightest provocation or imagined infraction, not to mention enforced cross-dressing for the day we misbehaved. Yes, it's true. As a result, I approached that school year with a little trepidation. Not an auspicious beginning. The writing was on the wall, the deck was stacked, and I was not looking forward to what was going to happen. I just knew it couldn't go well.

I wasn't disappointed. The white shirts and ties were okay; I could take the tie off after school and the shirts never stayed white for long. But the list of rules, the one I never saw, must have been as long as the Bible. Worse was the way the rules were applied. During that year I developed a deep understanding and appreciation for the words "capricious" and "arbitrary."

Funny thing about school in those days. If you did what they wanted, acted like they wanted, and didn't talk back or stand out you would be okay. But needless to say, I didn't do what they wanted, didn't act like they demanded, talked back, questioned, and stood out. Not the best plan, but back then I had no plan B. Looking back, I know I could have just gone along with the program. Maybe it would have been easier, but at the time that just didn't feel right or honest. Not that I was ever mean or a bully or didn't do my schoolwork. I just didn't conform to their idea of how a kid in Catholic school should comport himselves. I didn't even get close.

The first hint of what was coming started with my initial entrance into my homeroom. I walked through the nearest door only to be told I had entered through the rear door of the room, a rule violation. When I pointed out to the nun in charge that there were no labels or indication which door was the front or rear, or instruction on door entry, I got my first detention. We fought that battle the whole year I spent there. But it got worse. There were some good teachers who treated the students like people, but most of them seemed to have been trained to run the school like a concentration camp—and of course they were the guards.

I got in trouble for using the wrong door, for having my tie tied wrong (it was a clip-on), for talking in study hall, and all kinds of stuff. Once I even got a detention for questioning the virgin birth of Christ. The Sister was not amused when I pointed out that the Bible was, after all, written by people who could have gotten it wrong. It got worse when I asked how we knew that Joseph and Mary hadn't just gotten it on, in the biblical sense, of course. Bingo, another detention.

It got so bad I had a seat reserved for me in detention hall by other detainees who were unlucky enough to become victims of the nuns' capricious and arbitrary discipline. But don't think that Ron was slacking while I was racking up my detentions. We were in different classes, but I frequently saw him after school heading to his detention hall. At the end of the year, the principal made a point of mentioning our poor attitudes to the other students. But when I heard what she had to say, I had my only regret that school year. Not about what I had done, but rather that I hadn't known that I was only two detentions behind Ron. If I had known, I could have made an extra push to get the school record for the number of detentions in a year.

Like I said, we were a little different. Flaunt the law, you say; I say a healthy, normal, and appropriate exploration of boundaries and norms of school behavior. Chew on that a while. Could it be? Did they get it wrong? Probably not, but I wasn't the only one to contribute to my delinquency.

My tenure at the school culminated in either a blaze of glory or a shameless disregard for authority, depending on what point of view you took.

It happened like this.

Because of the overall trend in detentions, our principal decided that she would convene a peer "student court," where selected students would sit in judgement of their less fortunate brothers and sisters—their peers—aided and guided by a token nun or two with the dispositions of a pair of pit bulls, of course.

Lucky me, I was the first victim. I was sent up due to my large number of detentions for talking in study hall. Inevitably I only got more detentions when I pointed out to the teacher that silence wasn't really essential to study and we could learn from each other by talking and collaborating, appropriately of course. Didn't fly very far. Another afternoon in detention. Many detentions. I wouldn't give up and she wasn't going to lose. At least I got a head start on my homework.

Anyway, court day came. By then we scofflaws were calling it student kangaroo court. Naturally the court members were the chosen few: basketball players short on smarts, honor society members who never got in trouble, and your basic kid that sucked up to the principal. As you can tell it was a well-rounded and impartial court composed of those students that were "good citizens" willing and able to make fair and impartial decisions.

It did not go well, for them. I may not behave, but I'm not stupid. The composition of the court did not include a defense attorney, even though they had a prosecutor who was a basketball player that I knew was smart as bait and a judge and jury that was in the principal's pocket. They even had a sergeant-at-arms, another basketball player whose claim to fame was picking on kids smaller than himself and not getting called on it by the teachers. I guess they thought they needed a sergeant-at-arms because I would feel so bad I might go postal or try to hurt myself or maybe assault the court if the decision went against me, even though we all knew that was what would happen. After all, what could be worse than talking in study hall?

So, there I was. I was directed to the dock and ordered to be quiet by one of the token nuns while my crimes were read into the record. But I'm not a quiet guy and figured I really didn't have much to lose, so I interrupted the proceedings and pointed out the lack of a defense attorney while the charges were being read. They studiously ignored me and kept droning on about dates and times and talking in study hall and going in the wrong door and talking back to the teacher and a general statement about my utter disregard for rules and authority. After a while I got tired of what was going on so I spoke up again. I did not make any more friends when I asked if they were indeed acting as a court or rather an inquisition, since it was painfully obvious that I was not going to be given the opportunity to defend myself. That didn't go very well. I got yelled at by the principal, who was attending to lend her authority to the proceedings, and they moved on with the farce.

Did I mention that I was supposed to be silent, repentant, grateful for the life lesson, and maybe even embrace the chance to redeem myself? Well, that part of their program went down the drain. But really, what did they expect anyway, contrition or repentance or maybe crying and throwing myself on the mercy of the court? Or, knowing what kind of people I was dealing with, flagellation or maybe crucifixion in the grand Catholic tradition, or having me fed to their mean little dog?

After the reading of the charges, they convened their jury while I stood alone in the dock waiting for the verdict. Like we all didn't know what was going to happen. They clustered together like a gaggle of geese or, more appropriately, a murder of crows, whispering and being very obvious that they were ignoring my presence while being painfully aware that I was watching their every move. After their very brief and not very spirited deliberation, they delivered the required verdict with a beaming principal standing by nodding in approval. Big surprise. I was guilty. Of everything. And there was no excuse for my hooliganism or behavior. Needless to say there was no hung jury or dissention; the verdict was unanimous. So, I had to stand there and listen to that pap.

The jury foreman (he and I did not get along) gleefully delivered the verdict. Then the principal stood up and started to speak and it all went to hell. She should have known better. After all, what did I have to lose? The fix was in and my goose had been cooked before I even walked through the door, so I decided to go down fighting. I interrupted her and challenged her role in the proceedings. After all, they had billed it as a court of my peers in an effort to deceive their less astute victims into thinking that the proceedings and results would be fair.

I declared that she had no business giving any input due to the fact that she was in no manner a peer of mine; rather she was my superior in the school structure and this court was supposed to be conducted by my student peers. Then I suggested she stop making pronouncements on punishment that were supposed to be decided by my peers. It got very quiet and she looked so mad I thought she would pop. She had it all: a red face, clenched fists, and a look that would curdle cheese. Right then I knew what some of those martyrs felt like before they were sacrificed, but no way was I going to back down. I knew I had the moral high ground and I was going to keep it, even if it cost me, and I knew it would. That principal did not like to be challenged.

Then it hit the fan. It really hit the fan. She did not like what I had done. She knew nobody could keep word of my act of defiance from the rest of the school and she didn't like that one bit. She blew up, called me a bunch of names a nun shouldn't know, and announced my sentence. Court pau. All that was missing was leading me away in leg irons.

She decreed that as an appropriate punishment I would have to write an essay about what I could be doing instead of talking in study hall. She must have lost sleep trying to find a new and creative way to intimidate and embarrass me for my sins. She further decreed that the essay was to be delivered by me to the whole school—reviewed and approved by herself, naturally, to ensure that I would not make a mockery of my conviction. Then the administration of the punishment in front of an assembly of the whole school, elementary through high school, who would be there to marvel at my flagrant disregard for authority, witness my shame, and learn fear from my disgrace. I guess they liked to discipline students by making them think badly of themselves. Maybe it worked most of the time, but not that time.

I duly wrote and read my report to a glowering principal, who kept tapping her hand with a large, thick ruler—I knew she wished she could have been hitting me instead, so I kept my distance. I'd been on the other end of a nun's ruler before. Not much fun.

I got the essay approved and she scheduled the assembly, telling me I'd better show up or she would hunt me down and bring me in if I didn't. I believed her. She was not happy with me. There were a couple of other victims scheduled for punishment that day also, but I don't remember much about them.

I do remember the little reminder the principal gave the assembled students that this was punishment, it was not funny and any laughter or unruly behavior by the audience could result in severe punishment or expulsion. Naturally the student kangaroo court was up there on the stage lending their stern visages and illusionary authority to the event.

When I walked up to the microphone, the first one I had ever seen up close, all I could see was a gym full of faces, each one looking at me. I was nervous and scared, and I thought I was going to puke. But God does work in mysterious ways. Somehow, as I stood there stalling and fiddling with the mike and after a couple of thumps that make those cool mike sounds and "Testing, testing, testing" to delay a little longer, I had an epiphany. I know it sounds corny, but what else could it have been but an epiphany, a real, probably-sent-from-above-to-comfort-me-in-my-time-of-need epiphany. So, regardless of how I got there and how bad it was supposed to make me feel, I realized it was *my* essay, that gym full of students was *my* audience, and that moment belonged to *me*, not a bunch of kiss-ass students or a witch of a principal.

I started, "Fellow students." Somehow that must have been funny because I could see the smiles, hear the coughs, and finally a smattering of chuckling. I realized that the students who came to see me punished also knew what a joke it was, so I put the pedal to the metal. I guess I can be funny. Halfway through the first paragraph the chuckling got louder. I hit my stride in the third paragraph and now most of them were laughing. But I knew they weren't really laughing at me, they were laughing for me, because I couldn't, and we all knew it was just a big joke.

It got way better when the principal lost her temper, grabbed the mike, and started screaming at them to stop. Well, I made it through the essay and she could never blame me for what happened.

But even though she never intended it that way, she showed me that I didn't have to be afraid. Just be myself. Like I said, God….

Well, you knew it was coming. I didn't get expelled, but my dad was informed that I would not be welcome in their school again. Which was ironic, because later that summer when the school got the results of some kind of national educational test we had taken, they offered me a scholarship. Seems I had scored in the ninety-fifth percentile of the nation in the test. Someone who wasn't the principal must have figured I had some potential and, if properly motivated and docile, could be a credit to the school. But there was a catch, I had to promise to behave. But the cost was too high, I couldn't make that promise. I would have had to keep it.

Just so you don't get the wrong idea from all the fun I mentioned above, let me assure you that attending that school wasn't all fun and games. The Sisters had some odd ideas about how to motivate their charges. One of them was to separate each class into two sections. One was the overachievers, or at least the ones the nuns considered good citizens and worthy students. The other section was the "others," or those who were not great students, those that challenged authority, and any other student that didn't fit the mold. But they were determined to drive those square pegs into the round holes.

Another of their strategies was to rank each section's students in their homeroom by the student's academic ranking when report cards came out quarterly. Starting with the highest academic achievers in the front row and on down to the last seat in the last row. Then movement within the class was dictated by our behavior in class. I guess they hoped the "others" would be putting forth their best efforts in the hope they could achieve enough to move up to the other section. Yup, I was in group number two with the "others," but that's where all the fun students were so it was pretty good most of the time. But after every report card I would be moved up to second or third seat in the ranking, which shuffled me into the group who really cared and tried hard but couldn't understand someone like me. Not very comfortable, but usually about a week after we got shuffled, I would be battling it out for the last seat in the last row, the bouncer's seat, the one where anyone sitting there could see everything that was going on in the classroom and nobody was behind.

Occasionally another student would act up and the nun's response was quick, if not always appropriate. One incident I recall happened when another of my classmates was accused of something he didn't do. He wasn't a rocket scientist, hence the placement into our crowd of misfits, but he was not a liar and he certainly wasn't a coward. When the nun told him to come up to the front of the class so she could single him out and ridicule him, like they did with a lot of us, he refused. She got a little steamed, but when she tried to pull him up to the front, she realized he outweighed her and she couldn't budge him. We tried to tell her she had made an error, but like a lot of adults in those days she had made her mind up and just wasn't going to change it, even if she had it wrong. She eventually discovered her error but, go figure, she stayed mad because he had flouted her authority.

Sometimes the nuns would make a sweep through the restroom, which was only a problem because they were women and they went into the boys' restroom without making sure it was empty first. I did not endear myself to the principal one day when she swept in while I was in a compromising position. Well the old bod shut down. No way I could continue. She proclaimed in a loud voice that it had been reported (hearsay) that we were eating our lunches in the restroom. Really? I probably shouldn't have told her we didn't come there to eat our lunches, but to get rid of them. Another detention, another boring hour after school.

But wait, sometimes the nuns also entertained us. Not on purpose, but there were moments, very different moments. Like the Catholic cowboy.

It happened this way.

There was a nun, a very old nun, usually nice but with a temper. She taught science, which was all right, but she had a habit (yup, pun intended) of falling asleep mid-word in the heat of the post-lunch afternoon. Usually we let her have her nap; she never flunked anyone and, like I said, she was usually okay.

That day we were sitting quietly watching her sleep, when a large man approached the windows that looked into the field above. The room was sub-surface so we had an odd point of view. So, this guy comes into view. Nothing very unusual; we could see out and others could see in, that was normal. What wasn't normal was this guy, who looked like he was in his twenties, was dressed in a red striped shirt, shorts, a cowboy hat, cowboy boots, and had two cap pistols on his belt. That wasn't all of it. He was galloping up astride a broomstick with a horse's head on it slapping the reins and having a grand old time. (I can sense your disbelief, but this really happened.) Well, he saw us and pulled back on the reins while he was slapping leather. He got both guns up and was shooting, ducking, and weaving, coming ever closer to the window above the sleeping nun. When he got there, he ducked down behind the sill and popped up shooting, then ducked back down. That's when one of us—this time it wasn't me—started pointing and shooting back silently. Then all of us reprobates joined in, pointing and silently shooting. The cowboy in the red striped shirt was putting up quite a fight. Not deterred by the number of his foes, he soldiered on, at least until I guess he decided he got shot. He let out a loud shriek, grabbed his chest, and dropped out of sight. That's when the nun woke up from her nap. She usually took a couple of seconds to figure out where she was and get her bearings. But this time what she woke up to was a bunch of kids pointing their fingers, at her, or so she thought, and making shooting motions. I couldn't blame her for being upset under those circumstances.

Our foe grabbed his trusty steed and galloped off when he heard her start screaming at us, enraged at our impudence and disregard for her authority. She had her back to the window, so she never saw him. Things calmed down when a more level-headed nun came in to see what was going on and actually listened to us, better yet she knew about the Catholic cowboy. She lectured us on taking advantage of someone who was not quite up to speed. But I didn't feel too bad; he gave as good as he got, and at least for a little while he got to play with someone. But I guess they made sure it wouldn't happen again; we looked for him but he never came back.

My last hurrah at St. Joe's (hah, they never liked us to call it that) came during the year-end class picnic at Kolekole Park. Kolekole is a really neat park outside of Hilo on the Hāmākua Coast, off the main highway and down a short winding road, tucked away between high hills on either side and fronting a stream with a waterfall. In those days we could swim and do other things when we picnicked, so first we climbed up the hill on the town side, broke off the tops of ti plants and used them to slide down the hill, bouncing off anything in our way, until we hit the bottom. When that got old, we ran over to the stream and went swimming. It was great. We could tuck ourselves behind the waterfall and get the nuns worked up trying to keep track of all of us. They did not swim, especially in their habits. It went sideways when one of us found a faint trail near the waterfall and a few of us less obedient types climbed up the muddy slope to the top of the waterfall.. From that vantage point, we could see everyone at the picnic and we made enough noise that they certainly saw us. But that got old and we climbed back down. I was really dirty, so I slid behind falls for a while. I guess I missed the part where the nuns saw me up on the top of the waterfall but not after that and—knowing I wasn't wearing glasses and how blind I was—started praying on their knees for my safe return. I really didn't mean to scare them so badly, but when I disappeared they started looking for my body, convinced I had fallen and slipped under the water to my death. I think they were happy when I appeared all clean and washed. At least they didn't blame me for doing anything but leaving the picnic. I always wondered if they ever went back to that park with a bunch of rowdy kids again.

There was one incident involving another kid from school that didn't turn out that well. Up above the town on the Wailuku River above Rainbow Falls, there's a spot called Boiling Pots. It's named that because the river runs through tunnels and caves under the surface, and the water rising up under this pressure looks like it's boiling. We all went there and mostly we were careful and stayed away from the boiling areas. After all, just downstream was Rainbow Falls with its grim reminder of the possible consequences: a cross that commemorated the death of a serviceman who had foolishly jumped off the falls and landed on the rocks below. He did not survive.

One day at Boiling Pots, a kid who couldn't swim very well got caught in one of the "pots." From what I hear, he had gone down a couple of times and it wasn't looking good. But Sammy, one of the guys from our school, saw what was happening and jumped in and pushed the other kid up until he could be pulled to safety. But then Sammy was pulled under before they could help him out. He disappeared, and some divers recovered his body later. We all liked Sammy, and we weren't surprised that he did what he did; he was that kind of guy. We missed him a lot.

After I left St. Joe's, I did have another brush with the school, although not intentionally. One night when I was a teenager hanging out and surfing in Hilo, two of my good buddies asked me to help them put something into the back of a car. Being a good Samaritan and a loyal friend, of course I helped them. I found out when we got there what was going into the trunk: a nun's gravestone they had lifted from one of the cemeteries in town. Well, I did help them put the stone in the car, but then I made myself scarce. I knew there was no way this was not going to go badly. I found out later they decided to end their school year with a strong statement. They put the stone on the grounds of the school, just outside the teachers' lounge. I heard it looked pretty real, with a mound of fresh dirt and all. Naturally they were found out, got in trouble, had to take the stone back, and were chastised in the church paper. But for once I dodged the bullet. They never ratted me out or said who I was. I was just mentioned as "that unknown delinquent from out of town." Those were friends; misguided, but friends.

But my fun in school wasn't restricted to Hilo.

When I got back to Ka'ū in the tenth grade it was like I'd never left. Nothing much had changed. Much later, when meeting with a bunch of my classmates for coffee, one of them mentioned the ninth grade initiation and asked me how it was for me. She seemed surprised to realize I hadn't been there. I wasn't, I was in Hilo, dressed in a white shirt, tie, and slacks. Guess where I would rather have been?

CHAPTER 35

Come Dancing

One thing we did a lot was have dances at the gym. To be honest, aside from the occasional crush I had on some of the girls from school that never went anywhere, I had no girlfriend and wasn't sure what I would do if I ever had one. Remember, small town, not much to talk about. So I was really shocked to find out one day, after I had walked a girl home from the library at night, that she was pregnant and we were going to have to get married. Wow, even for Pāhala that was out there.

But I did like to take my sweaty palms and teenage angst to the dances. They were really fun and a place where we could mostly safely practice our courtship behaviors.

Aside from the occasional slow dance (you know the ones where the guys try to dance as close to the girls as they can, while the girls try to stay as far away as possible—awkward!), one unique thing about Pāhala was that we danced in rows. Rows of boys on one side and girls on the other facing each other and just dancing away. Sometimes the couples would dance from one end to the other between the rows, sometimes we would take turns. Never saw that anywhere else I've ever been.

There was one other thing. I found out that some of the more enterprising lads had found a secret way to climb from the boys' bathroom over the canec ceiling in the gym to get a glimpse of the girls' bathroom. Not my kind of action. Just not cool. But for a while they made the trip. I never did, but it must have been kind of risky. We found that out the night when one of my classmates broke through the canec ceiling when he made a misstep. We could all see him, and all of us guys knew what he'd been doing. We could see dim faces and grasping arms as he swung back and forth screaming for help. But alas, none of his friends wanted to go down with him or be revealed, and he fell. He wasn't hurt much, but at least one of the teachers figured out what was going on and made sure it didn't happen again.

We had all the usual events like proms and homecomings, and we all participated. It was lots of fun and I did enjoy them a lot.

Pāhala participated in interscholastic sports as well. I've heard that at one time Pāhala was the smallest school to do so in Hawai'i. I believe it. I hardly ever watched, since I had no future in sports in Ka'ū. So even if some big event was happening, I bowed out.

CHAPTER 36

PSAT

I've always known that I'm smart. I'm not trying to brag or be arrogant, I just am. However, I also get bored easily and am not very motivated and, as you can tell, my judgement is sometimes questionable. But I read a lot and remembered what I read. I never really put much effort into school. For years, all I ever read on my report cards was "John can do much better if he would only work up to his potential." I could never figure out how they knew more about my potential than I did, but that's the way it was.

Nobody ever asked me why I was unmotivated. They didn't care much about that, I guess.

Until my junior year, that is. That year, we had an interesting cast of teachers and one of them, the counselor, decided to make me his project. He was a good man, I liked him. He meant well and he wasn't a quitter. It was kind of like sparring; he'd find a button, push it, and I'd try to stay one step ahead. That was the situation for most of the year, until one day he thought he had me. That day he asked me to drop by his office. He told me he had just gotten the results of the PSAT and he wanted to go over mine with me. Normal counselor stuff. No danger, I thought.

When I got there the stage was set. He had two sets of papers face down on his desk, a smile on his face, and a "gotcha" look in his eyes. Then he turned one of the packets over. It was my test results. He explained that I had scored in the ninety-fifth percentile for the whole country; I had scored higher than ninety-five percent of all the students that had tested. He went on to tell me what a huge accomplishment that was and how proud I should be of myself. I guess it was kind of special, but I didn't feel any different.

Then he turned over the other set of papers, my report cards. He asked me, "What's wrong with this picture, John? How could someone as smart as you get grades as low as the ones you are getting?" That was a good one. He thought he had me trapped.

I guess animals would gnaw off a limb to get out of a trap, but thankfully I didn't have to go that far. I agreed with him. What else could I do? There was something wrong, dreadfully wrong, and something needed to be done to remedy the situation. I could see he thought he had me, and I really felt a little sad when I suggested he talk to my teachers to have them raise my grades. I explained that it was only reasonable, after all, how could I have achieved those magnificent scores unless I was learning more than they were giving me credit for? It made sense to me.

I stopped being a project, but to his credit, he never seemed to hold it against me and we remained friendly until I graduated.

CHAPTER 37

Da-vine Intervention

I had run-ins with some of my teachers in Ka'ū. Maybe my fault, maybe theirs, but the path of education always had some bumps for me. One of the teachers I never really warmed to was my algebra teacher. He was an odd duck; not the most personable guy and wont to writing long algebraic equations on the board and losing himself in them, forgetting he was there to teach. He would calculate, erase, mutter to himself under his breath, and forget he had a class full of students.

We had a point of contention. He was all about processes, but I have always been about outcomes. I could correctly answer ninety percent of the problems posed to us in class. I just didn't do it the way he wanted, my brain just didn't work that way. He would get mad. I would ask him why it was important and suggest that if I could repeat my results, what did it matter? But it mattered to him. One day we were going at it again, and after a while he sent me to the vice principal's office.

When I got there the vice principal was out, for about fifteen minutes the clerk said, and since she saw me more often than I liked she told me to just go in and sit down. I sat down next to the old PA system that hadn't worked for three or four years. Bored, I pulled out the cabinet and looked in the back. Lo and behold, there was a tiny piece of wire with a loop just visible poking out of a back corner near a terminal head. I hooked it up to an empty terminal nearby. I just couldn't believe someone else hadn't tried that already, but still I went ahead. Then I plugged in the PA and turned it on. I never expected the soft, PA-type *puu-waa* and static crackle that announced that it seemed to be functioning. So I thought, what the hell, might as well go for broke. I flipped the numbered switch for the classroom I had just left. That way if it worked, it could only be heard in that room. Then I got on the microphone and talked in a weird voice. I said I was God and told the teacher I was watching him and he needed to be nicer to his students.

I really didn't think it would work. After all, there had to be electricians and other people who had worked on the PA and tried to make it work, even if they had declared it defunct and left it in the office as a monument to something, or maybe nothing. But just in case, I carefully detached the wire, tucked it way back out of sight, put the switch back to off, and unplugged the unit.

A little while later the vice principal came in and we talked. He was a great guy; it was a good day when he got promoted to principal. He more than deserved the promotion. I unfailingly respected him. He never made assumptions and always heard both sides of an issue before deciding what to do. He was always fair and I never had a problem with what he decided, even if it didn't go my way. We were just talking, waiting for the teacher to arrive. He asked me if it would be too much trouble to just try it the way the teacher wanted. I was about to agree—it was a reasonable request and if he thought it would be fair I could do it. But then the teacher burst in and declared, "It was him! It was him! He had to have done it."

I said nothing, just tried to look interested but innocent. It got really interesting when the vice principal asked what he was talking about and the teacher reported that God was talking to him from the air, telling him to be nicer and he was being watched. Then he claimed it had to be me on the PA.

That's when the vice principal told him to cool down and explained that the PA system had been broken for three or four years, so it couldn't have been me. I guess that only left God. But the teacher kept on, so the vice principal told him to go ahead and try the PA if it would make him happy. Luckily, I hadn't been on the PA for long; I guess it hadn't heated up or it had enough time to cool down. Luckier still, he didn't see the wire when he looked in the back, after plugging it in and fruitlessly trying to get a response when it was turned on. He kept toggling the switch. I was told to go back to class, the vice principal and teacher were going to have a little quiet time.

When I got back to class, they were all still commenting about how God had talked to our teacher from the air. He was out for three or four days and we got a sub. But fair is fair. That wasn't a real nice thing to do, so after that I did try to use his processes even though I liked mine better.

But you'll never convince me that process trumps outcome.

Maybe a little bit about the teachers in Pāhala would be appropriate right about now. Generally, these teachers were good people who really tried to help us kids learn. There were some that I consider examples of the best that we can be. I remember them fondly and I hope that if any of them ever read these words, they'll know they had an impact on my life that's lasted till today.

They were teaching in a small town east of nowhere and west of nothing. A lot of them were young and from the Mainland with no car, which really limited any non-school opportunities. A lot of them just didn't understand the culture or the language (pidgin) we used for the most part outside of school. But they hung in there and did their best. Most of them were moving through on their way to someplace else, but while they were in Pāhala they really tried to be part of the community and a positive influence on the children they taught. But sometimes things went a little sideways. Slippage, I like to call it.

CHAPTER 38

Reading Class

By the time I was a senior in high school I had exhausted the Pāhala Library. Our librarian had started searching the library system and was bringing in six to seven books a week from other libraries throughout the state for me to read. I really respected and appreciated her. She was nice, and she went out of her way for me. I'd pick the books up on Friday when she got her shipment, and usually I'd return them on Tuesday and wait anxiously for my next batch. But I was never disappointed. I love to read, I always have, and always will. There is nothing like the feel of a book in my hand and a tale to immerse myself in for a while.

In my senior year the state Department of Education established a mandatory experimental reading and comprehension course that we all had to take, and it lasted all year. What we got was cards with short stories in different levels of reading and comprehension with a timed quiz for each story. Then we would grade ourselves using another card with the answers.

I didn't think it was that hard. A week after we started, I reported to the teacher that I had finished the material. What do you think she did? You guessed it. In the best tradition of a rigid, uncompromising teacher, she instructed me to do it again. I did. Third week, ditto. By the fifth week I had memorized all the cards, so I sat in the back, shuffled the cards, pulled one out at random, repeated the story from memory and followed with the answers to the quiz, out loud. Don't get me wrong, I'm not a genius, but it just wasn't that hard and I was bored.

She was, predictably, not happy. She felt I was mocking her. Maybe I was a little, maybe a lot, but I was not happy either. I explained that I felt I had done what I needed and I just couldn't read the same stuff for the rest of the school year. I was going crazy. She replied that that was the curriculum and I had no choice or I would flunk.

Flunk reading? Me? I spent every spare minute I had with my head buried in a book and she knew it. Insanity or power mad teacher? You pick. I even tried to come up with a solution and suggested she give me a list of books that I could check out of the library to sit in the back and read quietly. I even volunteered to do book reports. That's when she went postal; I was challenging her authority. The way I saw it, I was questioning her judgement, not challenging her authority. But I guess for her that wasn't okay. She got so mad she grabbed me and pulled me out of my seat and out the door. When we got outside, she pushed me up against the classroom wall. Then she got about two inches from my face and yelled, "Do you know what your problem is? Do you?"

After being manhandled and sprayed upon and smelling her stale cigarette breath, I was not in a conciliatory mood. I replied, in my best teen-with-an-attitude voice, "No, I don't."

She yelled, "You're a smart ass! A goddamn smart ass!"

I didn't help the situation when I responded that I would rather be a smart ass than a dumb ass that kept reading the same stuff over and over for a year. Off to the principal's office I went, again. I sat down and said hello, then she stormed in screaming to the principal that she couldn't take it anymore and telling him what a smart ass I was.

One thing about our principal, he was fair, he was everything I hoped for but rarely got from most other adults. He waited her out, then asked me what my side of the story was. I explained about the class and that I had completed the work already, but was being made to keep doing it over and over. I guess I got to him when I told him I had done the whole course at least five times already, all of the course, every damn story and I knew them by heart.

It didn't go better when he asked the teacher if what I said was true. She reluctantly agreed I had mastered the material. After all, what could she say since I had volunteered to recite any of the readings along with the answers to the quizzes from memory? She knew I could, that's why I was sitting in the office.

Then things got a little more interesting. She sulked when he told her that we all knew that I didn't really need a reading class. She started fuming when he further said there really was no need to make me repeatedly do the course work for the rest of the year if I had already finished and mastered what was required. Then it went into postal territory when he suggested she give me a list of books and I could sit quietly in back of the room, read in class, and do reports on the books she gave me to read for the rest of the year.

She hit the roof and accused the principal of colluding with me to undermine her authority, then started to go off on what a punk I was and proclaimed that he was just encouraging my insolent behavior. Of course, she said what I needed was structure and discipline. No doubt *her* form of structure and discipline, which to me meant rigid and uncompromising. I got to leave then. I don't know what happened in that office, but when she came back, I learned what they meant by the expression "If looks could kill." That was the year I got to read and do reports on the great books of the Western world. *Don Quixote*, the *Iliad*, the *Odyssey*, and the rest of them were way more interesting than those damn cards.

She graded the reports fairly and never admitted I was right. But that was okay, I never reminded her she was wrong.

Detente!

CHAPTER 39

A Contender? I Think Not!

Not really, not even close. Remember: asthma, glasses, overweight. But that didn't stop me from trying.

PE was pretty much the same year after year. We followed the schedule of other sports. We'd play football, softball, track in the same cycle as the other sports. It got pretty predictable and boring. The positions in physical education mirrored the teams Kaʻū had: the pitcher was the pitcher, the quarterback was the quarterback, and on and on. But change? Not a chance, even after I suggested to one PE teacher that since we were supposed to be having fun and learning things in PE maybe we could rotate the positions among all the students. Blasphemy, he told me. It just wasn't done. Then he asked me if I thought I was a pitcher or quarterback. I guess it didn't help when I replied that I didn't know, I'd never gotten a chance to find out. I didn't bother to ask again.

I was never much good at sports. I just never cared enough to really give it a hundred percent. So, of course I was always the last one picked for the teams in PE, and when I played softball I always got the field behind first base where hardly any balls got hit.

Mostly elementary school PE was a blur, but I still remember that awful moment when a slow, high pop fly I was trying to catch somehow slipped through both my hands and hit me square in the glasses. They broke and it became a big deal that my safety glasses had saved my eye. (Until they found out I hadn't been given safety glasses after all, but after that it died down.) I never got much better at catching or shooting basketballs or any of that other stuff. That's the way it went until I went to Catholic school in Hilo and got on the track team. Of course I had visions of glory and being blessed with a letter jacket and basking in the resulting glory. But it didn't go that way. I was assigned to run the mile and the half mile. I didn't have any problem running the distance, but I actually was the slowest runner at any of the meets I attended. I even got lapped a couple times, to my shame, but I soldiered on hoping that perseverance would compensate for talent. But no dice.

When I went back to Ka'ū my streak continued. But there was one ray of light. One day our PE teacher wasn't there and a substitute teacher took over for our normal mind-numbing hour of softball. But something was different. After my first time up to the plate and after watching me, he took me aside and suggested that I would do a lot better if I stopped trying to kill the ball and just hit it solidly instead. Wow, that was good advice. I started hitting the ball further than anyone else I played with, then I got good at aiming it where I wanted it to go, so I was having a grand time with a thrill every time the bat hit the ball with a satisfying and solid *crack*. It was so much fun I thought I could go out for the baseball team, since my dreams of glory were still lurking, as was the hope. But when I showed up for tryouts, I was told I didn't have to bother, the roster was full and they didn't need any more players. I got no reply when I pointed out that they just had about two more than they needed and certainly there was room for someone who could hit like I could. But no, shot down in flames.

But do I learn? I guess I really am an optimist. One day Pop—after watching me run to fetch a couple of cold beers for him and one of his cronies—suggested I might want to go out for long-distance running. Sounded good; I never wore out or got tired running, I just wasn't a sprinter. So I went out for the team. But there had never been a long-distance runner in our school, so the coach didn't appear to know quite how to train me. I guess after a while he got tired of my questions, so one day he told me to just run—anywhere, just anywhere else. So I ran. First, I ran up the main road into the cane fields, then down the back road to the main road, up the road to the mill and around to the main road the other way, and eventually back to the school field. By then everyone had left. When I got back, my coach asked me where I had been, so I told him what I had done. It hurt when he told me I was lying, so I told him he could kiss my—well you know—and I quit the team. I guess he must have been more than a little embarrassed when other people in the town started asking him about his training regime. Seems that truck drivers and others had pretty much seen me run the whole distance and they asked why I was so far afield. But I guess it would have been too much to admit he was wrong and look for a better track fit for me. So I didn't expect him to admit he was wrong, and I wasn't disappointed.

But third time had to be the charm. My senior year, I was asked by a couple of friends to go out for the football team. They were on the team and they were really short of players. By then I was a good candidate. I weighed about 180 pounds, most of it muscle I got surfing and doing other physical stuff.

So I showed up for the first practice. It went okay, although I did feel kind of silly yelling at a dummy and pushing a bleacher with the rest of the team. I thought it would be fine. I wasn't trying to be a quarterback or anybody important, just one of the guys who got in the way and rushed the other quarterback. Simple, just the way I like it.

But I guess it wasn't simple to some of my "teammates." The next day at school several of them came up to me and made a point of telling me they were going to "get me." When I asked them what that meant they told me that they were mad because I hadn't bothered to go out before and they were going to make me pay. Their chosen method, which they shared with great glee, was to use their cleats to grind my feet into the sod, which they told me would be easy because I would be practicing in tennis shoes since they would need to order shoes if I made the team.

I asked them why they thought it would be a good thing to cripple one of their own teammates, especially as short-handed as they were. But their response was something they left unsaid. It still doesn't make any sense to me. I guess that was one of the unwritten, unknowable, arbitrary Ka'ū rules that I kept bumping into.

But I figured I could ask the coach for an old pair of the right kind of footwear and soldier on, since I knew they had a box of old shoes in the corner of the locker room. So again I went to practice and it went okay for a while, until one day the coach, who had known me since I was in second grade, yelled at me, "Haole boy, go scrimmage!" Funny, he called everyone else by their name; maybe there were too many syllables for him to say "Japanese boy," "Hawaiian boy," "Portuguese boy," or "Filipino boy" when he called my teammates. But I got to be "haole boy." I guess that was not one of the neutral uses of the word that time. Not being the fool, I walked over to him and said I would be happy to, if he could loan me the proper footgear. It did not reassure me that some of my teammates were making grinding motions with their cleats on the ground and looking very intently at me the whole time. Not surprisingly, given my history, he ignored my request and yelled, even though I was right next to him, "Haole boy, I told you, go scrimmage!" Again I declined, but I was getting a little tired of the whole mess. The next thing he said was the last straw. "What's the matter, haole boy? You chicken shit or what?" That did it. I told him, "I guess I am, but you're an asshole," and walked off the field for good.

That pretty much ended my athletic career at good old Ka'ū High. I just went surfing instead. Funny, when they formed an interscholastic surfing league, they tried to get me to represent the school. Hah, I told them where to go. I wasn't going to pimp the thing I valued the most for them; they didn't deserve it.

There were other sports and other sportsmen, but there was one I'll never forget. In our town, there was a man who was a little delayed. Not a mean or bad person; we always talked to him and he was pretty friendly. I'm not sure what he did most of the time, but he really liked sports. Not watching sports, but being involved. Whenever he could, he would stand off to the side of the field and watch whatever sport we were doing in PE. We could always tell something was up with him when he started rocking back and forth and jumping a little. After he couldn't take it anymore, he'd dash on to the field and grab whatever he thought he wanted to do and imitate the players. We learned very quickly to let him have his way. He did not like it when anyone tried to stop him, and he was strong—real strong. So we just let him play until he became distracted and left, happily. That was better for everyone. But one day, one unbelievable day, he showed everyone what he could do. We were playing touch football and he was over on the sideline. We all knew what was going to happen, so we kept an eye on him until he dashed out and grabbed the football. We were throwing passes, so that's what he did—only his pass, his perfect pass, went from about one-third of the way from one goal post all the way over the other post. We all watched that perfect spiraling pass just seem to go on forever. Then it landed in the bushes on the other side of the field and he left. I think the coach almost cried. Talk about visions of football glory.

There was one other incident involving the sportsman. Some of the town bullies thought it would be fun to see if they could get him to have sex with a girl who was developmentally delayed. Bad mistake, real bad mistake. He might have been a little slow, but he knew right from wrong. He told them no. They persisted and he beat the crap out of all four of them. Later I heard there were mutterings from the losers about criminal charges and lawsuits. But that went nowhere, especially when everyone found out what they were up to. They left him alone after that, and for as long as I knew him I'd always say hi and spend a little time with him if I saw him around town. I guess you don't have to be a rocket scientist to know right from wrong.

CHAPTER 40

The Knocks on the Door

Like most teenagers, I never gave much thought to what was going to happen once I graduated from high school. I just lived day to day. When I was fifteen, Ron and I were at home one evening when there was a knock on the door. Not an usual thing in Pāhala. For a kid, or at least for Ron and me, a knock on the door at night is almost always a harbinger of dire events.

Not that we didn't ever get knocks on our door, even in Pāhala. The last time before that had been about six months earlier when, to our surprise, we answered a knock on the door one Saturday morning to find two genuine blonde goddesses standing on the porch. They asked if they could come in, and naturally Ron and I willingly agreed. When they did, they sat down very close to Ron and me in our living room. Then they turned on their charm, exhibiting their well-filled sweaters in the heady testosterone-rich atmosphere, and explained what they were doing in Pāhala.

They had been sent to canvas the town to sell magazine subscriptions to the locals, which they claimed was to fund their college educations. Mind you, these weren't even magazines we'd want—just drivel and trash, at least from what I saw on their list. They batted their eyes and wriggled parts of their bodies and did their best to talk us into believing that we *wanted* to spend money we didn't have on magazines we really didn't want. They didn't even offer us surfing or hot rod magazines, which was our speed in those days; just magazines about teen idols and sewing clothes, and the like.

Ron was all over it. He was looking through their catalog, trying to impress them with the wisdom and breadth of his potential selections. I didn't say much after I saw the list, as there was nothing there that I wanted. But I guess I still managed to look alert and interested, because one of the girls kept trying to sell me on those magazines. The problem was I wasn't interested in the magazines, just the peddlers. They were very easy on the eyes. I could see they thought from the glazed look in Ron's eyes they had hit the mother lode and were ready to seal the deal. But then I asked the one talking to me the magic question, the elephant in the room question, the "What's in it for me?" question.

Don't get me wrong, I'm mostly not cynical or mean, I'm just not a fool. I asked the blonde goddess who was brushing her sweater against my arm, holding my sweaty hand and gazing into my glazed eyes and trying to convince me I really needed lots of magazines I didn't want and couldn't pay for, "What's in it for me?"

She asked me what I meant and kept on trying to convince me that giving up my money so she could have a bright future was a kind and wise investment. Then I asked her again, "What's in it for me?" Of course, she tried to explain like I was a dolt who just wasn't getting it, that she would be able to pursue her dream of college, and in return I would get the magazines (that I didn't want or need). So, after being enlightened, I asked her, "What else do I get besides subscriptions?" Funny, she knew right away what I meant that time.

Of course, she got offended. In fact, they both got offended. Then, one of them asked me what kind of girls did I think they were? I knew what kind of girls they were. They got really mad when I replied that they were the kind of girls who used their looks to sell crappy magazines in nowhere land to hicks who thought they were getting a deal. When I asked them what the difference was, they left. They left in a hurry and didn't look back.

Ron was not happy. He thought the one he was talking to had really liked him. Right. But for better or worse, they were gone. At least I had the memory of that well-filled sweater pressed against my arm and a faintly lingering scent of a pheromone-laden perfume to haunt me. Better than nothing, I guess.

But back to the second knock on the door. It was a busy year—two knocks. I answered the door to find two of Kaʻū's three local policemen on the porch. One of them asked—in that weird, official cop voice they only used if someone was in trouble—if Ron was home. I thought that was kind of odd. After all, they could see him behind me, so I had to say yes.

I called Ron, who was trying to slink away unnoticed, when one of them said, "You better stay, John. We think you should hear this too." Then they pretty much told Ron that his time in Pāhala was over. It was time to join the Navy or Army or some other organization, but whatever it was it was going to be somewhere else.

I guess by now you've figured out Ron was kind of a rogue. Normally he was pretty good at staying under the radar, so he hardly ever got in trouble, except for the time he lifted another kid's bike on Halloween and hoisted it up the school flagpole. I was there when they came to accuse him, and I'll never forgot the look on their faces when they told him he had been seen and he better turn over the bike. It must have really hit them when he replied, "That bike?" and pointed to the bike at the top of the flagpole. I guess they just let it go as a boyish prank with no harm done. He kept skirting the law most of the time he was in Pāhala. Rowdy enough to have a good time, good enough to leave alone. But he finally stepped over the line.

I guess it was the last straw when Ron and some of his cronies had been drinking (underage, of course) and decided to steal and drag a section of the school's bleachers seven miles down the main road, then set up on the beach at Punaluʻu to watch the waves. Of course, they didn't bother to take it back, and as in any small town someone had seen them and was willing to talk.

Ron, no fool, joined the Navy the next week and left for boot camp. After that, I kept a very low profile. I missed Ron, but life went on.

Much later when he and I spent a week in Kona together we talked about his departure. I was really shocked when he told me he had always been proud of me and knew I was really smart. But that just wasn't for him. He had always struggled in school and when he left, he was in the same class as I was. I never teased him about it and never felt it was fair, but there was nothing I could do. Then he told me that in the Navy they had figured out that he was dyslexic and without help he had actually done better than they would have expected. They helped him get his GED and he could move on. When he told me that, I felt really lucky that someone had figured out I needed glasses when I was a kid. Who knows how I would have turned out otherwise?

A little side trip here.

Ron was always a little different. Mind you, it was a good different. He could always do things I couldn't. One of the things he did best was listening. He had no problem sitting down with people who knew things he didn't and listening to them tell him about the old days, how they lived, and how they solved problems. That has always been a struggle for me, even now. After all, Pop told me years ago that I could never learn anything with my mouth open and he'd been right, again.

Here's one example of what Ron learned and applied: One day when he lived near Volcano Village, he was helping a friend clean his house before moving. One thing the friend wasn't taking with him was a collection of old oil paintings, so Ron asked for them and was given the paintings for helping. When I saw them, they were stacked in one corner of Ron's living room, leaning against the wall. So I leafed through them and commented on how terrible they were. Ron agreed, but he showed me one of them and said this one is worth big bucks, and he was going to trade it for money and a family heirloom for his daughter.

So I asked him how he knew the painting was so valuable. He showed me the signature of a very famous Hawai'i painter, then told me that this was that artist's earliest known painting. Of course, I asked him how he knew that, but his reply made more sense than I would have expected. He pointed to the landscape and said, "There was an earthquake in the 1800s and that point of land sunk into the ocean, so the painting was made before that happened." That's how he knew. He remembered something someone had told him and recognized it in the painting. Later when I asked him how the sale had gone, he showed me a whale fishhook that once belonged to one of the buyer's ancestors and told me he had gotten that plus $5,000. He said he was going to try to find his friend and split the money, but the fishhook was his.

Back to our story.

Ron left to join the Navy and another year went by, with no knocks on the door, I might add. Pop and I were having dinner one night. He asked me what I was going to do after high school. The superb career counseling we received at school consisted of our gym teacher who—after demonstrating how to lie on a table and pull up our left knees to more easily pass gas (really)—advised the guys that the best option for a career was to join the military and learn a trade (other than killing people), then come back and work on the plantation. Clearly, he wasn't encouraging college as a choice, but I asked anyway. That's when he summed up his presentation with a loud, "Shut up, Walters—I wasn't talking to you!" I'm still not sure if it was a compliment or an insult.

Still, I told the old man I planned on going to college, just as he had.

I was floored when he agreed with me and even volunteered to pay for my education, which I had never really expected. The euphoria of the moment lasted about a minute, until he explained that, of course, the only college he could afford was Brookings in South Dakota. He said I could live with relatives, wait tables for cash at the college, and eventually I would graduate.

I wasn't thrilled. I knew he was serious, but I'd lived in Hawai'i all my life. I loved it then, and still do; sun, surf, and beaches. That's the way he raised me. Not in a place with snow, mosquitoes, and, worst of all, no surf. Knowing how he worked, I asked him, "What's behind door number two, Pop?"

One thing about Pop, he always had a plan, and a plan behind the plan, and a backup for the plan behind the plan, even though we never got that far down the plan ladder.

He replied that door number two was that, since I was going to be sixteen the next day and just coincidentally there was a Naval Reserve meeting that night in Hilo, we could drop by and he would sign the papers and I could join the reserves. That way after two years of active duty, I could use the GI Bill to go to college anywhere I wanted. You guessed it: I took door number two and embarked on my career in the Navy. All one year, eight months, twenty days, and fourteen hours of it. But that's a tale for another time. Suffice it to say, the leopard does not change his spots.

CHAPTER 41

Motoring Madness

For years we referred to my father as Mr. Toad. Not because of his looks, but for his inclination to drive everywhere with foot planted firmly on the accelerator and then plastered to the floorboard of whatever he was driving at the time. Don't get me wrong—he was a good driver and only had one accident, which he always claimed was not his fault. According to him, his snappy, fire engine red 1966 Pontiac Tempest forgot the way home after a quiet evening of introspection and meditation in Hilo at the Elks Club. Scratch one car. His leg was broken in two places and he waited in the car for three or four hours for someone to come by who could help. He was a very tough man; help finally arrived. He was the only person who was ever transported in the town's ambulance, an old wartime Dodge.

Our cars were a series of chrome behemoths. Pop liked his cars, and he liked them big and with big engines. Usually he bought Pontiacs—he really liked his Pontiacs. Usually, he got them secondhand. I guess having five kids really cut into the budget, but he did okay; he always had a machine with a big engine that worked, and that could accommodate all of us.

About engines and cars that didn't work: When I got my license and got my own cars, mostly used cars, they sometimes weren't the paragons of motoring dependability I would have liked. So one night, Pop and I were talking and I asked him what I should do if one of my cars just stopped working and I had to pull over. His reply has given me pleasure for years and it turned out to be great advice. He said, "Simple. Use the dumb haole look." When I asked him what he meant, he said, "It's easy. Just pull over, lift the hood, and stand there looking into the engine compartment scratching your head. Someone that knows more than you will pull over and take care of it." He was right again. More than once I've had to pull that out of my toolbox and it worked every time. People in those days helped each other out and they certainly knew stuff I didn't.

We mostly had station wagons—huge, long vehicles that rode and drove a lot like a boat. Pop always wanted the biggest engine he could get and he liked to drive fast, like everyone else back then. Kind of makes you wonder why everyone was in such a hurry since there wasn't much to do and not many places to go. Maybe the hurry was what they wanted to feel. Anyway, after a series of wagons that are kind of fuzzy to me, he got his first new car that I knew about: a brand-new, spiffy Pontiac Bonneville station wagon. It was a great machine and the one I learned to drive with, which was a chore when it came time to park it since it was so long. I still remember trying to parallel park it during the road test for my license. Even though I tried to talk to the officer about fishing, as everyone suggested, after a couple of abortive efforts to squeeze that car into a space designed for a Volkswagen, he told me to give it up and practice more. I guess he saw that I was serious because after another week he told me I was good enough and that I should drive by the station and pick up my license.

That car could scoot! I think the engine was 389 cubic inches of go, the same engine that was in the GTO. It had a normal carburetor, but Ron took care of that for Pop. Ron and I had made a trade for a car we couldn't fix, couldn't drive, and couldn't move. Real smart. But it did have one redeeming feature. It had a brand-new Carter AFB carburetor, which was twice the size of the one on the Bonneville. So we made a trade: the car we couldn't drive, move, or fix in exchange for the removal and installation of the AFB on the Bonneville. We threw in the old carburetor, since Pop wouldn't be needing it. So that's what happened. Everything went pretty much as it normally did, except for the next time that Pop, in a lead foot moment, wanted to pass a much slower car. He pushed his foot to the floor and I guess we were all surprised. With a very loud growl, the car lunged forward like a starving tiger. Pop just reveled in the moment, blowing by the other guy and motoring on toward Pāhala. But when things slowed down, he mentioned that he didn't remember the car being so fleet of foot, must be the gas. Ron and I just kept silent. He

Little helpers.

never looked under the hood so he never found out. But he did notice something else. When he opened that baby up, we could watch the gas gauge move toward empty real fast. But that wasn't a problem, since gas back then was a steady fifty cents a gallon with full service.

We motored on with that station wagon until he got his 1966 Pontiac LeMans. I really loved that car, not that I am a car-loving type of guy. (After all, my favorite vehicle without exception is the 1950s-era Jeep station wagon.) But that LeMans, in fire engine red with a 327 cubic inch engine, had it all. Fleet of foot and a timeless beauty. Too bad it forgot the way home from Hilo one night.

Then we got the last car Pop had while I was in Pāhala. This time he went all out. He got a Pontiac Grand Prix from a friend who was a dealer in Hilo. My theory is that the car didn't sell because most sane people would be afraid to drive it. Not that it was a bad driving car, it's just that it was so fast; once it got going, it was scary. It had a 428 cubic inch engine and a speedometer that went to 140 miles an hour, and it would go that fast and more if it was pushed until the needle hit the turn signal light. Guess how I know that? Thankfully, the roads were not very crowded back then and there were lots of straight sections. What a beast.

It was delivered while he was in the Pāhala hospital recovering with the pins in his leg. It just about killed him that I drove it before he did. I had to drive it down to the hospital every day and move it around so he could see every bit of that car to be sure I wasn't abusing it, or his trust, and that I was taking care of it. We finally got over that and he very happily got behind the wheel and continued his motoring ways. There was one change though. If he had spent a little too much time in quiet conversation and introspection, I got to be the designated driver. I think we both felt a little better about things after we made that change.

But that's not the story I wanted to tell.

I guess Ron and I had a bit of Mr. Toad as well. We had vehicles of our own to play with. Not the passed-down plastic bikes or wagons we were often "gifted" with that lasted no longer than the first excursion or ride. No, we had well-used but sturdy chrome-plated beasts that could withstand the worst abuse a child could dish out and come back for more.

The bikes usually were just about invulnerable and they had fenders, real seats with springs, and wide, easy-to-grasp handlebars. They also had coaster brakes that we could rush pell-mell down a street and hammer down to screech to a halt, leaving a little smoke and plenty of rubber as a memento. They had one speed and were heavy and slow uphill, but on the downhills they were unstoppable.

We also had one of the legendary little red wagons for a while, but it came to an untimely and premature death when Hurricane Dot swept by Pāhala back in 1959.

It happened like this.

As the hurricane was passing, Ron noticed the very brisk winds that were sweeping across the length of the football field. A light went on when he remembered one of the age-old formulas for fun and motoring madness. Wind + wagon = speed. Bigger wind + wagon= more speed. Again, he somehow talked me into being involved. By then I should have known better. I had sworn off any more experiments after the last disaster, but I backslid and succumbed to the dual blandishments of speed and danger. I guess it's a guy thing.

Ron collected the red wagon and an old army blanket. The plan was he would steer and I would hold the blanket up to be a sail. It didn't take long to figure out that was not a workable plan. I just kept getting blown over and the wagon didn't move.

Then Ron upped our game. He got three sturdy broomsticks, kept the army blanket, and procured some rope. The grand plan was revealed. We were going to make a sail, like one of the old sailing ships, and sail like Vikings across the field. I have to say, it sounded good. We braced the mast, tied the blanket to the crosspiece, and secured it with two more lines from the bottom corners tied to the wagon.

That's when I asked Ron what the third stick was for. He explained it was our brake and, as I would be sitting in the back holding on to the two lines, I was also the designated brakeman. Naturally, Ron as the oldest and most experienced was steersman, pilot, and captain. I got to be the crew, the whole crew, responsible for our safety by dragging the stick to slow us down when the order was given.

Ron got in the front to steer, and I got in the back to hold the lines and brake if necessary. Ron gave the signal and we unfurled the sail. I grabbed the two lines to keep the sail tight, and away we went. But neither one of us expected what we got. It worked, which probably surprised Ron. I know I never thought it would get off the ground.

We started off at a crawl, then proceeded to a stately pace, advanced to a fast clip, and shortly thereafter we were racing totally out of control. Ron was trying to steer, but we were weaving from side to side and I could tell the wagon was out of control. I couldn't see anything as I was behind Ron and holding on for dear life. But I could feel the wagon going faster and faster. First Ron yelled, "Faster, faster! Hold on!" Then he started yelling, "Brake, brake, dammit! We're going to crash!" At least I thought that's what he said. What he didn't know was immediately after we started, I had tried to slow us down, but with two hands and three things to do, the stick had been ripped out of my hands. It was gone, along with our only chance to slow down, and there was no way I was going to stick my feet into that mess. Finally, after we hit a bump, I felt the wagon going airborne.

Somehow, every time I encounter disaster it seems the space-time continuum distorts and time is expanded. It all happens quietly and in slow motion. Maybe it's because the universe wants to squeeze every last bit of fear and disbelief out of me before the inevitable crash and burn. If so, it always works.

I watched it happen kind of detached from reality, almost like an observer. The front of the wagon lifting in the air, Ron screaming, "Brake! brake!" and the slow roll to the right at high speed. Next, the awful nosedive into the grass. Then things sped up. I don't know what happened to Ron, but I got tangled in the wagon and crushed it, leaving a twisted, broken mess on the field.

Ron came over and looked at the carnage. His only comment was that our sister, whose wagon it was, sure wasn't going to be happy. We decided that silence and innocence was our best defense, so we dragged the wreckage back to a corner of our yard and hid it under a pile of mango leaves. That time it seemed to work. Probably because nobody found it till it rusted out and even if they had seen it, could anyone imagine we would engage in that kind of lunacy?

But wait! Ron wasn't done. While we were salvaging whatever we could from the wreckage, he had another idea. He grabbed me and ran over to a slight hill on the windy side of the field. Guess what? He had discovered that the wind going across the school field was creating a really strong updraft at the top of the hill. We stood there for a while letting the wind blow on us. It held us up when we leaned into it. And when we opened our mouths, we felt the wind puff out our cheeks while we moaned like banshees. Great fun!

Then Ron had big idea number three. There was no stopping him once he got started. Reverse parachuting. He figured there was no reason why we couldn't use the updraft and the army blanket like a parachute, but instead of going down, we would go up. I guess by then I was punchy; it sounded like a great idea. He grabbed two of the blanket corners, one in each hand, wrapping them around his fist to secure them. I did the same. Then we stood just below the top of the hill and he yelled, "Three, two, one—open!" and we opened the blanket into the wind and up we went. It worked, it worked too well. I got scared about a second later and about eight feet into the air, I let go, but Ron hung on, and for once he was the one that took the hit and landed hard. He was shaken, but okay. As soon as he knew he wasn't hurt, he started yelling at me that we could have gone twenty or thirty feet into the air. But he was silent when I asked him how we were supposed to get down. He hadn't quite worked that part out yet. But still, it worked.

CHAPTER 42

Amusements and Diversions

We tended to make our own toys, so when skateboards became the latest thing Ron and I, with no money between us, made our own. Funny thing about money. We never had a lot, but it seemed to be enough. If I remember correctly, our allowance was a quarter a week. We got to keep the money we got for Christmas and birthdays, but for years, any other money we got, we earned for ourselves. I used to pick ʻopihi, sell coral on the beach, and hire out as a yard boy for ten cents an hour. But the good part was that stuff didn't cost as much back then. A candy bar was five cents, a soda as low as seven cents (for the Hilo Soda Works brand, still the best sodas I ever tasted), and comic books cost twelve cents, or fifteen cents for the *Classics Illustrated*. It didn't take a lot of money to be happy. We just had to be creative and use what we had wisely.

It wasn't hard to make a skateboard. All we had to do was find a pair of worn-out skates and take one each, split them apart and hammer them flat, then nail or screw them to a suitable board in the front and back, push off, and have fun. Too bad Ron procured the first skates from an old pair that didn't belong to him. But they weren't being used, and when I found out they weren't Ron's, it was too late to do anything but forge ahead. But we did let everyone use the skateboards, which kept things okay. Shortly thereafter, all the children in our family and some other kids had skateboards. We'd spend hours circling the tennis court when nobody was using it and rode down the long hill on the main road in town when there were no cars.

They did have their limitations. If you rode them a lot, they tended to get real thin on the outside edges of the wheels and the bearings, which were never meant to take the abuse we dished out, didn't last very long, and often gave out even though we learned early on to lubricate them so they lasted longer. The problem was they usually gave up the ghost at the worst possible moment. Revenge maybe? Like the time we were racing down the long hill and a wheel passed me on the left. I just had time to laugh at the fool who was riding without a wheel and didn't realize it was me before I went down—hard. I still have the scar. They also had a tendency to lose control and weave back and forth uncontrollably if we went too fast, but with no brakes we'd try to crash into something soft. No helmets, no pads, but lots of fun sprinkled with liberal amounts of road rash and blood.

Later Ron and I used some of our savings to purchase real custom skateboards from a guy in Hilo who was building them with all the bells and whistles available at the time. Big money, fifteen dollars each, but well worth the price. What a difference! Rubber wheels that were smooth running and actually flexed to turn the board, which looked like a real surfboard. Just about that time, the plantation had paved a steep section of road in a new subdivision where there were no houses and where no one was working. We had it great for about three months, until the construction started. Head dips, cutbacks, and all the surfing moves for hours and hours. It doesn't get any better than that.

CHAPTER 43

The Bicycle Built for Two Fools

We also had bicycles and tricycles; mostly well used, but functional. We'd ride the trikes in the tennis court because of their turning radius, and because it was the only safe and even place to ride them. But we'd ride the bikes everywhere: up into the cane fields, down the old road, and once as far as the beach, seven miles away and mostly downhill.

Once, Ron was even part owner of a bicycle built for two that he and some chums were building. They had talked someone into welding two bicycle frames together that sort of looked like the beginnings of a bicycle built for two. It had handlebars, seats, and pedals when Ron had it, but nothing else. It didn't last long but it went out in a blaze of glory.

I rode it once with Ron, its first and last flight. Somehow, he convinced me (again) what a great thing it would be if both of us pushed the bike up to the band building one weekend. The plan was that we would start at the top of the school near that building, ride down the sidewalk through the school, speed across the road, and jump the small hill that bordered the football field, after which we would coast onto the field until we stopped.

Of course it didn't go that way. You'd think I would learn, but I was as hot to trot as Ron was. Oh, it started out fine. We pushed the bike up and started out from the band building, proceeded down the long walkway from the building, picking up speed on the slope through the school, then raced down the sidewalk towards the road.

Oh, did I mention there were no brakes? Ron had neglected to inform me of their absence when working me up for the ride and selling me on his grand scheme. He later told me that he knew that if he told me there were no brakes I would never have gone along. Foolish me, I assumed that little detail had been taken care of. I should have known better. His plan was that I would slow down and stop the bicycle with my feet, even though they couldn't reach the ground. I guess I thought (rightfully) that only a fool would ride that thing down a hill without a reliable way to slow down or stop. I was having a grand time speeding down the hill with the wind in my hair, until I tried to put on the brakes and the pedals kept spinning around the wrong way without any effect. We kept picking up speed and almost missed some of the turns, we were going so fast. As we raced on, I tried to decide whether to bail out or keep going, while Ron concentrated on keeping us upright and heading in the right direction. He kept yelling at me to slow down, the fool. I would have done it if I could, but no chain, no brakes. I never bailed out. I was too terrified to jump and knew that if I did, I would get creamed. There were no good choices. I was too scared to jump, but too scared to stay. So I mindlessly hung on till the bitter end, hoping for the best. I should have bailed, or at least closed my eyes. When we crossed the road, we made the jump just as Ron had said we could and went airborne, and it looked, for a very brief moment, like everything would end well. But Ron's euphoria and my relief didn't last long. When we landed after making the jump, the weld joining the two halves of the bicycle separated, and the bike broke in two pieces that parted company along with its riders. It must have been hysterical to watch. Ron took a nosedive into the grass as I flew over him, crashed onto the field, rolled a couple of times, and finally stopped—dazed, scraped a little from the grass, but miraculously unhurt. Ron of course just got up, brushed off the dirt and grass, and walked over to the wreckage. I left him there to figure it all out and walked away. I was finished. I never saw that bike again.

It didn't end there. I guess both Ron and I had motoring madness in our blood. We moved on to bigger and faster machines, but none of them seemed to provide the oomph or lunacy as those we rode in our younger escapades.

CHAPTER 44

The Phantom Rider is Out There

Long before there was the character Ghost Rider in the comic book of the same name, we had one in Ka'ū. I bet you can guess who assumed the mantle.

From time to time there would be other haole kids from the Mainland in our school, usually just until their parents got other work elsewhere—anywhere—and escaped. Ka'ū was not one of the great urban centers on the Big Island and most people who weren't raised there were just passing through on their way to someplace else. When I was about seventeen, another kid lived up in Ocean View Estates, a godforsaken jumble of lava and more lava that had been made into house lots with plenty of empty streets. He was a little older than me and had a much more powerful dirt bike than my Yamaha 80. He used to drive at full speed through the empty subdivision on the roads in the unimproved sections at night. Not a good idea. Sadly, one night he miscalculated and went off the end of one of the roads and into the lava at about eighty-to-ninety miles an hour. They found him, after they heard the crash, by the shine of his headlight into the sky. Real sad. He was a quiet but nice guy.

At the same time, I was buzzing into Hilo on Friday night and back to Pāhala on Sunday evening on my Yamaha 80. Because it was so clear in Ka'ū at night, at least when it wasn't cloudy or raining, I could see the road clearly without using my headlight. So I'd turn it off and race as fast as I could on the winding road through Hawai'i Volcanoes National Park and on down to Pāhala. Real cool. Super adrenaline rush.

I didn't often pass another car coming home from Hilo. When I did, no problem. I would just move over to the right side of the road from the middle (I rode on the white line), turn on my light and, after passing the car, turn it off again and keep going.

I thought little about it until I was up at the shopping center one day and heard two guys I knew talking about "the haole boy's ghost riding the highway." When I heard that I kind of perked up. Seems that, since the accident with the kid from Ocean View Estates, people had been reporting seeing a phantom motorcyclist. He would appear out of nowhere, his lights would flash, and he would vanish. Go figure.

They knew I always rode that stretch of road on Sunday, at the same time as the sightings, and on a dirt bike. But instead of connecting the dots, they asked if I had seen the ghost. Of course I said no, and when they were speculating why not, I suggested that since we were friends, he wouldn't haunt me, everyone knows that, right? Naturally, they thought that made sense and agreed that must be the reason and no more was said, but lots more happened.

I put it to you, what could I do? I sure didn't explain what was happening. Oh no, that would be too easy. Instead, I kept right on riding without my lights, turning them on, then off, and disappearing into the gloom.

In my defense, nobody asked me if I was the one doing it, but after a while I was in too deep to confess. If I had, I would have been in real trouble. Nobody really wanted to lose a good ghost story and find out it was just a punk kid fooling everyone. Truthfully, I didn't really want to stop anyway.

It went on for a couple more months, but like all good things it finally came to an end. I decided to pack it in one night after I passed a car and did my thing. This time I heard the brakes as the car stopped, then they turned around and came back up the road. Well, I knew if they caught me, it would get ugly, real ugly. So I turned off the road, without my lights, onto a small trail leading into the lava field. When I got into the trail as far as I thought would be safe, I killed the engine and rolled the bike behind a big rock and lay down beside it, hoping the crackle of the cooling engine wouldn't give me away.

It was so quiet I could clearly hear drunken voices talking about finding that damn haole ghost and sending him to hell, where he belonged. I could also see the beams from the flashlight they were using to scan the roadside. Luckily, I had been able to get about a hundred yards in before I hunkered down. Not a very comfortable situation. One of them came down the trail about halfway to where I was hidden, but he went back when he finished his beer and threw the can into the lava.

After a half hour or so, punctuated by much drinking of beer and swearing, they gave up and took their beer and flashlights down the road. Of course, I waited another hour in the cold to be sure they weren't trying to lull the ghost into a false sense of security before I left for home, with my lights on.

Over the next couple of weeks, I kept the lights on and waved to everyone I passed on the road. Then somehow, the consensus evolved into the theory that the spirit had passed on because of prayer or some other divine intervention.

It sure was cool while it lasted. But I never told anyone in Pāhala that I was the real Phantom Rider.

CHAPTER 45

"See you in court, kid!"

I bought the Yamaha 80 when I was sixteen. It was a trusty and dependable steed, from the first day I motored up to the house until I left for active duty in the Navy. But it also figured in some interesting events and my last brush with the law in Pāhala.

When I got the bike I duly applied for and received a learner's permit, but I guess the police in Pāhala didn't have a protocol for road testing, and one day the policeman I respected the most in town stopped me as I was motoring around—practicing, of course. I was kind of surprised when he handed me a license. Apparently, the officers stationed in Ka'ū had been talking and the consensus was that since I hadn't killed myself or been in an accident, it would be okay to give me the license. Like I said before, old-time policing.

But my last brush with the law was not a real good example of that kind of police work. Remember, I had been put on notice, not for anything I did, but more because I was Ron's brother. Guilt by association, I guess.

But anyway, one day in school when I was a senior there was one of those police knocks on my classroom door. And again, in that weird cop voice, I heard, "We'd like to speak to John Walters." Not even a "please." So I followed the two officers (I guess they thought I was a dangerous criminal and they needed back-up) to the counselor's office, with the eyes of everyone we passed on us, wondering what was going on.

When we got there, we sat silently. I didn't know what they had in mind, but I was trying to remember if there was anything I needed to worry about. At that time, there was nothing. Just the dirt bike I had left on the side of the road the week before up by the volcano. I couldn't drive it because a critical nut had fallen off the back suspension; I had to get another one and then retrieve the bike before it would be safe to drive. Shouldn't have been a problem. Everyone knew who owned the bike, and nobody could drive it off anyway.

I guess they got tired of trying to wait me out, so one of them, the one that never liked me, the one that "suggested" Ron should leave town, asked, again in that weird cop voice, "Would you like to tell me about it, John?" So, believing it was about my bike I replied that I just needed to get someone to drive me up and I would move the bike. It wasn't a real big deal.

That's when he tried to lower the boom and said, "You know that's not why we're here. You'll be better off if you just tell us about it." That's when I knew I had them. I knew I was clean, but I sure wasn't inclined to be conciliatory. So, in my best teenager-with-an-attitude voice, I told them if I knew what they were talking about I'd be glad to tell them about it.

Of course that didn't go over very well. One of them growled that I damn well knew what they were talking about. But I held out and eventually it came out when one of them said, "We know that you and Reggie were up at the volcano slashing the tires on the tourists' cars."

I have to say, that was a shocker. I've never been a saint, but I never even considered being a vandal. It just made no sense to me, then or now. But still, I held my ground until they said they had a witness who had positively identified me. Go figure. But still I held out and asked them for more information on what their "star witness" had told them. Then one of them read from their report, in that weird cop voice again, trying to make it sound official and ominous. Kind of like: At 1200 hours on whatever day it was, two youths identified as myself and Reggie were witnessed driving around on my bike up at the volcano lookout and in the immediate vicinity, and slashing the tires on several tourists' rental cars.

But the devil is in the details. After a pregnant pause, while they waited for remorse and guilt to hit me (I was trying to drag out and savor the moment), I asked the big question: "What day was that?" Of course they thought it was a desperate attempt to stave off the inevitable confession. But this time it didn't go their way, not even close. Sometimes, in spite of the law, there is justice.

When they repeated the date, I asked, "Did any of you geniuses check to see if I was in school that day?" Of course they hadn't. So I let them have it: "So you're telling me that myself and Reggie, who I don't hang out with, took our three hundred-plus pounds of youth, got on my bike, drove twenty-five miles up to the volcano at about ten miles an hour (that's about how fast I could have gone with that load, and they knew it), slashed tires for an hour, then rode twenty-five miles back, all during our lunch hour? I was in school that day and only went home for lunch. Get your witness and I'll see you in court." I knew they couldn't say that time had been distorted just to make me a vandal, so I figured it was safe. Besides, I didn't know if I'd ever get another chance to be innocent.

Damn, that felt good. I knew I would pay somehow for my defiant attitude, but sometimes you just have to bring the hammer down. Our interview ended with dire threats of doom and destruction for me down the road, sprinkled with hints of incarceration and other acts of legal reckoning. But nothing more happened, and I never even got an apology. But I made damn sure not to give them anything else to use against me for quite a while.

CHAPTER 46

Work

We always had chores when I was growing up. At first little ones, then bigger. We were pretty lucky, my mother had someone come in to help her with the washing and other inside-the-house stuff. We mostly worked on the yard, the huge yard. In Pāhala all of our houses had big yards, but the last one we lived in as a family had a huge beast of a yard that had to be mowed and raked endlessly, along with other work, depending on what fruit was in season. There were mango, pear, avocado, banana, and guava trees growing in or around the yard and various shrubs and flowering plants surrounding the house.

We mowed the yard weekly. Our mower was a secondhand model with a blade that spun under the cover. It wasn't the kind that wheeled itself, so we had to push it the whole time. And it was kind of finicky; it was hard to start and liked to take frequent breaks. But even so, we had some moments. Once, Ron saw me moving the mower from one side of the concrete walkway that ran through the middle of the front yard from the street to our front porch. Because the mower had a tendency to stop, I'd approach the walkway until I could get just the front tires onto the concrete, then lift the front of the mower and run the damn thing off the walkway at top speed.

Easy money, that is until Ron decided to play bigger, smarter brother. As I made my approach and was ready to lift the front of the mower on to the walkway, he screamed, "Stop, you stupid kid! You're going to get hurt!" So I stopped. After all, he was bigger than me.

While he was yelling, trying to instruct me in the proper method, he chose to demonstrate by reaching down and lifting the front of the mower. Too bad it was still running. Luckily, he shaved only a little line across all of his fingernails on both hands—just a little sliver of a line, but still scary.

Needless to say, I had the good taste not to comment; it wouldn't have been polite, or safe. But after that, he left me alone when I was mowing.

We also had to feed the animals and, in mango season, raked up hundreds of pounds of rotten fruit from under the two mango trees in the yard.

We pretty much kept up the same chores until I was fourteen and my parents divorced. After that, it was fish or cut bait. I learned to cook, wash my own clothes, and keep the house minimally—or at least sufficiently—clean.

Things stayed pretty much the same until I was sixteen, when the dream of easy money lured me to Lāna'i to pick pineapples. I can still hear the radio ad that ran endlessly just before summer vacation, promising that if I signed up I would "have fun in the sun while you earn." Sheer genius, that ad. But I really wanted a dirt bike and the only way I'd get one was if I earned the money myself. There were almost no earning opportunities in Pāhala. The plantation jobs went to the graduating seniors, so we others just had to make do with whatever we could find to do to pick up spare change. Sometimes I could get a couple of dollars picking 'opihi or selling coral to tourists at the beach, but that wasn't even close to the $400 that a dirt bike would cost. My mother had located one in Honolulu and the guy who was selling it was willing to wait till the end of summer for his money, so off I went. Just so you know, there was not much "fun in the sun" while I earned. We'll get to the money part later.

When I first got to Lāna'i I lived in a schoolroom that had been converted into a barracks, with upper and lower bunks separated by tall lockers to make sections where four workers lived. It was the first time I had been away from home. Perhaps not auspiciously, I weighed about two hundred pounds, wore glasses, and was terribly out of shape. At least there was no sugarcane and my asthma took a vacation that summer.

But I really wanted that dirt bike.

Living in the barracks was like living in a zoo. It was hard to sleep and there were constant fights, since many kids from all over the state were crammed into a very small space. Adding to the chaos were the young members of Mainland football teams and church groups who had been recruited for their own fun in the sun. I can only speculate what kind of "tropical paradise" ad was running back where they came from. Most of them went into culture shock or what we called "rock fever" as soon as they arrived. But I guess they had to stick it out. Someone had to pay for the airfare.

Did I mention we got a hefty $1.08-and-a-half cent an hour. Yup, that's right, $1.08-and-a-half cent an hour. About $8.64 a day for an eight-hour shift in the fields, $43.20 a week, and $166.80 a month, less food and keep. What a deal!

The Mainlanders didn't really blend in very well. Quite often they would get little beetles we called sesame seed bugs in their ears and run screaming through the fields until the *luna* (supervisor) could catch them and dose their ears with oil. Sometimes there was trouble with communication. They just didn't get that saying "What?" in response to a comment was essentially an invitation to fight. They didn't thrive, and sometimes they didn't survive.

We all lived at the school that had been converted into the rough barracks. They separated the classrooms into cubicles by lining up rows of four metal lockers about six or seven feet high, one for each inmate, and putting two bunk beds in the space that this created. It was okay, but it was noisy and the food was terrible. But I guess it was the best they could do and we managed, mostly.

One day after work one of the Mainlanders was getting a little out of hand in the barracks. He was waving one of the large knives we used for weeding and yelling he was going to kill us all. Nobody knew, or more likely was willing to say, what had had happened to him. But something had to be done. Somehow, the guys I bunked with decided I was the best one to talk him down. After all, they said, "Haole-to-haole is the best."

I sidled over and asked him to calm down and put the knife away. I calmly told him he was scaring everyone and nobody wanted to hurt him. That was okay, but foolishly I had put out my hands out in front of me; I guess I thought I was making calming motions. If so, he didn't get the message. He really did put the knife away, but he put it away in my left hand, the one he stabbed, the one with the scar. That really pissed me off, so I pulled a row of lockers over on him and, when he was pinned and screaming, took the knife away, and made myself scarce. He couldn't get free, so later on when the police came to take him away, I slid out the back while they came in the front. As it turned out, he couldn't ID me and of course nobody else saw anything. So I got a scar, a knife, and a story. He got to go home.

After that I'd had it with dorming, so three of the guys on my crew and I rented a duplex for a lot less money. No meals were included, however, so we had to supply our own food. Mostly what we ate was rice and anything else that was cheap. Vienna sausage, Spam, chicken; you know, the basic food groups—starch, fat, and salt. I still get a whiff of nostalgia when I see or smell a can of Libby's beef stew.

We never ate breakfast. For lunch I'd get up when the 4 a.m. whistle blew, wash rice in my kau kau tin, throw in a can of Vienna sausage, warm it all up to infuse the rice with the delicate flavor and enticing aroma of the Vienna sausage, and when it was done, grab it on my way out. I ate a lot of half-cooked rice with burst Vienna sausage, but hunger really is the best appetizer. Dinner was whatever we could scrounge up or canned food sent by sympathetic family members, always accompanied by lots of rice. By the end of the summer, I'd lost about fifty pounds. It just seemed to disappear. Go figure.

I worked on the day shift. That meant I would get up, cook lunch, then make my way down to the truck yard by 5:30 or 6:00. At the yard I would muster with my luna and work gang. Then we'd get into one of the pineapple bins on a truck and away we would go to the field we were going to pick that day.

There were several kinds of fields. The easiest, and most productive, were the one- and two-year-old fields. Those plants still produced lots of fruit and the rows weren't overgrown yet, so it was easy to walk through them. But the summer help got the three- and four-year-old fields that were overgrown and tangled, grew high, and were not that productive. We called them the Jungle, and for good reason.

While working, we had to wear protective gear because the leaves of the plants would shred, poke, cut, and really hurt us without it. We wore leggings over our jeans, work boots, jackets, and special sleeves that we pinned over the jacket sleeves for additional protection. We didn't have to wear helmets, but we had big brimmed straw hats and goggles for our eyes, either the ones made of something resembling mosquito netting that made us all look like flies or the green plastic ones that made everything look red when we took them off. All that gear was heavy and hot, really hot. A gallon canteen was issued to each of us and sometimes we would go through two gallons of water during a workday, it was that hot.

Of course, we had to get all the gear from the company store, on credit, before we could start working.

Picking pineapples isn't rocket science. Each worker gets a row and is expected to pick all the pineapples on both sides of the row. The trick was to pick all the ripe, or almost ripe, pineapples in your row. Sounds simple, but it wasn't. We followed a boom with a conveyer belt that loaded the pineapples into hoppers on trucks that were replaced as we filled them. The speed of the trucks was set by the luna, who liked to move fast. All day they kept yelling, "*Mansu!*" or "*Hyaku!*" which I think means "faster." All day we were pushing through the jungle, trying to spot all of the pineapples, pick them, and keep up with the boom.

I quickly learned there were two ways to pick pineapples, or "pine" as we called them—one for when the luna was watching and the other, more efficient way when he wasn't. The approved method was to hold the crown and "flip" the pine, using the weight of the fruit to break off the crown, which we dropped. Another way, which was much slower, was to hold the pine in one hand and twist the crown off with the other hand, which would always result in falling behind the boom. The other, unapproved method was to "bang boom," or remove the crown by tapping the fruit right at the base of the crown against the rubber bumper, leaving the fruit on the conveyer belt. Very quick, but if done wrong, bad for the fruit. But it was about twice as fast and the only effective way to keep up with the boom.

It was hot, dusty work on a normal day, but sometimes we would be sent to fields that had names like the Oven or the aforementioned Jungle. I quickly learned that those names meant something, and it was best to pay attention so any extra prep could be done to make it easier.

Every day after my shift, I went home exhausted and worn out. "Fun in the sun while you earn." Sheer genius.

It wasn't all work. Lānaʻi City offered a tiny library, two stores, a theater, one restaurant, and a bowling alley. Everything was dispensed at a premium and cost at least three times what it would normally cost on the Big Island, which was probably twice what it would cost on Oʻahu. I don't know what I would have done without my weekly care package from my father. I could always depend on at least four cans of Spam, eight to ten cans of Vienna sausage, and a couple of cans of Libby's beef stew.

I never went to the bowling alley. It wasn't my thing, the food was expensive, and the tough guys liked to hang out there looking for fights with easy victims.

We did go to the movies now and then. It was quite jolly—a small, hot and stuffy theater filled with screaming teenagers. Most of the films were at best B-grade, but it didn't cost much. The theater was so old that the ceiling was made of canec and had many holes. During the lulls in the bedlam, we could hear disturbed rats running back and forth over our heads. Once, one of them got it wrong and fell through a hole onto an unfortunate moviegoer. We got to see the whole thing. First the skitter, then the blob falling through the air from one of the holes, then the mad rush to vacate the area, and the screams of those unlucky enough to be in the vicinity of the panicked and enraged rat—all to the cheers and jeers of the rest of us in the theater. That's entertainment! At least it was better than the movie, which they kept rolling. I guess they had to keep to a schedule. Nobody even checked to make sure that no one was hurt. All that entertainment for a quarter. What a deal.

If we were feeling flush, we would go the single restaurant in the town and for a dollar buy a hamburger with the owner's "special secret sauce." As he told it, he had been offered $5,000 for the recipe (probably just a mix of mustard, mayonnaise, and relish), but he wouldn't sell out. Regardless, it was a pretty good hamburger and it was so nice to eat something that didn't come out of a can and that I didn't have to cook myself.

On Saturdays and Sundays we could stay in town or go to the beach. The plantation ran trucks from the town to Mānele Bay during the day so that we could get in some recreational time. One thing about Lānaʻi, it's got great beaches, and in the summer the bodysurfing at Mānele was great. If the swell direction was right, we could bodysurf down one side of the beach along the rocks. Or if it was not that good, we could always "body whomp"—just take the drop and tuck under the break at the bottom. It could get really interesting on a big day with bodies, waves, and the bottom coming together with painful consequences. It got even funnier when the guys from the Mainland, who had never seen the ocean, let alone bodysurfed, ventured into the break. They just wouldn't listen when we told them they could get hurt. After we'd beat ourselves up on the shore break, the plantation folks would pass out lunches and we'd lounge around the beach or catch a truck back to town.

Sometimes we would take excursions to the other side of the island. That meant climbing into an empty truck with a couple of adults and driving to the northern shore facing Maui. The view was great, but the real attraction was Shipwreck Beach. There were carcasses of various kinds of vessels littering the beach for miles. The wind blew onshore there and any boat or ship that lost its anchor in the channel would run aground if nothing was done to save it. But the main attraction was the huge freighter that still rests about one or two hundred yards offshore. Of course, we were told that the ship was off limits, but that didn't stop us. Some of us just waited till the adults had walked down the beach to where they couldn't quite see us and started out for the ship. We figured we could claim we hadn't heard them if push came to shove. The current was pretty stiff, so those of us who decided to swim out had to really be able to swim. It was not easy to make the trip. Most of the guys punked out as soon as they got into the current. I swam out with about five other guys. Not a real challenging swim for us, but not easy. For a ship, they sure made it easy to climb up, since there was a length of line hanging over the calm side of the ship near the stern. Once aboard, we explored the rusty hulk. Mostly there was nothing left, but it was fun running around wherever there was enough light and no holes in the hull through which we could hear water—all the while listening to the rudder move back and forth, *clank, clank, clank*. There was a large hole in one of the holds where the hull had been breached, and we stayed away from that. It was too dark and scary and probably had a kraken. After we had our fill, we slipped into the water and swam back. They never even missed us but we were still the envy of our less adventurous friends.

After a short three months of summer it was back to the real world, following a stop in Honolulu to pay for the Yamaha and arrange to have it shipped to Hilo. I got home tired and happy to be there. I think even Pop missed me; he sprung for a Dairy Queen lunch while he was watering at the Elks Club.

I probably didn't mention that I had broached the dirt bike concept to Pop before I left. He took a stand and told me if I got one of those things then I shouldn't bother to come home. I knew he really didn't mean it, but when I picked it up and drove it home, he was not happy. So, I had to buy a helmet and get insured. It got better later when I reminded him that with the bike, I wouldn't be pestering him to use his car.

I have to say that bike was worth every exhausting hour I spent in the fields, and I had a great time riding it around the island.

So, I guess in the end it really was fun in the sun, and I earned it. I also learned a lot about growing up and being responsible for myself and my work. It was so much fun that I went back to Lānaʻi the next summer when again there was no work in Pāhala.

CHAPTER 47

Working on the Old Plantation

In due time, despite the challenges, I graduated from high school. Not with honors, but I thought I did okay. I've always liked to learn, but grades didn't interest me much. I never believed they really measured how much I learned anyway, just how many hoops I could jump through. One other downside unique to Pāhala was that I had been taught early on it was best not to stand out in the crowd. My experiences made me believe that to excel was to get your ass kicked, at least for me. I mean how many people can say they got beat up because they pronounced "film" correctly, instead of saying "filum" like everyone else, or because they knew what a valise was. Gotta love those standardized tests written for and by people who never seemed to realize that one size really doesn't fit everyone. But anyway, for me, doing has always been more important than winning.

Graduation was a surreal experience. The day before graduation, I was a punk kid, but as soon as I graduated, I somehow became a man. I didn't feel different, but at every graduation party I dropped into I was plied with copious amounts of beer and obliged to make a toast with scotch or some other hard liquor, which until that night was strictly illegal and off limits. Go figure. I did not feel good the next day.

When I graduated, I was in the Navy Reserve, waiting to go on active duty. But my Navy test scores were so high I had to go to training, and reservists were low on the priority list, so I had to wait. It took a while, and Kaʻū is no place to be without money for gas, beer, and the other essentials that I needed as a newly minted adult. With no other options that I could see, I followed the grand old tradition in Pāhala of moving from high school graduate to plantation field hand.

Luckily Pop had some connections. I was hired, but there was a catch. Isn't there always? I got to work, but I couldn't join the worker's union. It seemed that because Pop was management, labor thought I was being imbedded by management on some kind of secret assignment to spy on them. Hah!

This union attitude created some interesting problems. You have to remember, Pāhala is not a large community. All of the workers on the plantation had known me since I was a kid, so they probably could figure out I wasn't a saboteur, spy, stealth agent, or anything similar. But old habits die hard. According to my father, the sugar workers had gone on strike in 1958 for quite a while. The strike probably was justified, but Pop worked the numbers and found out that based on the length of time they were out and the amount of the raise they finally received, most of those workers ended up losing way more than they gained.

In any case, one day while I was working there was a strike vote. I didn't know so I showed up for work. I guess they didn't tell me because I wasn't in the union. When I got there, I was the only worker in the yard. They had all gone to the Pāhala Theatre to be agitated by the union or something. One of the managers drove by and let me know what was happening. He told me to wait until the vote was over. After an hour or so I could see the other workers walking up toward the yard. When they got near, I asked the closest one whether we were going to work or not. I didn't think anything of it, I'd known him most of my life. To my surprise, he took a poke at me, yelling that I was a spy and he wasn't going to tell me anything since I would just tell my father. I backed off and told him I wasn't a spy and I just wanted to know if I was going to work or surf that day. Again, he tried to hit me, yelling and swearing at me. By then I'd had enough so I punched him. He went down and the other guys pulled us apart before it went any further. In the end, we went to work. That wasn't so bad—everyone respected me because I didn't back down, and they figured out I didn't care about the big picture, just my paycheck. The worst thing about the incident was that I really liked and respected the wife of the guy I punched; she sewed my surfing shorts and I saw her every time I went to the shopping center. I figured she already knew what happened so I went up and apologized for hitting her husband. I was really relieved when she patted my shoulder and said she wasn't mad, that he'd had it coming for a long time and I had done everyone a favor. He and I got along after that. No apologies, but we were okay.

My first assignment was probably the hardest work I have ever done in my life. I was assigned to the "cut seed" gang, which went out into the fields identified as seed cane and cut it into two-foot lengths to be used to plant the next crop. Sounds simple. It wasn't, not even close. Cutting cane is not for the weak or faint of heart. Cane will cut you like a razor if you brush against it wrong, so there is lots of protective gear. It's hot and the cane fields have rats, huge cane spiders, and lots of other insects that are not happy when their homes are disturbed or destroyed.

First, there is the gear.

Most important is the cane knife. Cane knives are more like short, blunt machetes with a hook on the upper part of the blade. There is a lot more to them that meets the eye. When I was working, there were two kinds of knives used by the planting crew. All of the knives of the cut seed gang were cut down so that they were about half the width of a normal knife.

Also, there were two kinds of tempers the knives had. One was called soft tempered because it wasn't very hard; it was harder and better than the one that came with the original knife, but not much harder. In use, they wouldn't hold an edge long, but they were easy to sharpen with a sharp file I kept in my back pocket. Also, if I hit a rock, the edge would not chip but just fold over a little, and with a little filing I was back in business in no time. Like the better knives, they had also been cut down to be about half the width of a normal cane knife, which made them lighter and faster. Lighter and faster is good; not so hard to swing and faster gets through the cane easier. That's the kind I used. I guess Pop knew what I was going to be doing, so he had procured me a soft cane knife that he gave me before I reported for work.

The second type of knife had what they called a blue blade, I guess for the color of the temper when the blacksmith finished working it over. Those knives were for the professionals. They were also narrower and lighter than the usual knives, and had been worked over by the plantation blacksmith to have a really hard temper that held an edge much longer than the soft-tempered blades. But they had to be sharpened with a hone or a stone, not a file, and they were more brittle. If they hit a rock they chipped, and the edge had to be resharpened. The guys who had them tried not to chip them, but when they did, they were not happy. It was important because we had a seventy bundle-a-day quota, and anything over the quota meant a bonus, not much, but back then money was worth a lot more.

We also had to wear aluminum shin guards, leggings, gloves, long sleeve shirts, hard hats, goggles, and boots, and most of us also had extra thick sleeves that we pinned to our work shirts to keep our arms protected. Lots of gear. And very hot. Very, very hot.

Cutting seed meant that I had to bend over and cut a stalk of cane right at the bottom. After it was cut, I had to drop it into a bin near me that was made of welded rebar, to which earlier I had added a length of wire with small loops on both ends across the bottom. Then I'd cut the cane into lengths about the size of the bin and pile them in until it was full, pull the wire tight and twist it to close the bundle, dump it, and keep going. The first day I thought I was going to die. I had to turn in my shin guards already because I'd missed so many times and hit them so that they were beaten to a pulp. The other guys on the crew thought that was really funny. But I still had my legs and eventually I got better.

I was not designed by nature to be a seed cutter. My torso is really long and I don't bend very easily, even at 180 pounds and no fat. It was really a struggle keeping up. I don't think I ever got a bonus, not even close. The luna knew I was doing my best and I worked hard all day but I just didn't have it in me to be a good seed cutter. One of the worst days I had, at any job, ever, was the day they set me up in a row that was further in than the others. I guess they were trying to help me, but that meant that in the September heat in Kaʻū, I was locked into an oven. The cane on each side held the heat in my row and prevented the wind from cooling me off. I thought I was going to collapse. I drank two gallons of water that day and still had lost ten pounds when I got home. But I kept going and I kept trying. At least I got along with the other guys on the crew. They knew I was trying to pull my weight, and since everyone had their own quota, if I didn't make mine it didn't affect them, so we were okay with each other.

That's one of the things I appreciate most about working on the plantation. If you did your best and pulled your weight just about everyone left you alone or tried to help you get better. We really were in it together and unless someone was sandbagging or slacking it wasn't about how much you could do, but more about your attitude and effort. That's something I always tried to remember and do the same with people I worked with. Funny how much better working is when nobody is picking at you or telling you to do better without showing how it's done.

This probably is a good place to explain that in my experience there are two types of people at work.

The first kind are the ones who feel they worked hard to figure out better ways to do things, so therefore that knowledge belongs to them and they either refuse to share it or dole it out in little bits that never really connect. They seem to take pleasure in watching others struggle, especially if they know ways to make things easier. That always seemed, to me, to be kind of mean and pointless.

Then there is the second type. The kind of person who feels that we are all in the same boat, and anything that can be done or shared to help someone else is the right thing to do. If that means giving away knowledge and sharing experiences without expecting anything in return, so be it. That's how I've tried to be my whole life. I never saw the sense in hoarding information or ways to do things when I can make someone else's life a little easier.

We would alternate seed cutting and *hāpai kō* (carrying the seed cane bundles from the field). We would pile them into hoppers to be dipped in a mixture of fertilizer and insecticide before they were taken to the planting crew. I figure that's where I paid the bill since I was a lot bigger and stronger than the guys on the crew. Most of the other guys could only pack one bundle and they sometimes were pretty far from the hoppers. I could pack one seventy-pound bundle on each shoulder and carry them all day, so I made sure I grabbed the farthest bundles and tried to save them some work. I think they appreciated that I tried to pull my weight doing whatever work I was good at.

I guess sometimes I do get lucky. One day we had caught up with the need for seed and there were no hoppers that needed loading. That day they assigned us to *hoe hana* (work with hoes). Our job was to go into fields that had been planted with the planting machine and make sure all of the seed cane was completely covered. When they gave me my hoe it was an epiphany. An agricultural implement I didn't have to bend down to use. That day I was a hoeing fool. It felt so good I just kept going and never got tired. The next day I was told that because of my talent for covering seed I was being transferred to the planting crew. I think they were just happy to find something I could do, but I didn't care. I put down my cane knife and picked up my hoe.

Just so you know, there are differences in hoes, just like cane knives. Back then there were two kinds of hoes we could use. One looked just like most that are available today—a length of handle and a blade attached to a humped rod.

But back in the day there was another kind. Those hoes were designed with a socket so the blade slipped down the handle—a better angle for working—and a blade that was made of better steel. On those hoes there were also different lengths of handles, so the hoes could be adjusted to the height and strength of the worker. That's the kind I used. I'll still take a hoe over most tools, hands down. In the right hands, they will do almost everything a shovel or pick will do, and better.

The planting crew, where I stayed until I left the plantation, was quite a bit different for me. Instead of working bent over in heavy protective gear, I got to wear a work shirt, jeans, boots, and my hardhat. Way more comfortable.

The planting crew worked with a Caterpillar D9 that had been converted to a planter by attaching plows, a holding bin for seed cane, conveyer belts, and a hydraulic system to raise and lower the bin to gravity-feed the seed cane into chutes behind four plows that cut the furrows. Along with that, the machine fed fertilizer into the rows. So, the cane fills the bin, which raises and lowers, and the seed cane is fed by hand through the chutes to drop into the furrows in the rows just behind the plow. The plow bits normally were straight up and down, but if they hit a rock, the plow would shear a retaining bar of iron and swing up until someone cleared it and it could be lowered and resume planting. I was the someone who walked for eight to ten hours behind the machine, straightening the seed cane and fixing the machine as necessary.

It was great. Clean air, lots of exercise, and a job that wasn't rocket science. Most days we would get into one of the Jeep trucks with bench seats and they took us up into the fields. When we got to the field we were going to plant, we would get ready for work while the machine was started up. Because it was so large, a small donkey engine was used to start the D9. There was a *thump, thump, thump* that began slowly, then sped up until it was up and running. Often, when we were in the upper fields and the air was still and cold, the machine would blow large smoke rings with every revolution of the engine until it started running.

At that point we would start plowing and planting. It was hard work walking in dirt or mud six to seven inches deep all day, but I was in great shape and it didn't bother me at all. Most days we would work till lunchtime, then have an hour for lunch, then work again till quitting time.

Lunch was kind of interesting. We all brought our lunches in our kau kau tins. I used the same one I'd had on Lānaʻi. Two containers; the small one for meat or main course, the larger one for rice. But I had to be different: Every morning I'd fry a pack of hot dogs and four or five big potatoes, eat about a third of it for breakfast, and the rest was lunch. I liked it and I never got tired of my menu.

Normally, the gang would eat together, with everyone putting their main course in the middle to be shared and eat some of everyone's food with their rice. On my first day, when they asked me over to eat lunch and I saw what they were doing, I put my big container of hot dogs and potatoes in the middle with everyone else's. They took one look at it and told me they weren't interested in my food, and that I didn't need to eat with them anymore. Not in a bad way, just not what they wanted to eat. After that I'd wolf down my lunch, grab a couple of empty fertilizer bags, break them open to a clean layer of paper, lay one on the ground, and use the other for a roof, and sack out till lunch was over. It was okay with everyone. The crew was mostly older Filipino guys and even though we liked each other, we didn't have much to talk about.

We did have our bad days. One in particular stands out. It had been raining for about a week and the ground was wet and soggy. Most other crews had been sent home to wait it out, but our luna was kind of stubborn. The older and more experienced guys told him it wasn't a good idea to plant in the kind of weather we were having, but he just had to go. So off we went. Everything went pretty normally, until we got about twenty or thirty feet into the field. Then the machine started digging itself in deeper and deeper. When we saw what was happening, the driver tried to back up to the road. Not a chance. The more the driver tried to get out, the deeper the machine dug into the mud. After a while the mud was about three or four feet deep, up to the top of the tracks. Everyone bailed out, waded through the mud to the road, and tried to figure out what to do. I just stood by. I knew this was going to get interesting. Sure enough, it did. They decided they couldn't leave the machine buried in the mud and brought in two smaller Caterpillars to drag it out. Then they had to figure out how to connect two thick cables to the hook in the front of the planting machine, which was about three or four feet under the mud. Someone had to take them out and drop the cables onto the hook and close the top latch. Guess who got volunteered? I guess it was only right. I was taller, younger, and could hold my breath for about two minutes. Off I went, with everyone standing off on the road offering me useless advice and feeding me the cable as I struggled through the mud dragging the cables one at a time to the planter until I was above the hook. Then I tried to hook them over using my feet. No dice. Then a hoe. Nada. I tried letting them sink but they didn't, and in the end the boss decided I would have to go down and do it by hand. Oh joy, the claustrophobic kid, diving in mud. I took off my shirt and wrapped it around my head to keep the mud off my face and out of my eyes and mouth, grabbed the looped end of the cables, and went down. Luckily the mud was not real thick. I was able to lift the latch, hook the cables, and lower the latch on the first dive. Lucky break, I would have been too scared to make any more anyway. After I got the cables on and secured the latch, I pushed down but I didn't go up; my feet went down further into the mud and there was no solid bottom I could reach. That's when I panicked and stuck my hands out of the mud and started waving them madly in the air. Luckily some of the guys figured out I needed help, waded over, and pulled me out, sans boots and really muddy, but alive.

Then the machines took over. They told us to get behind a hill and started to put a strain on the cables to the planter, with the planter's driver ready to assist as he could. It seemed to be going well until we heard a ripping sound and a loud *twang* when one of the cables broke and whipped into the hill we were hiding behind. Mud everywhere, but I didn't care, I couldn't get any dirtier. But at least the remaining cable held the strain until the planter had started moving up toward the roadway, and the other machine was able to tow it onto the road, where we left it for another day. On the way home, I kept sliding off the bench because of the mud and pretty much got everyone else dirty. But we were all happy to be finished and unharmed. When I got home, I yelled for someone to come out and hose me off. It took me about fifteen minutes to get decent enough to take a shower. The next day it was still raining. Funny thing, we didn't plant.

But all in all, it was great. Sometimes they would send us off to cover seed. On those days I could work my way in front of the rest of the crew and just enjoy the peace and quiet. Sometimes we could see nēnē geese flying overhead and could often hear them honking off in the fog and mist.

Before I left the crew to go into the Navy a couple of things happened.

The first was my fault and not very bright of me. One day when lunchtime rolled around, it was way too muddy to put out my shelter, so I moved it onto one of the stacks of cane that had been dipped in pesticide. Bad move. Even worse, I discovered I was extremely allergic to the pesticide, which caused a rash over my whole body that itched, and itched badly. (I never could stand to itch. I'd rather hurt than itch any day.) They wanted me to soldier on, but I insisted on being evacuated to the hospital. No help there; the doctor told me the only thing he could think of was for me to sit in cold water until the rash went away. It itched so bad I spent a cold November night in our bathtub, up to my neck in freezing water. In the morning, I looked like an albino prune, but at least the itch was gone.

The other incident is one I still consider divine intervention and an example of the legendary but rarely experienced *bachi*. Just before I was due to leave for active duty in the Navy, I was assigned to the road gang. Road gang duty was pretty simple. The roads on the plantation took a beating with all the cane trucks running on them all the time. They needed rehabilitation frequently, or they would just become quagmires and slow everything down. After the road was graded and leveled, a truck would lay down a layer of hot tar. Then the road gang, two workers with square shovels, stood in the back of a dump truck and fed gravel into a device that spun the gravel onto the hot tar. While we were shoveling, the dump truck bed lifted up to keep the gravel coming down. Not only did we have to keep up with the pace of the truck, but we had to stand on shifting gravel and keep shoveling. Not that difficult, but when I got to work, I found out my partner was the football coach. Yup, the same one that had called me chicken shit for not wanting to have my feet shredded. Not wanting to cause trouble, even though he kept giving me stink eye, I just kept to myself and shoveled the gravel into the hopper, until I noticed that macho boy, who was quite a bit older than me, was matching me shovel for shovel. When I sped up, he sped up. If I slowed down, he slowed down. That's when I knew I had him, and I felt it was only just that I return the same kindness and consideration he had shown me earlier. I kept increasing the pace little by little and he kept matching me shovel for shovel until he was exhausted way before our first break. I tried to act more worn out than I was, but he didn't get it. He was so interested in making a fool of me, he made a fool of himself. Well, by lunch he was so tired he just crawled off and slept for the hour while I sat around and talked story with the crew.

I guess after lunch he got his second wind because he was puffed up and ready to go, and he started hammering as soon as he got into the truck. That was his second mistake. Again, I started slowly increasing the pace, and he just had to keep up. That went on for about three hours and he looked like he was ready to collapse. So, for another half hour or so I pretended that I was just barely able to keep up with him, and he increased his pace, figuring he would make a fool of me and make me look like a slacker.

All day long the other guys had been watching what was happening and had tried to get him to be reasonable, but he just didn't get it. He kept muttering about "chicken shit haoles" and "punk kids" and other complimentary phrases I won't repeat, to preserve decorum, of course. The last half hour I just poured it on and started doubling my output. Then he lost his pace and just couldn't keep up, but he never stopped trying to show me up. It was kind of sad, and futile. He just wasn't going to accept reality. Even though he could barely lift his shovel, he kept trying to keep up. But he just couldn't and I blew by him and kept going—stroke, stroke, stroke. I really wasn't even tired. While this was going on, I hadn't said a word to him all day, just ignored his snide comments and stink eye and kept working. But just before quitting time, as he was going down for the count, that little demon that lives in me piped up and said, "Come on, man up! Do I have to do all the work? Why don't you do your share? What's the matter? You chickenshit?"

I guess that was the end for him, and it was also the end of the day. They had to help him into the truck to go home. I still wasn't even tired and mentioned that I was going surfing after work. I even asked him if he'd like to go along to show what a forgiving kind of guy I was, but of course he didn't. In fact, he never spoke to me again, ever. I guess he knew how to hold a grudge. No loss. But my grudge was gone, and as far as I was concerned, we were even.

I guess we all have a little of that revenge demon lurking in our soul, and on that day, there was no listening to the angel that preached kindness and forgiveness. Instead I was listening to the bad little guy inside, who kept telling me it was time to bring the hammer down.

But it sure felt good to get a little back from that guy, and I learned a valuable lesson: It's bad enough when someone else makes a fool of you, but it's even worse when you make a fool of yourself.

CHAPTER 48

Swimming Lessons

When I was a little over five years old my parents sent me to swimming lessons. They knew we would be spending lots of time around the water and wanted all of us kids to be able to swim. They made sure that we were able to hold our own in the water by enrolling us in swimming classes as soon as they could. What they ended up with was a bunch of kids who could swim like fishes and were comfortable in any kind of water that was even remotely safe, and were smart enough to stay away from water that wasn't.

I went to swimming lessons at the Hilo Yacht Club, which was out in Keaukaha near the ocean. It had a saltwater pool, very large and really deep at the deep end. It had low and high diving boards and an attached clubhouse where the adults spent time while the kids swam. Funny thing, though, I never knew anyone in the club who had a yacht. The closest thing was my uncle's P14, a fourteen-foot fiberglass boat that we used for fishing in Kona.

I was taught to swim by a lifeguard. I never knew his first name; to me, he was always Mr. Keliipo. I remember him as a tall, big man who was good at what he did. He was firm but kind and was able to get me to believe I could do whatever he asked. But it didn't start out so well. When my mother dropped me off at the pool for my first lesson, after introductions he looked me over and proclaimed, "John, you can swim." Not wanting to get him upset, I explained that, no, I couldn't swim, that's why my mother had signed me up for classes. He told me again that I could swim and again I tried to explain. Then he said, "Let me show you." We were standing near the deep end of the pool and without another word he grabbed me by the neck and shorts and heaved me into the deep end. I went down, but I came back up and started to panic, but he didn't. He let me thrash around for a while, until I realized I wasn't going down but was somehow managing to stay up. Then he told me to start pulling the water toward me with my hands and kick with my feet. When I did, I started to move toward the edge of the pool and safety. When I got to the edge, I pulled myself up onto the deck, gasping. That's when he told me again, "See, John? I told you, you can swim. I can't teach you that, but I can teach you how to swim better." After that I just did whatever he asked and tried to pay attention to the lessons. After all, I could swim; all I needed was instruction on the finer points of swimming. I found out later that he had taught hundreds, if not thousands, of kids how to swim.

CHAPTER 49

Nīnole

We spent lot of time near the ocean. We'd spend some weekends and vacations in Kona, but most of our beach time was spent at the black sand beach at Nīnole—or Punaluʻu, as we all called this beach. If you were a kid who loved the water and spent every minute you could swimming, spearing, and exploring, Punaluʻu was a great place to be.

Punaluʻu was seven miles from Pāhala, four miles down the highway and three miles off the main road. Back then, as you drove down the road to the ocean, coconut trees and a black sand beach came into view. When you parked at the bottom, off to the left you could see the old wharf that had been destroyed by the 1946 tsunami. By the time we moved to Pāhala, all that was left was the concrete skeleton of the wharf, with rusted fragments of steel scattered around. At the wharf, there was a flat platform and part of a concrete pillar separated from the shore bridged by a single railroad track (you can still see it on Google Earth). We used to climb over the track to the pillar and spend hours jumping off, climbing round again, and jumping until we were tired. Sometimes we would play bang make! in the tunnels and other hiding places in the wharf, even though it was falling apart. It was full of small places where children could hide for hours, if the wasps and scorpions didn't chase us out. Off to the right of the wharf, between the two sandy sections of beach, was a small peninsula of lava with little tidepools filled with small fish and freshwater springs. Further on was the largest section of beach, then beyond, a short rocky area and beyond that a shallow rocky reef next to the pavilion, which stood on a high point of lava to the extreme right of the beach.

It didn't stop there. Rocky shoreline extended from the beach toward Kona until it reached Johnson's Pond. The pond was named after its owner, a rather cranky and abrupt man. Along the shoreline there were tiny offshore islands that people fished from by bridging the gaps between the islands and the shore with ropes, to which they tied short fishing lines and hung baited hooks to catch the *ʻulua* that swam in the strong tidal currents between the islands and the shore.

There were two ponds. One was smaller and filled with brackish water and cut off from the sea. It was populated by an ugly fish we called *bunog* and also mullet. Mr. Johnson jealously and zealously guarded his fishponds and was known to take potshots with his .22 rifle at poachers when he was able to catch them. He never hit anyone, but he sure scared lots of kids. It was at the little pond that I discovered one of the least known and most effective methods of mullet fishing. It appeared that mullet can't discriminate between firecrackers and food items. If a carefully timed and lit firecracker was thrown into the water in front of a hungry mullet, it would be swallowed whole. If the firecracker went off, the mullet became food. Too bad Mr. Johnson caught me. At least he didn't shoot me.

Beyond the little pond, the ocean met the outfall of a mountain spring in a rather large lagoon. The water in that area had to be the clearest, coldest water I've ever seen. Reeds grew along the edges of the pond where the spring emptied into the lagoon. There was a small grassy area alongside the water and off to the right, an island made of tall green reeds. Over the years we had opened up tunnels below the tangle of reeds above. The tunnels were small and dark, and, once you started swimming into one, there was no turning back. There were breathing holes just at the edge of our endurance—basically the duration of one deep breath. But it was great fun to swim out in the freezing water, duck under the edge of the reed island, and kick and pull in the mostly dark tunnel until light and safety appeared.

Around the corner in another channel was a much deeper and spookier area that always seemed to be gloomy and dark except right at midday. It was said that people had seen sharks cruising in the lagoon. I never did, but I was never sure they weren't waiting just around the next corner, making every foray into that area scary and much more exciting than the other areas. Up on the cliffs above the lagoon, a heiau overlooks the water and the coastline back to the beach. On the other side of this heiau at the bottom of the cliff is a short, sandy beach with a small island outside and high cliffs on the right, where huge waves came in from the deeper water to crash on the reef in the shallows.

The island was a short swim away from the beach, but it was not a trip for the fainthearted. The currents were very strong and there were also huge stingrays that circled the island and charged at small critters (like children) when they swam in the water near the island. I've never gone to the island when there wasn't at least one ray that first circled then charged at me. They never hit, but it was scary just the same. We learned to swim quickly to and from the island or we paddled on logs or other floating objects. You may wonder why we bothered to go to the island at all, but on this particular island we could pick cowry shells off the rocks in the cracks that fractured the body of the island. We could pick all we wanted; there were hundreds, but we had to be careful and watch what we were doing, because the island was awash at high tide and eels and wana lived in the same places as the cowries.

Beyond the main beach at Punaluʻu, on the left as you passed the old wharf and continued on past Johnson's Pond, were portions of the king's road, lined by smooth rocks leading along the shore. Toward Volcano, the path winds its way to Kamehame, which has a small beach with a high cinder cone behind it and a shallow reef in front. Spearing was especially good there. On the way from the main beach, there is a deep crack in the lava filled with fresh water. The water is deep, clear, and cool and tastes very good. We used to stop there and swim in the pool to take the salt off our bodies after swimming at the beach. In the pool were small fish and shrimp that we could watch if the sun was up above the crack. Otherwise, it was dark.

There also is a pavilion standing at the other end of the beach from the lei stands that serviced the tourists. It's made of lava and concrete and has a kitchen and bathrooms. One of the local wags had dabbled in graffiti, about six feet high on one side of the structure. When I first saw this, I asked the guy who was surfing with me what angle the graffiti artist had in mind—45, 90, or maybe 180. He looked at me like I was crazy and asked what I was talking about. The graffiti was apparently meant to read "Kanaka Angels," but it didn't. We both had a big laugh when he finally got my point. Emblazoned in six-foot-high, spray-painted letters were the words "Kanaka Angles." I still wonder who put that one up.

Behind the pavilion on the hills behind the beach is a small chapel with a graveyard. There were a number of houses set back from the shoreline and a concession stand on the beach that sold trinkets and sodas to the tourists brought in by the tour buses that circled the island.

In the '50s before the 1960 tidal wave, there were numerous three-plank canoes and canoe sheds built on the beach above the high tide line. When the waves hit, these were washed away and never replaced.

At one time there was a painting at Honolulu's Bishop Museum of a Nīnole resident who'd been caught in a tsunami and washed out to sea, after he went back home between waves to retrieve a bag of money. The next wave destroyed the house, and he was carried out to sea hanging onto a door. After a while, he was spotted surfing back to shore on the door, money bag in hand. A wave washed him ashore, the story goes, and he ran for the hills—escaping with his life and his money.

The sand in this area was black, and in summer the heat waves shimmered six feet high off the beach. If you didn't run fast enough to and from the water it would blister your feet. The water was cold, alternately layered fresh and salty, but it was clear and clean and there were fish, crabs, and eels to hunt.

Punaluʻu could also be a dangerous beach, as there were strong currents off the point to the left beyond the wharf. The best diving was off the point, but it was only safe during slack tide because once the tides started running it was too strong to fight. There were stories of three men who had tried and died trying to fight their way into shore after starting back too late. Oddly enough, the only people I know who survived the current were the doctor's wife and her two children. They survived because they weren't strong enough to wear themselves out fighting the current, and so they let it carry them out beyond the reef until they were in front of the beach, and then swam through the reef to the beach.

One other thing about Punaluʻu: The water was cold and somewhat hazy because of the many springs that fed out of the mountains into the bay. We could see the difference between the fresh and salt water, and once I even dove to one of the openings and grabbed a small mouthful of water. It was pretty fresh and drinkable. We were told by some of the old-timers that back in the day fresh water wasn't easy to come by, so people with no other access to fresh water would dive or lower a calabash to where the spring was, fill it, and pull up fresh water that way.

CHAPTER 50

Fishing Fool?

There were lots of regulars at Punaluʻu. Since there wasn't much to do in town and no TV until sometime around 1960, people went to the beach on the weekends. At the lei stand there, I could earn a soda by stocking the Coke cooler—not an easy job when the bottles had to be lined up in the tracks just so, to be sure that the cold ones arrived at the service end first. Besides lei, the stand sold souvenirs made out of local stuff like the seeds of *haole koa* and Job's tears. We could also pick ʻopihi and sell them to the owner of the lei stand. Five whole dollars for a gallon of large yellow ʻopihi. That would cost maybe $200 now, if you can get them.

On Saturday and Sunday people would fish, swim, picnic, and generally unwind from the frenetic urban life that Pāhala offered.

Each weekend one elderly man used to park his car by the wharf, set up his folding chair, put out his cooler with a sixpack of beer next to his chair, put up an umbrella, and throw a line in the water. I never saw him catch a fish, and he was never upset when we kids got too close to his line. But he looked happy and he was at his station every Saturday and Sunday for years.

When I got a little older, I stopped one day and asked him how come he kept fishing even though he never caught anything. He looked at me kind of funny, then he laughed and told me I was the first person to ever ask him that question. He asked me if I could keep a secret. He knew me, and knew he could trust me if I promised, and I agreed. He lifted his line out of the water. I could see there was a weight attached, but no hook. When I asked him how he expected to catch a fish without a hook, he replied, "That's the secret." He told me he hated fish; never ate them and wasn't interested in catching any.

Then he asked me a question, a really good question. He asked me what people would say if all he did was sit on the wharf with his cooler and umbrella sipping on a cold beer and did what he really like doing, just watching people having fun? From where he set up his chair, he was up high and could see the whole beach, with kids swimming and playing, the surf and all the good things that happen when people are happy and having fun.

I could tell him in a heartbeat. The few intolerant, busybody, gossiping, and mean-spirited people who lived among us, who saw him and didn't understand what he was doing and what he valued, would slander him and talk about him behind his back, always saying that they had "heard" that there was some nefarious reason he sat there and just watched.

His neighbors and mine, not all of them, but enough. Don't get me wrong; there were way more good people in town than those that loved the dark side, the gossip, the whispers, and the side-eye looks. I guess there must be some of those assigned to every town to make the rest of us look like saints. They would never understand or believe that he just enjoyed watching people having fun. He agreed with me, then he told me that he'd never been questioned but had received lots of comments on his perseverance and tenacity. He'd also been told often to never lose hope, that even though he was an unlucky fisherman, someday he would get the big one if he only hung in there.

That was one smart guy, and he knew his neighbors. He "fished" for many more years and I've never broken my silence, until now. But for years, whenever I saw him sitting on the pier, I'd ask him how it was going and he always said, "Da fishing is great!"

CHAPTER 51

'Opihi

As I said earlier, we could pick 'opihi to earn some cash, so we often hiked down the coastline looking for the mother lode. Make no mistake—'opihi picking is not for the clumsy, timid, or stupid in Ka'ū. It's dangerous, and the 'opihi are never easy to come by or easy to get into a bag. Most of the coastline we hunted was just cliffs and the ocean below.

Our equipment consisted of a thin-bladed butter knife (borrowed from our kitchen but rarely returned) and an empty rice bag slung over the shoulder, on the left side for right handers and on the right for the lefties to make it easier to flip the 'opihi into the bag.

The theory was to climb onto the cliff like a crab without being washed out to sea and, when an 'opihi was spotted, to quickly slip the blade of the knife under the shell and flick it into the bag. Sometimes it went like that. Often it didn't, and I've watched many 'opihi drop into the depths when it missed the bag.

Remember, we were alone and there weren't any adults around, and we had been weaned on tales of 'opihi picking gone bad, of pickers washed off the cliffs who just disappeared. And there was the guy who fell into the surf and was scraped by a shark as he desperately rode a wave up the cliff to escape its sharp teeth, until he found a handhold where his friends could grab him and pull him to safety. He'd been lucky, but it didn't always end that way. Back in those days, adults would try to stop us from doing dangerous things by scaring the crap out of us, but it didn't work then and probably doesn't work any better now.

But sometimes they were right. One day I was prospecting with a friend and we spotted the mother lode, dozens of big 'opihi high up in a crack in the cliff that looked like I could get to it with a little careful climbing. I was just getting ready to edge out on the cliff and climb up to them when I heard someone say, "Watch out, haole boy! Don't go there." When I turned around, I saw one of the older pickers who always came back with lots of 'opihi and never seemed to get hurt. He'd been sitting there quietly and I hadn't seen him, as I was focusing on the mother lode. I asked, "Why not?" since I wasn't sure of his motive. He just said, "Wait!" So I waited and nothing happened for about five minutes. I was about to ask him what I was waiting for, when a set of waves came in and blew a spout of water as big as Old Faithful right up the crack in the cliff I had planned to climb. If I had, I'd have been washed off the cliff into the surf.

After I thanked him, he gave me some of the best advice I've ever had. He pointed out that with all the 'opihi pickers that passed that spot there had to be a reason those 'opihi were still there—so before I put myself on the cliff and it was too late, it wouldn't hurt to just sit and figure out why nobody else had gotten them. He said it's better to spend a little time watching and thinking than to get hurt or die. The cliffs in that spot were about twenty feet high. If I'd been washed into the ocean, I would never have been able to get out on my own. Ever since then, before I go into the water, I take a little time to look things over, and sometimes, just sometimes, when a little voice in my head says don't go, I don't. There's always another day.

CHAPTER 52

Deep Divers and Surfing Fools

We come from a long line of folks that liked to swim. Pop was a great diver in his youth and even expanded his horizons by fabricating a hardhat diving helmet that he used to clean the swimming pool back in Brookings, South Dakota.

Fishing wasn't the only thing to do at the shoreline. Every Saturday and on Sunday after church we would load up the car, pack a lunch, and head off to the beach. It didn't take much to entertain us, a couple of old inner tubes (better yet, one per child), a diving mask, fins if we had them, spears, and our *paipo* boards. Ron and I, being the oldest, were constantly trying to discover ways to dive deeper and stay down longer. We would practice in the bathtub, timing each other to see who could stay under longer. We would train at taking in huge breaths and holding them in as long as we could. At the beach we would tow rocks out in our tubes and let them carry us down so we didn't have to waste effort. In short, we would try anything that kept us on the bottom longer. We got scared a lot and our ears hurt when we went down too fast. So we got smarter.

We tried the snorkel extender (we were going to make a lot of money with that one when we patented it). We taped eight feet of water hose to a snorkel, tied it off to a tube. and tried to suck air down. No dice. Then we tried using a bicycle pump to get air down to the diver. Again, no go. Our final and most foolish effort was the result of a picture in a diving book of the first diving bell, an air-filled device lowered from the surface to the depth at which the diver wants to dive. It was elegant in its simplicity and appeared simple enough to make. We liberated a large bucket, lugged it to the beach, and rigged a sling with rocks to hang underneath. We towed the bell into about thirty feet of water, our limit at that time, and filled the sling with the rocks until the bucket started down. It looked good, it wasn't leaking, and when we peeked underneath, we could see the shimmer of air. Ron really thought this one would work. He was so sure, he tested it himself, insisting on making the first dive. He huffed and puffed, hyperventilating until he was ready. I guess it's here I point out that we were barely able to touch bottom and come back to the surface in water that deep, with no air to spare.

Well, from the top it looked good. Ron dove down, reached the bottom, and stuck his head into the bucket. Nothing happened for a few seconds, then Ron exited the bucket and scrambled wildly for the surface. Arriving just in time and out of breath. It seems the air had shrunk and the level had risen just past nose-level in the bucket. According to Ron, when he stuck his head into the bucket, the air was right about eye level and the bucket was too small for him to turn his head sideways. Neither of us felt like trying to retrieve the bucket after all that work. Maybe it's still there. After that, we just trained until we could dive sixty to seventy feet deep without too much trouble.

We also surfed, of course. Before the days of the boogie board, we used to make our own paipo or body boards by nailing a skeg and a handrail to whatever plank of wood we could scrounge up. We surfed in the area near the wharf when there were waves. It was always good

Pop (on the left) with his homemade diving helmet, ca. 1940s.

for a short ride when the swells came over the reef and broke in the deeper area near the beach. But we mostly surfed in the shallow, rocky water fronting the pavilion. We'd jump into the water off the rocks and wait out near the edge of the shallows until a likely wave came through, then all of us would paddle and kick madly until we caught it. We rode straight in toward the beach until our knees or the skeg hit the rocks, then we'd turn around and paddle or crawl, depending on how deep the water was, until we were outside and do it again. Sometimes the end of the ride was a bit more painful, when instead of a rock, you'd hit a wana. That hurt bad. It also didn't help that everyone else wanted to pee on your knee to help get the wana spine out. Good thing I never got one in my head. Still the old "pee on the knee" was the best and fastest way to treat a wana spine injury.

Tubing took up the rest of the time after we got tired from diving and surfing. Somehow there isn't a more calming and relaxing thing to do at the beach than drift back and forth in the waves sitting in the tube, just washing in and out, in and out. Picking up the odd bit of shell or sand-smoothed glass was tons of fun.

If we got too salty, we could walk over to one of the brackish pools near the edge of the water and take the edge off the salt by hunting for jumping jacks, a quick little fish that's nearly invisible and hard to catch. Or we could pick pipipi, a small black snail, off the rocks. Some people eat them. I did once, but I've had bigger treats than digging tiny boiled snails out of their shells with a pin and eating them. Takes about a hundred to make a mouthful.

Sometimes we would look for a short coconut tree, climb up, and throw a few nuts down. It's quite an experience to shinny up a tall tree until you can get a hold of some fronds, then climb up to the very top and sit there with a view of the beach and the hills and watch everything that's going on. It's also quite an experience when you get to the top and find out a rat has taken up residence in the tree and is really unhappy you came to call. All those helpful rings on the tree when you go up leave scrapes and bruises on the way down, especially when you're in a hurry.

When the sun started to go down, we'd pack up the gear, hotfoot it across the beach, and drive home. Worn out, but much happier than when we arrived.

CHAPTER 53

The Eels

One of the least wonderful things about being an older brother has to be taking the younger children along when you go somewhere. It was as true then as it is now.

Ron was constantly being told to take his younger siblings along on his diving trips. He wasn't very happy about that, but he was pretty good about not losing us or letting us drown. By that time we all could swim like little fishes and were in little danger of drowning. Still, it was quite a handicap to Ron's spearing that he had a smaller and clumsier following that he had to watch every minute to keep out of trouble. Nevertheless, he did take us with him, if he had to, and he kept us out of trouble, mostly. There were a couple of exceptions that stand out in my memory.

The first episode happened when Ron had been spearing from the wharf towards the main beach. A couple of us were tagging along behind, just taking in the sights. Ron didn't often look back to be sure we were safely right behind him. He was looking for the fish in front of him, he said, not the kids behind him. It was a rare occasion when he gave more than a quick glance behind to see what might be happening to us. We always figured we were on our own when we went spearing with Ron. That wasn't a comforting thought, since I couldn't see and wasn't trusted with a spear, and the other siblings weren't much better.

Whatever the case, Ron just happened to take one of his obligatory glances behind that day, checking us out for safety and well-being, when he saw a rather large *puhi* (eel) emerge from its hole. The puhi opened his mouth and swam rapidly towards my younger brother's fluttering white foot (probably because it looked like a dying fish or something just as edible). All I saw was Ron turning around and shooting his spear right at me. I thought I was dead. I thought he was going to spear me and cringed waiting for the impact. The spear passed maybe an inch from my shoulder—I think I actually felt it go by—and toward the eel. None of us had even noticed it until the spear hit that eel right behind its head. A perfect shot! The eel died right where it was and sank back onto the rocks. That had to be the shot of Ron's life, the best shot of his spearing career, and also the luckiest. If it had been off even an inch, someone's foot would have been lunch—not to mention that Ron would have had to explain why he shot me. Ron dragged the eel to the beach where we all gathered around it, senselessly prodding the carcass with sticks, until someone took it away to use for fish bait. That eel was three or four feet long. If it had latched on it wouldn't have been able to let go, as its teeth point back. The only thing to do would have been to cut it off, so if it had made it back into its hole, whoever was caught with those teeth could have been held under and drowned.

Another time, Ron had somehow convinced me to be his bag boy when he went spearing one night. I can't remember how or what he threatened or bribed me with to get me into the water. He knew how nearsighted I was, and he was always calling me spastic. And at that time it was true; I couldn't see and I was clumsy. In fact, I'm still afraid of diving at night. I guess desperation knows no limits when the moon is up and the water is calm. We geared up on the beach, where he gave me directions and a burlap bag. Of course I couldn't understand the directions, and furthermore I had no fins, no spear, and only the bag and my mask to protect me from the creatures of the night sea. But somehow, he got me into the water and we headed out. Shortly thereafter, I found myself in the dark, holding a bag full of dead bleeding fish, and listening to Ron say, "Follow me. There's nothing to worry about." Somehow to this very day those words uttered by just about anyone strike fear into my heart. Of course, there really was something to worry about. Think about it for a second. I was bait, just bait, and the whole time as I struggled like a dying fish, I was convinced that the next thing I saw would be a shark, up close.

Ron dove and I followed for about an hour. The routine was simple: He would disappear with the light, spear a fish, then scream insanely at me until I caught up. He would deposit the bloody, struggling fish in the bag and swim off again. All this time I wasn't getting any more comfortable out there, what with no light and lots of fish blood in the water. The moon was no help at all, it just made things even scarier. Ron kept going further afield in search of fish, leaving me in the black night trying to keep my head above water and swim after him with the bag, wondering what would sting, bite, or eat me while he was gone. Finally, the last little bit of courage I had left ran out. Ron had called from some distance away for a pickup. I was laboring towards him with a full bag through the rocks in the dark. Suddenly something bumped my mask. Thinking it was a rock, I tried to push off, but there was nothing there. So I started forward again. Meanwhile, Ron was screaming at the top of his lungs to hurry up, he had spotted another fish. I'm not so sure he had. Ron was no fool; he didn't want to hang on to a bleeding fish in the dark. Something bad might take notice and decide on a nighttime snack. He didn't have anything to worry about; nothing was going to happen to him, it was going to happen to me. I bumped something for the second time and still couldn't feel anything in front of me. By then I was pretty close to panic.

Meanwhile, Ron had tired of yelling and had come back to get me. Then, just as his light swept through the water in front of me, something bumped into my mask again. Only this time I could see what it was: a huge eel, and I was looking right into his mouth. It didn't move, and I was so scared, I couldn't either. We stayed that way, mouth to mask, until Ron's approach with the light scared it away. When I told Ron about the eel, he said I must have been seeing things. There was no eel; *he* hadn't seen one. I didn't care what he thought. I'd had enough and swam to shore as fast as I could. But I left the bag with Ron. Odd, he came in right after me; said an eel tried to get the bag. I told him he must have been imagining things; *he* hadn't seen any eel. One good thing came out of that trip: He never asked me to go night diving again and I never volunteered.

CHAPTER 54

Honomalino

If Punaluʻu was the bread and butter of beaches, Honomalino was the cake.

We spent lots of time in the water around the island but my favorite spot without exception was my uncle's beach house at Honomalino.

Honomalino was about fifty miles toward Kona from Pāhala. As the story goes, in the 1930s my uncle Budgie (yes, he was nicknamed after the bird, but I never got the backstory on that one) who had been diving that coast for years, made a bid at a land auction and got two house sites in one of the most beautiful places on earth.

He built his house with help from carpenters who dropped off his lumber and equipment from a steamer and camped in the bay until the house was finished. The main house was pretty much a large room with a small kitchen off to the side and an indoor bathroom that my aunt insisted he put in if she was going to stay there. The house was designed by my uncle Hubert, who really did a great job. At the house there were two kinds of water. Fresh water came from large water tanks that filled up when it rained; that water was used to drink. The other kind was brackish water from a well under a coconut grove, pumped into a smaller tank for use in washing and for outdoor showers. We always had to remember in the kitchen, "Left is right, right is wrong," because the left faucet turned on fresh water, and the right, brackish.

There was a path lined with concrete stepping stones between the *naupaka* plants and the grove of coconut trees on the right that provided shade to a boathouse, which stood down at the shore near an old house site.

The house at Honomalino.

To get to Honomalino, we first packed *all* of the provisions we would need while we were there; piled into the station wagon and drove over the long curving and bumpy road through Nā'ālehu, Wai'ōhinu, Ocean View Estates; then a pit stop at Manukā State Park and on until we reached the turnoff to the small, one-lane road that winds its way back and forth down from the main road past the coffee and lava fields until it reaches the end of the road, Miloli'i.

Miloli'i has been called the "last fishing village." I'll buy that. When we went there as children it was a small and very isolated town, very insulated from the rest of the island. In Miloli'i there was no drinking water that didn't come from a water tank and no electricity that didn't come from generators, and everyone had an outdoor toilet.

Back when I was a kid, you see, many homes were without indoor toilets. Instead they had outhouses, little shacks off to the side of their homes with a door, some kind of seat with a hole in it, and a pit below to hold whatever was dropped from above. Most likely there was an old Sears catalog with a hole punched through it hanging next to the seat. The protocol was simple: Do your business, tear off a couple of sheets of paper, wipe, drop into the hole, sprinkle some lime on it to keep the smell down, and exit. All normal, and that's the way it went for years. The Sears catalog was best because not only did it not stain, it wasn't too rough and you always had something to read. The telephone book was too thin and not only did it not last long, the ink would smear. Toilet paper wasn't unheard of but was considered a frivolous expense when the catalog worked so well. But things changed, as they often do, and not for the best. Sears updated their catalog to a glossy paper and things went south from there. Not only was it slippery, it was impossible to get completely clean because of the slick surface. So toilet paper took over, except in places where it was too expensive, then it was the phone book or some other less desirable catalog.

Miloliʻi always seemed a friendly place to me. There was a wharf in the town that we used to jump off from the top of the wall into the cool, clear water, over and over until it was time to leave. There was one store, owned by a family in the town. This was a small, one-room shack with a limited selection of in-demand items. The prices were high compared to the rest of the island but, considering the distance and difficulty in transporting goods and keeping the store stocked, it was pretty fair. Besides, the next store was about fifty miles away.

The store also sold gas that we pumped ourselves from the old pump out in front. It had a glass reservoir showing how many gallons were pumped into it before we poured it out. The owner of the store was always friendly and willing to share stories and tell us how he caught *ʻōpelu* and other fish.

Two things come to mind when I think about him. The first was that he could tell the difference in taste between fishes that were speared, hooked, or caught in a net. One day he told Ron and me that how fast a fish died made a difference in the taste, and he offered to demonstrate if we would catch three *manini* using these three methods. It took us a while, but finally we had the three fish and hiked the trail to Miloliʻi, where we cooked the fish and offered them to him. Damned if he wasn't able to tell us, and just from a little taste. As he explained it, it depends on the amount of adrenaline that goes through the fish as it dies. The speared fish dies quickest so it is the least bitter, the hooked fish is a little different, and the netted fish struggles the longest, so it tastes the most bitter.

Pop in the boat.

The other thing he told us was not to fool around with any very large *kākū* (barracuda) if they hung around close to people. He said that if a *kākū* did that, it was because it was probably an "'ōpelu mama" that needed to be left alone, because it helped the fishermen by herding 'ōpelu into their nets. He further explained that the 'ōpelu mama was a *kākū* caught as a small fish and had had its teeth pulled—so to eat it had to be hand-fed a mash of sweet potato or squash and 'ōpelu until it had grown large enough to release back into the ocean. Each time they were fed, the fishermen would tap a paddle against the side of a canoe as these fishes' unique dinner bell. When the fishermen reached the fishing grounds, they would locate a school of 'ōpelu, tap the side of the canoe, and the kākū would herd the 'ōpelu into a tight ball,. The fishermen would then take as much as they needed, then hand-feed the kākū to reward them for their effort. I saw lots of big kākū, one at least six feet long, but was never able, or willing, to get close enough to see if they had teeth, and I never got to see them in action either. They were spooky fishes. They would hover in the clear water just beyond the length of a spear, but if we went down, they went down. If we swam toward them, they backed off the same distance. If we swam away, they swam toward us.

I never heard of one biting or otherwise hurting anyone, but once there was a very large kākū that was hanging around the buoy inshore where children were swimming. I don't know how the men decided it was a threat, but they decided it had to be taken out. I know they knew about the 'ōpelu mamas and had never gone after a kākū before, so they must have figured it wasn't tame and all those little feet might be too tempting. After much discussion among the men, Pop pulled down Unc's CO_2 speargun. That speargun was something else. One cartridge, one shot. Sometimes we would use it to shoot coconuts out of the trees, but this time it was used on the kākū. Pop, Ron, and I swam slowly out to the area where a kākū had last been seen. Sure enough, it was there, and looking pretty big and scary. Ron was carrying a spare spear and I had a couple of CO_2 charges, just in case. Well, Pop swam toward the kākū, who didn't move, then he waited until it turned broadside and fired a spear. The gun erupted with a huge bubble, and when it cleared there was a cloud of blood and scales. Pop had hit the kākū dead center. The weight of the spear pulled the fish to the bottom where it wriggled loose and swam off, leaving a fist-sized chunk of flesh on the spear. It couldn't have survived, but that was one tough fish.

In the Miloli'i area, we could still see the ruins of koa outrigger canoes along the road that ran through town from the wharf to the schoolyard, where the trail to Honomalino started. Mostly the fishermen there used what we called three-plank canoes. These actually are outrigger canoes built using three long planks of wood, one for each side and another for the bottom. They were about twenty feet long and the outriggers were made using galvanized pipe and branches from the *hau* trees that had just the right curve. They were long and pointed in the front, with a square stern on which they mounted outboard motors for power. In those days the canoes weren't fiberglass but were painted inside and out, and the paddles were made out of plywood. There wasn't a lot of room since the canoes were narrow and each had a fish box in the middle between the outriggers, but they sure were stable and seaworthy, and cheap to build. When they weren't in use, they were pulled up on the shore on wooden rollers and covered with coconut fronds to protect them from the sun and at least a little from the rain.

In town there was a covered open-air area for working on fishing nets, three-plank canoes hauled up on the pebbled beach on the way to the schoolhouse, and a small park at the end of the road. Beyond the park was the trail to Honomalino. From the edge of Miloli'i the trail worked its way past little white sand-fringed inlets with a couple of derelict sampans, up a short hill past a graveyard, through a section of kiawe forest along the coast, down the king's trail, then over the stile and through the lava fields to the back of the house at Honomalino. This route was just about a mile of mostly lava and kiawe.

Kiawe trees grow everywhere on the Big Island and line every trail and beach access, which isn't so bad—the shade is nice. What is bad are those thorns. They are long and sharp, and when one gets in your foot it sticks around.

The hike to Honomalino was a real trek, especially wearing rubber slippers and carrying a couple of paper sacks overflowing with food, and draped with other gear in the midday heat. The sacks always ripped, and we'd have to carry armloads of cans and heavy stuff in our shirts and arms. Sometimes we'd have to make two trips. But if anyone was already there and the boat was in the water, we'd load everything into the boat in Miloli'i to be ferried over to the bay and could hike the trail and meet them at the beach to carry everything up to the house.

It sure was a relief to arrive and drop everything on the porch, then dash off to the beach before we were told to help set everything up for our stay. Usually the adults would spend a little time unpacking and putting the food away, and when we'd blown off a little steam, they would put us to work. First, we would unlock and slide back the big door that covered most of the front of the house. After that we would ferry out the tables and chairs for the patio, along with folded cots for sleeping. Then we would unlatch the shutters that covered the windows and pull them up and tie them up. Then we would rush around madly trying to kapu a bed or special cot where we would pile our clothing and gear. Then, after a brief lunch, we'd grab our gear and head to the beach again.

The beach has changed a lot since the 1950s when I first saw it. Now it is pebbled and the sand is dark and has moved up the beach. But back then it was a wide, clean white sand beach that extended into the water and out into the middle of the bay. The beach gave way to rocks on the far end of the bay near the jeep trail that ended at the houses.

Back then there were only three houses in the bay—a house up in the kiawe behind the two that my uncle owned. Along with the main house, there was a smaller one, basically the same kind of layout—one large room, a kitchen, a bathroom, and a large porch and a boathouse near the beach in a coconut grove. The coconut trees at Honomalino served several purposes. First, they provided shade. Even in the worse summer heat it was possible to slip into the shade of the trees and feel a lot cooler. Second, they provided coconuts. Of course we had to climb them, but at the time we were well able to climb to the highest trees, twist the coconuts we wanted off the stalk, then drop them below.

There was one other interesting use for the coconut tree. It's not something we did often. It wasn't good for the tree, or the men who did it. They would climb a tree, select the emerging immature frond, then tie half hitches around the frond and bend it into a U shape with the tip down. After that they'd cut off the very end and tie a tin can with cheesecloth under the cut. Then they would climb the tree every day and harvest the juice that had dripped, keeping it in a mason jar until the frond ran dry. By then the drippings had fermented into coconut swipes and they would mix it with orange or another juice and get hammered. Nothing like a bunch of tipsy men acting like teenagers. What was strange is they always had some other kind of store-bought booze, but I guess they wanted to maintain quality control or something. I tried some once. Not for kids or the faint of heart. The damn stuff would peel paint or curl toes depending on the application.

We also used the fronds to cover the patio, make hats, and one other thing—catch crabs. Yup, you read that right, catch crabs. ʻAʻama crabs, to be exact. ʻAʻama are relatively large for Hawaiian crabs. They are black and very fast, and live on the rocks near the surf zone, moving up and down with the tide. They don't normally swim unless they're trying to get away from something. We could eat them raw as *poke*, although some people cooked them, and we also used them for bait.

We caught them using a bamboo pole about seven or eight feet long. We would strip two palm leaves, keeping the long flexible rib in the centers, then lash these two ribs on opposite sides of the bamboo pole, tying either a shred of the coconut or a very, very fine fishing line between them with a loop that drooped down a couple of inches.

Then with pole in hand we would sneak up on a bunch of ʻaʻama crabs, pick one, and loop the very thin line around one of the crab's eyes. Apparently the crabs couldn't see this thin line, so they mostly just sat there unless we moved too quickly. When the line touched the crab's eye stalk, it would pull its eyes in, which secured the line. Then a quick jerk and grab and we had another crab. It's not that hard once you know how, but getting there is not easy.

We'd also hunt ghost crabs at night to use as bait, which was a lot easier. All we had to do was bury a tin bucket in the sand, put in some bait, and come back later. The buckets were always full.

The water supply for both of my uncle's houses came from two water tanks made of redwood. The largest was next to the kitchen of the lower house. It was huge and had bands that held everything together, which we could climb on if nobody was watching. The water ran off the roof of the house into gutters, then into the tank. It was the only fresh water available. There was another, smaller freshwater tank that we pumped water into from the larger one. It was up higher, so there was some water pressure and it handled the overflow from the big tank if the rains were heavy, which wasn't often. There was also a brackish water tank that was filled from a well down in the coconut grove. It was pumped from the well to fill the tank to use for washing and non-drinking purposes.

Electricity, when we used it, mostly for an hour or two after dark, was provided by a generator that powered the lights inside the house and out on the patio. All of the other appliances were gas, which powered the stove, refrigerator, and some lights. The gas tanks sat in the back of the house and had to be brought in by Jeep. Just about every night right after sundown a couple of the men and us older kids took flashlights and went to scare the spiders and scorpions in the generator shack. The mechanism inside was an old Caterpillar engine with a generator tacked onto one end. It was hard to start; it wheezed, burped, gurgled, and generally was cantankerous, but once it started it kept going. The house was insulated, so all we heard was a low hum below the sound of the waves until it was shut off, usually after an hour or so. Then the lanterns would come out and light the lānai with a soft glow until we crawled into our cots or beds and were lulled to sleep by the sound of the waves washing up and down the beach. But there were nights we stayed close to the house. It never seemed that anyone talked about it or made a real point of it; there were just times we didn't go outside at night. It just didn't seem like it would be a good idea.

When I was a teenager, Pop took one of the nurses from Pāhala out fishing; she had come from the Mainland to Honomalino for the day. I went along, and while they were fishing off the point I walked down the main beach. I was a little surprised when I stepped onto something that crunched under my foot and stuck to my heel. I was more than taken aback when I lifted my foot and found part of a human skull attached to it, so I peeled it off and ran down the beach to show Pop and the medical expert. She said it was probably a pig skull and dismissed my idea that it was human. Well, I showed her when I went back and dug around a little and found a jawbone. Now she believed me. I went back and dug around some more and eventually had two full skeletons stacked neatly on the beach. They'd been there a long time, probably since a wave of smallpox had run through the community. One of the older residents of Miloliʻi told me that victims had gone down to the beach and lay in the water to bring down the fever, but many of them didn't make it and died there. By the time we started going there the remains had mostly disappeared, but these must have decided it was time to emerge.

So I got a shovel from my uncle's house and started digging a hole big enough for all the bones farther up the beach, above the high tide line. It was hot, sweaty work, and after I'd been at it a while Pop and the nurse came over to see what I was doing. Pop got it, but the nurse asked me why I was doing all that work for some old bones. All I could tell her was that this was what I would want someone to do for me if those were my bones. Eventually I had made a new resting place for the bones. I lined it with coconut fronds and naupaka and I tried my best to stack the bones neatly in two piles with the skulls on top. I did say "sorry" to the one I stepped on, and I told them I hoped that what I'd done was what they would've wanted. Then I covered them up and left. Funny thing—after I did that I never felt uncomfortable at the bay, even on those nights we stayed inside. As I said, it's never a bad thing to show some respect and do the right thing.

Sometimes we would sleep down on the beach in the sand. It sounds great, but there were challenges. Bugs could and did crawl into our ears (we'd use cotton balls to keep them out or, if they did get in, pour oil in to flush them out) and there were mosquitos—big, hungry, noisy mosquitos. Somehow every type of mosquito there is likes my blood—even later in my life when the South Dakota mosquitos ignored my wife and kid in favor of my rich red blood.

It took years, but Ron finally solved the problem of mosquitos at the beach and was kind enough to share his solution. I've used it, and it works. We were camping once and the first couple of hours were miserable. I was hiding under a sheet, but still hearing that awful whine from the squadrons of mosquitos lusting after my blood. I guess Ron had had enough. He got up, walked into the coconut grove, and came back with a couple of dry coconuts. Then he split them in half and threw them face down onto the embers of our fire. When they started to smolder, he placed a half-coconut in each corner of our camp. It worked; no mosquitoes for the rest of the night. He never said whether he invented the technique or learned it, but damn, that was one ingenious solution for what would otherwise be a miserable night. He explained that as long as the coconuts kept smoldering, the smoke would drift over the camp and keep the mosquitoes away. And even if it did smell like smoke, that was okay—smoke doesn't want my blood.

Down from the house on the right was a boathouse, standing next to the stone and coral foundation of a house that had disappeared years ago. Off to the right of the boathouse, around the point as you faced the ocean, was a large shallow area that always seemed to have waves pounding its shoreline. The reef extended outward and there were long rocks that were exposed at low tide. We used to walk over to the shallows and try to catch little fish with bamboo poles, using shrimp for bait. Sometimes we would comb through the debris that lined the shore, looking for shells and other neat stuff to take home. On the left of the bay there were low rocks that led into a small, rocky cove, just to the side of the low cliffs that rose higher as they circled the bay. Dotted

Pop, Ron and John with a freshly caught 'ulua near Kailua-Kona.

here and there among the cliffs were short sections of beach, usually underwater at high tide, where turtles basked in the sun when the sand was exposed. The cliffs reached their highest point about two-thirds of the way around the bay near the spot we called Shark Cave. Nobody I knew had ever seen a shark there, but we still believed that a huge shark was lurking in the darkness, waiting to put the bite on us if we got too near. Even further beyond the cave was a fisherman's camp under a kiawe tree and a trail that passed some heiaus and fire-walking pits before it ended at Okoe Bay, the site of another sandy beach about four miles from Honomalino Bay. Okoe was smaller, rougher, and hard to get to, so we didn't spend much time there. But it was cool to hike to Okoe and climb the hills behind the bay to the top of the ti leaf slides, imagining what it must have been like to slide toward the ocean on a narrow wooden sled down a steep slope lined with ti leaves, with jagged lava on either side that would eat you if you made a mistake.

Once Ron told me he needed my help to get something. Of course I said okay without getting any details. So off we went, and we kept going, and going, over the trail to the end of the bay, then on to the lava flats out toward Okoe Bay. It was hot, humid, and we had no water, so I kept asking Ron if we were there yet, but he kept saying, "Almost." After about an hour we finally got to where he wanted to go. It was a spot in the middle of a lava field. There was nothing there but a big stone with an indentation on its side, like where an eye would be on a shark. Ron told me he wanted that rock and we were going to carry it back to the house and then he was going to take it home. Jeez, it was not a small rock and we were two small kids, but somehow we got it back to the house before dark. Then of course Pop told us that if we wanted it, we were going to have to carry it, so again we saddled up and when we left for Pāhala, Ron and I humped the stone to Miloliʻi and our car.

But that wasn't the end of the story. When we got to Miloliʻi and put the stone on the tailgate of the station wagon, Eugene Kaupiko, the unofficial mayor of Miloliʻi walked over to see what was going on. What he said gave me chicken skin. He said, "I'm glad the rock picked someone. We've been worried about it sitting there in the field for so long." He further explained that it wasn't an ordinary rock, it was a rock that represented a shark god, and it was still there because the person doesn't pick the rock, the god picks the person that will take care of the rock. When he said that, I looked a little closer and it really did look like the head of a shark, it even had a crease where the mouth would be. We didn't tell anyone, but both Ron and I treated that rock with a lot more respect. After he was picked, he had the rock for years up at his house in Fern Forest and every time I went there I would check it out in his front yard. But once, I went over and the rock was gone. When I asked where it was, he said that something told him to take it back to Miloliʻi. He told me that while he was parked trying to figure out what to do next, one of the villagers was walking by and something told him to give the villager the rock. When he did, he was asked where he got the rock; they'd been looking for it for a while, since they knew it existed but not where it was located. When Ron explained what had happened and what Eugene had told him to do, they all seemed to agree that it was okay—even though Ron wasn't Hawaiian, the rock must have had a reason to pick him. I guess so, he really valued and guarded that rock, but only he and I knew what it was supposed to be.

We spent most of our time at Honomalino in the water or on the beach. I can't even describe how clean and clear the water is. Just off the beach in the water, a shelf of sand extended from the surf line into the deeper water, then dropped off to about five feet deep. When the surf was up, we'd jump into the thin line of foam where the water was going out, then run into the water coming in and get spun round and round until we were tossed up on the beach, screaming, "Calcutta!" at the top of our lungs for some forgotten reason. If it was calm, we'd spend hours drifting back and forth with goggles and fins, picking up pieces of shell from the sand.

We also fished a lot, both with spears and from boats. Unc had a P14, a very seaworthy and capable boat—a little small, but solidly built, somewhat portable, and very seaworthy. I still think they were some of the most useful boats I ever saw or rode. It had a two-stroke outboard motor, probably about twenty to thirty horsepower, that ran on a mixture of gas and oil. Funny thing, just about every other engine around the place would give us trouble, but never the outboard. I know we only used one engine, and the men were really particular about keeping it running and dependable. Sometimes it was a long way back to shore, with no radio or phone.

It was always exciting to open up the boathouse that smelled of WD-40 (an aroma that still smells like Kona and boats to me) and pull the boat out on the small cart that sat on the railroad tracks running from the boathouse to just above the sand on the beach. We would take sections of tire and tubing and position them on the beach in front of the boat, then push the boat into the water over the tubes, moving them back to the bow as the boat passed over them until it was floating in the shallows. Then one of the men would start the motor and moor the boat to a buoy tethered to a large railroad wheel just offshore.

Then came many trips to and from the house carrying rods, reels, food, lures, and, most importantly, beer for the fishermen. Then it was time to set out over the ledge at the mouth of the bay and the coral heads in the ever-deepening but still crystal-clear water, straight out for about a half mile. We'd follow one of the current lines looking for anything that was floating, for birds and, most of all, for fish. Usually we'd catch mahimahi, ono, aku, or ʻahi.

Once Pop caught a big ʻahi about a mile out. It turned into a kind of an *Old Man and the Sea* thing. He wouldn't give up; the fish kept fighting and soon Pop had been fighting it in the fourteen-foot boat for three long, hot hours. My uncle had had enough and decided to just run the boat up on the sand and let Pop muscle the fish onto the beach. So they circled in front of the beach once, yelling at everyone to get out of the way, then in they came, full bore right onto the beach, as my uncle pulled the motor up out of danger. Pop sprang over the side clutching the long pole and ran up the beach until the fish was in the shallows, then he quickly turned around and threw himself on the fish, wrestled it into submission, and held it until Unc bashed its head in with a club. I have to say it was impressive, especially since the fish spit out the lure as soon as it hit the beach and was trying desperately to swim into deeper water and get away. Well, that one didn't.

Once, I was in a boat that lost a propeller and didn't have a spare. It was called the *Spooky Luky* and we kids were on an excursion beyond Miloliʻi. We were merrily motoring along when suddenly the motor started to race out of control. When the motor was shut down and with the motor pulled up, we discovered there was prop. There were also no spare or oars, so six or seven of us kids were given ropes. We jumped into the water and pulled the boat for about two miles till someone from Miloliʻi saw us and gave us a tow. Nobody even treated it like it was an emergency, just a little problem that needed fixing. We got a prop and a cotter pin on loan and motored back to the bay—tired, but proud that we had done our share.

We also used to take our spears and go down to the beach to look for anything we could spear that was edible. I don't think there's a spot in that bay I haven't swum to and dove around, except the Shark Cave, of course. It's a miracle we weren't eaten by sharks, since we'd swim about a half mile to the middle of the bay just to see if we could dive deep enough to touch the bottom, about seventy feet down. I never got a spear. I guess the combination of very poor eyesight and a hair-trigger hinge gun didn't really appeal to anyone but me. In any case, I usually carried the bag.

In those days we mostly speared with hinge guns we made ourselves. Surprise—they were actually made out of door hinges. Out of an abundance of caution, I am not going to say how we made them, because they were really dangerous and had hair triggers. When I lived in Pāhala there was at least one incident a year when an accidental discharge resulted in a spear through someone's arm or part of their leg. No surprise—they wouldn't get in the water with me if I was carrying one.

Even Pop got into spearing a little. He loved to swim; kind of surprising for a guy raised in South Dakota with nothing to swim in but a swimming pool. But I still have pictures of him diving and a newspaper clipping of the hardhat diving gear that he and another lad cobbled together to clean the pool.

He wasn't too excited about spearing. Mostly he went with my uncle and carried the burlap bag they would fill with fish and lobsters when they went night diving.

But the only thing I ever saw him bring back was a huge tako that he dropped a harpoon through one day. As he told it, he was really looking for puhi, so he could harpoon one and cut it up for bait. But as usual, things didn't go exactly as planned. He was cruising in about twenty feet of water and saw something moving on the bottom. He wasn't sure it was an eel, but decided, *What the heck, it's worth a shot.* So he swam over it and dropped his harpoon. (It was a real harpoon, made of galvanized pipe and rebar, weighing about five pounds.) The harpoon dropped and he could see it hit something. But when he dove on it, he realized that he had dropped the harpoon right through the brain of the biggest tako any of us had ever seen. When he dragged it up to the house and stretched it out, it spanned twelve or thirteen feet. It was huge! I still remember sticking my palm against the suckers next to the body of the tako, one sucker covered my whole palm. Of course, there were no cameras or pictures. Sadly, nobody would admit they knew what to do with it, so one of the men who had been drinking for a while took it to Miloliʻi to try to sell it to someone. A fool's errand, if there ever was one, kind of like taking coals to Newcastle. When he got back it was clear that he had been snookered when he admitted he had paid someone five dollars to take it off his hands.

Here's a diving tip. If you ever try to catch a lobster with your hands, always look at its antennae first. If one is pointing back and one is pointing out, there's an eel nearby, every time. If both antennas are pointing back, there is more than one eel nearby, every time. My uncle explained it once to me: Lobsters and eels can live close together, but the lobsters don't trust the eels and use their antennae to keep track of them so they don't become a meal.

Maybe Pop wasn't the greatest spearfisherman, but he sure could swim, and he was fearless. At night during lobster season, he and my uncle would head off into the night with an underwater flashlight and a burlap bag. Usually, about an hour later they would wade out of the water with a bag full of lobsters and *uhu* (parrot fish). My uncle would catch them both with his bare hands. The lobsters weren't too hard. He would just look into their hole, check to see where the eel was, and to see if any of the lobster's feelers were pointing behind, then a quick grab and another lobster went into the bag. As they told it, the uhu wasn't much harder to catch. My uncle would locate one sleeping in a balloon of mucus, then gently slip his hands around it, and that uhu ended up in the bag with the lobster.

After they were done, they cleaned out the intestines, threw the lobsters into a huge pot with boiling salt water, cooked them till they were bright red, dumped them into a galvanized tub with lots of butter, and then tore into them along with enough beer to wash them down until they were all comatose.

My uncle was one of the old-time divers in Hawai'i. It was said that he helped invent the underwater flashlight (the first one I know of was a flashlight in a section of inner tube with a glass lens) and was also the first to import diving masks (he got some in Japan after seeing the 'a'ama divers wearing them). He was quite the wag as well. I still remember watching some of the home movies he starred in that were taken in the early 1950s by a hardhat marine photographer. The first was a clip of a huge barracuda moving slowly through the water until our intrepid diver swam up behind it with a knife in his teeth and stabbed it repeatedly, after which it slowly sank to the bottom *hors de combat*. The effect was lessened somewhat by the visible line towing the obviously dead barracuda through the water. Still, he tried.

Then there was the clip that began with a puhi in its cave breathing in and out, its mouth agape. At first it was pretty hard to tell how big the puhi was since there was nothing else in the picture. Then the camera panned to a shot of a short, pudgy diver with a Hawaiian sling speargun, cocked up to the barb, diving down toward the eel, followed by a close-up of our diver spearing the eel right behind the gills and grabbing the spear on both sides of the eel's head. Then all hell broke loose. My uncle was just a shade over five feet tall, the eel was about seven feet long and pissed about being speared. All the film shows for about a minute is a short, fat shadow hanging on to a long, thin, sinuous shadow for dear life with sand billowing and obscuring everything. Then, as the water clears, we see my uncle swimming up toward the surface with a dead eel on his spear. What a guy!

Unc was a great guy and I remember a lot about him, but my favorite memory is the gifts he gave Ron and me for Christmas. Every year after I learned how to swim, like clockwork Ron and I got diving masks and fins for Christmas. Real masks and fins, made by Swimaster, the best there was at the time. For a kid who loved diving and swimming and the ocean there couldn't have been a better gift. Thanks, Unc!

We liked the Swimaster because the mask was simple to use and it equalized the pressure in our ears when we dove. All we had to do was push in on the bottom of the mask, up and toward our nose, then snort and our ears would pop and we could keep going. The fins were also Swimaster. We liked them because, unlike the fins that covered the whole foot, the Swimaster just looped over the back of our heel and was easy to get on and off but stayed put when we swam.

One tip I'll share is how to keep your mask from fogging up. Glass masks always did, but there is a cure. Just take a naupaka leaf (the plant with the small white flower that looks like only half a flower), spit into the mask, and rub the naupaka leaf around the whole mask. Then rinse it out and away you go. But don't forget the most important thing—tear off a very small piece of the leaf and leave it in the mask. No fog, every time.

Sometimes one of the fishermen from Miloliʻi would motor into the bay in his canoe and take Ron or me, or both of us, fishing. He lived in a one-room shack just outside of Miloliʻi on the way to Honomalino. He was not real talkative, but he was always friendly and liked to have Ron and me riding in his canoe when he fished along the coast.

Once, after a long day on the water, he invited me to his home for sugar water, so thinking he was offering me a soda, I said sure! We walked from the village to his shack, just one room with a bed, a kerosene stove, and a table with a couple of chairs. No refrigerator or running water, but he had an outhouse out back. He invited me to sit, and when I looked around all I saw was fishing gear, some jars, pots and pans, dishes, a couple of eating utensils, and a gallon jar with some money in it. When I asked him why his money was in a jar, he told me that was all of his money, every bit of it that he had earned from fishing. But I was even more surprised when I asked him if he wasn't afraid someone would take it one day when he was out. His reply was that if someone needed it that bad, they could have it; he wasn't worried, he trusted his neighbors. Then he took two clean jars, filled them with water from another jar, poured two to three tablespoons of sugar in each one, stirred them until the sugar dissolved and then handed one of them to me. "Here's the sugar water," he said. So I drank mine, he drank his, and we talked for a while before I hiked back to Honomalino. Even though it seemed kind of strange drinking sugar water, I knew he was giving me the best he had, the stuff he saved for himself.

He seemed to know every nook and cranny of the coastline. He took us handlining and showed us where to look for ʻopihi along the coast where he could bring his canoe near shore. He knew where the largest ʻopihi lived, the kind we'd have to dive ten or fifteen feet deep to find. We'd dive down with a butter knife and take them off the rocks. Some of them were huge, about five to six inches across. We'd have to be quick; if we couldn't get them with one swipe of the knife, we'd have to make lots of dives to pry the knife loose, as they clamped down if we didn't break the suction first. He would also throw nets, and one time he used a coconut frond to gather ʻoama (small *weke,* or goatfish) near the shore by having me swim outside the school, waving the frond until I was able to crowd the school inshore to shallow water. Then he took a red net, lowered it quietly into the water and used another palm frond to gently herd the ʻoama into the net, then into the bottom of his canoe. He would do this a couple of times, then yell to me that he was pau. He never took more than he needed for a couple of days.

Another time, we went to Kona for a work party. A work party was an excuse for the men to sneak away for a weekend to "repair and maintain," but mostly to fish, drink, and play endless games of cribbage.

A little bit about cribbage, which we called the "holy game of cribbage." If you want a game that moves fast, requires mathematical ability and luck linked with an effective strategy and quick thinking, it doesn't get any better than cribbage. All that, and it's played with a board and pegs that keep score. The dealer even gets an extra hand.

Usually Ron and I were taken along because we were willing to work, able to follow directions, and never complained about fetching endless cans of beer. On that trip, when we got to the bay we were intercepted by Eugene Kaupiko and a couple of fishermen from the village, who asked us not to go into the water or make any loud noises because there was a huge school of *akule* in the bay. So we kept out of the water, were very quiet, and just watched what was going on. First there wasn't much happening, then some canoes crept in slowly and started laying a huge net around the whole school of fish. They moved the net closer and closer in to surround the school. Then they dove down and moved the bottom of the lead-weighted net a little at a time, closer and closer to the school.

After the school had been fully enclosed, Eugene came up to the house and asked if Ron and I would help them move the net. It was hard work, and they could use all the help they could get. Of course we jumped at the chance to get into the water and see what was happening. So we grabbed our gear and jumped into a canoe with Eugene, who explained what he wanted us to do as we motored out into the bay. We were told to dive about seventy feet down and help close the net in by moving it forward a little at a time, until the fish were trapped in a section of the net. Damn, that was hard work, but both Ron and I were able to make it down, move the net a little and come up, over and over again. I got really tired, but never even thought about quitting. We were doing a man's work and were happy to be involved.

After two or three hours of this, we had moved the net into position and the men closed it up with the fish inside. What an incredible sight! Seventy feet of fish, thousands of them, from the top of the water to the bottom, shining and flickering in the clean blue water. Then the guys at the top started rolling the net up, kind of like rolling a sock down your leg. They took large nets and dipped and filled them at the top of the net and emptied the nets into a line of canoes that was ferrying the fish back to Miloli'i where the women were cleaning and getting the fish ready to dry. Like all good things, this came to an end when Eugene gave us some fish and thanked us, and we went back to the house and slept the rest of the day.

We always took a couple of guns along on our trips, usually a .22 rifle and my father's K22 pistol. We never got any game like goats or pigs, but we saved a lot of birds by thinning out the mongoose population. We'd sit for hours, potting the occasional mongoose in the rubbish dump, just down through the naupaka in sight of the house, mostly using dead mongoose as bait.

But we didn't always restrict our mongoose hunting to shooting them; there were other methods. Once, one of us even fished for mongoose. I still can't remember who it was, but whoever it was, it was an act of lunacy. In any case, he fished for the mongoose using a bamboo pole and a hook baited with a little shrimp. I think he thought it would be cool to have a mongoose for a pet and wanted to catch one without having to shoot it. So, he hung the baited hook over the edge of the porch and lurked, waiting for the big bite, until nobody was paying attention to what he was doing any more. That was a mistake because pretty soon we heard some squealing and yelling, and there he was with a very pissed off mongoose at the end of his line, well hooked through the cheek and trying very hard to get to the source of his pain. It was quite a battle; the mongoose fisherman yelling for help, the mongoose yelling for help, and the rest of us standing around watching the show.

Well, he got some help, but the mongoose sure didn't. When Pop saw what was going on, he was kind of irritated. After gabbing a pair of pliers and trying to bring the mongoose in to unhook it and let it go only to have it charge him viciously and repeatedly, he started to lose his temper. The comments from the peanut gallery sure weren't helping. None of the grown-ups standing around with beers in their hands wanted to help or had any practical solution, but they all wanted to tell him what to do. He just wanted to cut the line and let the damn thing fend for itself, but the soft-hearted mongoose huggers wouldn't hear of it because, as they insisted, the poor thing would get the line tangled and the hook would get infected and it would suffer for a long time before it died, or something like that. Of course none of them wanted to get into the pit with the mongoose. It was all up to Pop. Well, I guess they never saw what was coming next. I sure didn't.

Pop gave up trying to be nice and tried to club the mongoose with a rake, but even hooked it was too fast for him and by then the mongoose was squealing loudly, looked rabid, and seemed to have decided that Pop was the reason he was hooked through the cheek and hurting. So, it kept attacking Pop repeatedly and almost got him a couple of times. Pop grabbed the pole, gave it to Ron and told him just to hold the damn thing, and disappeared. When he got back, he was pulling the bolt back on an M1 carbine with a thirty-round magazine fully loaded. After telling Ron to move the mongoose alongside a coconut tree, he tied the pole onto the trunk and, after ordering us all to stand back well out of danger, he opened up and started pulling the trigger as fast as he could until he got a round into the mongoose. When it slowed down and keeled over, he gave it the rest of the magazine, just to be sure. When it was all over, he took the gun back, then came out and told us to pick up the pieces and throw them onto the rubbish dump. There was no more fishing for mongoose.

Sometimes the things we caught were a little more painful. Most times we kids would try our luck at casting from the beach, at least until we got tired of tangled lines and empty hooks. Casting the old reels took a lot more finesse than we had at that age. Once, Ron got his hook into the water quite a way out near the buoy off the beach. After it had been in the water for a while, he figured out he had "caught Hawai'i"—gotten stuck on a rock or part of the reef. No problem. He handed me the pole with instructions to reel as fast as I could when he tugged on the line. He swam out and I felt the tug, then started reeling. Right after that, I saw Ron rise to the surface and race toward the beach. He was yelling, but I couldn't make out what he was saying. When the hook got to the beach, I figured it out. Ron had been hooked himself and was yelling at me *not* to reel. He didn't get hooked in a finger, leg, or foot, but in a place that makes me wince every time I remember it and that decorum dictates I not name. Suffice it to say it was not only extremely painful, but also very embarrassing. It didn't help that all the adults were gathered around marveling at how anyone could get hooked like that. Finally, they marched him up the beach, cut off the barb, and backed out the hook. He healed and never really got after me for what happened. After all, I had just been following orders.

We spent a lot of time fishing and collected a lot of stories about the events we had witnessed. Here are some of them, in no particular order.

There never was a time that we didn't believe there were sharks in the water, everywhere. For me, especially since I was nearsighted and easily fooled, any stray object or splash was considered a threat. We were raised on stories of ten-foot tiger sharks eating turtle guts in two feet of water, gory stories of one of my uncle's relatives who lost a leg to what was called "a large fish" while swimming in Hilo Bay, the shark hunts in Kohala, paniolo stories of tiger sharks attacking cattle as they were swum out to the interisland steamers at Honu'apo, and Pop's story of the shark he passed one day in the mouth of the bay that was longer than the fourteen-foot boat he was driving.

Pop was also fond of telling stories about people he fished with in Kona. I knew most of them and they were a crusty bunch, prone to drinking the occasional medicinal beer or coconut swipes they had made to offset the deleterious effects of the sun, of course. They also played many games of cribbage while arguing endlessly about minute details of gear, methods, and memories of fishing expeditions.

Once, Pop was fishing with a couple of his cronies—a guy they called the Laplander and his son. Pop was at the helm, as he usually was, when the lines they were trolling with got tangled somehow. So they stopped and tried to decide who was responsible while they untangled the lines. Pop and the Laplander were so busy arguing that neither one of them was paying much attention to anything else. That's when Pop noticed a large object in the water drifting slowly toward the boat. It wasn't till it drew up next to the boat that he could see it was a whale shark—rare, but not unheard of in Kona. Pop claimed that his fishing party nearly jumped ship in fear when he suggested they stop arguing and try and catch that fish. He neglected to mention that a whale shark is harmless. I'm not sure they ever forgave him, especially since the Laplander always seemed to grit his teeth on his pipe when my father told the story to others—always with a little embroidery on the truth, of course.

Sometimes our encounters between shark and man weren't as humorous, or as safe. One day Ron and I decided to spear an eel for bait. We hiked down past the brackish well and over the lava to the shallows that fronted the house. Ron was carrying a hinge gun and I was carrying the harpoon that Pop got the tako with earlier, more for comfort and defense in my case. I really didn't want to spear a big eel, I probably would have been too scared, but I couldn't admit that, especially to Ron.

We started in the shallow water, where Ron passed up a couple of likely looking eels as "too small" even though they looked plenty big to me.

Finally, we split up to comb the area better. Ron went off swimming into deeper water. I spent my time aimlessly swimming around, half-heartedly poking the harpoon at small, well-hidden and impossible-to-retrieve eels. Things went on like that for a little while, until I popped my head out of the water to breathe and heard Ron yelling—loudly and for once, very clearly. What he was yelling sent a chill down my spine. It was "Shark!" and there was no doubt in my mind that he was serious, dead serious. Yup, no doubt at all. Luckily, I was next to a large boulder that, while isolated from the shore, still gave me lots of protection, since I was up high enough to be safe.

Ron wasn't so lucky. When I got to the top of my rock, I spotted him about twenty-five to thirty feet away—up to his knees in water on a much smaller rock, with five or six medium sized sharks circling him, very closely. Well, when I saw what was going on, I joined in and started to yell, "Shark!" as loud as I could and shortly the shore was filled with anxious family members. That wasn't much comfort; they didn't help very much since everyone was yelling different advice and no one seemed to know what to do, and the sharks kept circling.

That all changed when Pop got to the rocks. I have to say that the old man always had a plan, and mostly it was a good one. This time we needed the right plan, and we needed it quick. The sharks were getting bolder and taking passes closer to Ron, then circling out, then coming back in again. I figured he didn't have much time before they figured out he was an easy meal. But Pop got everyone else to quiet down and yelled to Ron to look at him and only listen to what he said. He told him not to watch the sharks, but to look at my rock and, when he said go, to move straight to my rock without stopping for anything. Ron said okay and threw his gear near the rock where I could grab it, all of it, that is, except the spear that he kept in his hand with the rubber stretched as far as it would go, cocked and locked.

Finally, when Ron said he was ready, Pop watched the circling sharks and when they were just ready to come back yelled, "Run, Ron, run!" And Ron ran, I mean he really ran. I still don't think he ever got more than knee deep in chest deep water. He was at my rock so quickly he almost knocked me off. When the sharks got back, he was safe and they had been cheated out of a meal. So Ron and I moved off the rock to the shore and stopped fishing for eels and started fishing for sharks. But we stopped when one of them grabbed the huge hook and rope we were using, ate the bait, and broke everything. After that we tried to get one with our .22s after making sure there were no boats at risk. No luck, but maybe there were a couple of sharks with small holes in their fins when we got through. There sure weren't any sharks caught that day.

On another day I swam back about a half mile from the Miloli'i side of the bay with my cousin and her husband. We had slowly cruised around the point and were nearly at the beach when I noticed everyone standing and waving wildly on the beach. When I lifted my head out of the water, I heard what they were screaming. Yup, it was "Shark!" I'm not quite sure what happened after that. Suddenly I was on shore peering nearsightedly at my cousin's husband stroking toward the beach at an amazing pace. I could just make out a huge fin cruising out beyond the breakers. The shark stuck around for a while, but for the rest of the day nobody seemed to want to go swimming.

We didn't see too many sharks inshore, but there was an incident out at sea that I still remember clearly, even after more than fifty years.

We were trolling toward Okoe Bay one afternoon when Unc spotted a huge group of birds in a frenzy, wheeling in the sky and diving toward a commotion on the surface. We sped toward the flock, because when you see birds over the water in Kona, it almost always it means there are fish below.

This time was no exception, except it wasn't aku or 'ahi. This time the fish were huge and sharky, and they were eating a whale. It was a scene out a of nightmare. We got a close-up of the huge black whale twisting and turning in the water, trying to get away from the feeding sharks. As the whale thrashed, we could see big sharks biting into it. They shook their heads and bodies back and forth until the whale flesh gave way and disappeared into the bloody frothing water. We didn't stay long. Nobody wanted to see the whale die and some of those hungry sharks looked longer than our boat. We turned around and trolled off the other way.

Unc put it best, and I've never forgotten what he said when I asked him once how I could tell if there are sharks in the water. He replied, "There's always sharks in the water. You just can't see them." He must have been right. He was right about most other things.

There were also people around from time to time that hadn't seen a real shark up close and personal. Sometimes their efforts to spot them were humorous, sometimes dangerous. Like the guy who decided he would slip into the shark laden waters with a bag of rotting fish parts tied to his swimming trunks, so he wouldn't lose them. Nobody could persuade him that it was a lunatic idea. He donned his shark bait and took his fish-belly self and swam around for two hours looking for sharks. Never saw one, not a single one, in the same place Ron almost got eaten. Maybe the sharks figured it was too good to be true—their dinner coming to them—and were scared away.

Most of the trips we took were as a family with other families. By and large, the children played together, the women watched the children, and the men did manly stuff like fixing things, drinking beer, and either planning, preparing, talking about, arguing about, or going out fishing. It should be pretty obvious the men had a whole lot more to do than their wives and kids.

Don't get me wrong, I like fishing. I've always loved the ocean and boats. But sometimes in a flippant moment I think there has to be a better way to get fed than by taking a noisy, smelly, cantankerous motor that has to be fed oil and gas that we have to mix, stepping into a small boat and filling it up with men and noisy children, and dragging fishing lines and lures back and forth through the water in hopes that a fish will be foolish enough to bite a plastic lure that doesn't even look like real food. Then, if a fish does bite, to laboriously winch it in using a device that can't bring in the line evenly without help and keeps giving line back to the fish so that you have to pull it back until it's near enough for some tipsy fisherman to stab with a sharp hook and hopefully pull into the boat to thrash madly and bleed all over everything until it dies. Yup, I guess there can't be much more fun to be had on Earth.

But sometimes on our fishing trips we experienced some not-so-typical fishing experiences. Like the day when Pop was shorecasting from the beach and someone was swimming a little farther out and spotted a school of weke. He tried to tell Pop where they were, but I guess Pop didn't quite believe him so he said, "If they're there, why don't you go get one?" So the guy went ashore for a bamboo pole, put some bait on the hook, then walked down to the beach, and swam out over the school. When he let the hook down, *bam*, he caught one of the biggest wekes I've ever seen. Pop never really forgave him. After he pulled his weke to shore and carried his prize away, Pop kept casting fruitlessly into the middle of the school with nary a nibble. I guess the bite was off.

We weren't averse to playing tricks on each other and sometimes on the adults. Only fair. Nothing gets your heart started faster than having something scratch down your back when climbing up a coconut tree and hearing a trusted adult yell, "Rat!" Not fun at all. So once, while Pop was fruitlessly casting and drinking down the beach, I found a hook and line fouled in the rocks down the beach near where he was. I spent a while trying to untangle the line, but I was getting nowhere when they called us for lunch. I was last out of the water but before I left, I put a piece of bait on the hook, just for fun. Imagine my surprise when I got back and there was a rather large *pāpio* hooked and dead on the line. Gleefully I surfaced and told Pop there was a pāpio under me, which was true. I just neglected to tell him it had already been caught. He, in his surly "I'm not getting excited and I'm not getting any bites" voice, replied that *if* there was a fish, I should get it. After that weke you'd think he would have learned. I can tell you he was astonished when I dove and surfaced with a huge pāpio in my teeth, shaking and wrestling it to the beach. He was not a happy camper, but he ate the fish. After all, like he said, it really was his fish, I just retrieved it for him.

Another time we had been trolling all day with someone from the Mainland who really wanted to catch a fish. Normally there would have been an aku or mahimahi, but that day, nothing. It was one of those hot, muggy Kona days when kids in the boat crawled under the bow to sleep and the beer didn't stay cold and last through the day. Pop was on his last beer and just about ready to call it quits when we finally spotted something. The men really didn't want to go back empty handed so he motored up to find that it was an inflated balloon fish on the surface. They decided, *What the heck, better than being skunked,* and the Mainlander was given the honor of gaffing it and bringing it in. Well, he swung down at the balloon fish, but he came up with an evil looking fish about four feet long. Over the side it went into the boat where it thrashed and snapped, trying to bite something. We were all on the bow of the boat or on the rail. That thing was scary; actually, it was terrifying. It was long and snakelike with a sail on its back and little dots running along its side. But that wasn't the scary part. The scary part was the teeth, the huge teeth, that made it look like some oceanic saber-toothed thing. It had a huge head and teeth that looked more like fangs. We could see them as it opened and closed its mouth, snapping at the air—long, sharp and scary teeth. Finally one of the men, probably my father, took a club and subdued it by beating its head in; he wasn't going to take any chances. We took the fish back and, since we had run out of food, made chowder out of it. Very strange flesh. Once it was cut up, we could just see our hands through the translucent flesh. Of course, no camera, but Ron pulled out the teeth and kept them for years. Funny thing, even the fangs were translucent.

Whatever happens to me in life, I'll always have the memories of those good times to take with me, and there are lots of times I'm lucky enough to get a whiff of nostalgia when I see a sunset or smell something that takes me back to those days.

CHAPTER 55

Cowabunga—the Exultant Cry of the Surfer

I've always loved the ocean. Seems like there can't be a better place to be, whether you're diving, surfing, boating, or just watching it from the shore.

I started surfing with a wood plank paipo board that Ron and I made with a handle and skeg nailed into the back end. These boards weren't pretty, but they were functional and could take a beating; really, the damn things were indestructible! They would take abuse that would have destroyed a less industrial board. They were heavy, but that meant we could duck under waves easily while paddling out.

I only used that kind of board at Punalu'u, in the shallows near the pavilion, but we sure had fun there for hours on the weekends and during the summer. We'd always leave the water with bloody knees and sometimes wana spines in our feet or knees, but it was worth the pain. The drill was easy. We'd walk down to a low spot in the small ledge that ran along the break, jump into deep water, then swim over to where the waves lined up and broke. When a likely wave rolled in we would do our best to catch it and, if we did, could ride straight in toward the beach until the wave died or we hit something and stopped. (That's why the skegs were so good: Not only did they provide a little steerage, they were also helpful for braking.) We surfed there for years, and I can't remember ever not having a good time. The waves were small and slow, but I guess everyone has to start somewhere.

Sometime between my paipo and longboard phases, a friend's father introduced me to a redwood and balsa surfboard from the 1940s that measured about fourteen feet. Sometimes he'd bring it to the beach so the kids could play with it in the surf. It really was brutal and more work than fun. We had to drag that huge and heavy board from the car to the beach over the very hot black sand. Then we'd have to decide who was going to paddle out; it usually took three or four of us because the board was so heavy and clumsy. Then we'd paddle out to some random ripple, arguing all the way. Once there, we'd pick a ripple and all paddle until the board was moving, then stand up, glide to a halt, and fall off. I'm not sure we ever caught a wave, but we had a lot of fun, until we had to take the board back to the car. Seems like we'd lose half of the kids somewhere on the way.

When I was about fourteen, I decided I was a real surfer—a longboard surfer. Ron had preceded me in succumbing to the craze that was sweeping the country at the time, and as usual I had to go along with the flow. Not that it was bad. Surfing music, surfing clothes, surfing magazines, surfing shorts, and all the trappings of a cult, based on nothing more than having fun in the water. What's not to like?

Ron had always preferred paipo boards over any other wave vehicle, but I decided I had to be a board surfer. After all, I had seen all those pictures in the magazines of surfers having fun on waves from two feet to thirty. How hard could it be? So, I took every penny I had and paid sixty dollars for an old, beat-up, waterlogged surfboard by a maker named Bragg. It was an eight-foot pintail made in California. It turned out to be some of the best money I ever spent in my life.

I had no car so I depended on Ron (when he got his license) and others for transportation to get me to and from the surf.

The first place I remember surfing with a board was about four miles out of Hilo, at a place called Four Mile, oddly enough. There was no beach, just lava to the shoreline and a snappy, hollow break with rights and lefts, short, fast, and hollow. The first time I paddled out I spent the whole session swimming, without much surfing. It looked so easy in the magazines. But my routine in the beginning was: Paddle out, take off on a wave, pearl (bury the nose of the board in the water), flip over the board, and lose it, then swim in, retrieve it, and paddle back out again—over and over and over. This went on, but after three or four incredibly frustrating surf sessions I learned that I needed to stay further back on the board, just enough to keep the nose above the surface instead of under it, and things went a little better. That wasn't as easy as it sounds. Boards in those days were kind of straight without much rocker in the bottom.

After I figured out how to catch a wave and not pearl, the fun really started. I could get to my feet with no problem, but a parallel stance is really not the best surfing stance I could have picked, especially since I had a tendency to lock my knees. I wish I could have seen myself; I probably would have died laughing. Lots more wiping out, lots more swimming. I was in great shape back then since I swam for hours chasing my board. Finally, someone took pity on me and suggested that I pay attention and ride with either my left (regular) or right (goofy) foot forward and bend my knees a little to take up the bumps. After that it was all practice, and I did get better. Not great, but better.

I figured out that on a longboard (and later on a shortboard) the weighting and unweighting of the rider on the board makes a huge difference, depending on how the rider's weight is distributed. But really, surfing can only be learned by paddling out and giving it a go. Eventually, I left Four Mile. It was good to practice and learn on, but there were bigger, longer, and better breaks calling.

CHAPTER 56

Surfing Kaʻū

Normally I surfed on my board outside at Punaluʻu Beach. Most often alone, very alone. Ron wasn't interested. He said the waves were too mushy for a paipo and he wasn't going out for the exercise. Nobody else had a surfboard or wanted to surf there if they did; too long a paddle, strong currents, and (it was said) sharks. To be honest, there were only three breaks at Punaluʻu that I could ride on a board: a short, fast, and hollow (mostly impossible to make) break at the left middle of the bay; a bigger, more consistent but mushy break just behind a reef at the right of the bay; and a small section that sometimes broke inside near the wharf.

Riding the break on the left was simple: Take off, turn, crouch, wipe out, and swim for the board, then out again for another wave. That wave was a challenge on a longboard. It was basically a wave that closed out, and I would try to get just a little ahead of it before it died out, and it was shallow—real shallow. The only way across it on a board was to stay on the face of the wave to keep enough water under the board so the skeg didn't hit. If I wiped out, I was on the reef and dancing with the wanas. Still, it was a skill builder and not boring.

The break on the right was easier, but mushy. What worked best was to take the long paddle out, then sit just at the inside edge of the reef until a biggish wave broke over it, then catch the white water, stand up and work the wave when it built up, riding as far as possible. I spent most of my time surfing that break since the rides were way longer than anywhere else, even though it was a long paddle and I sometimes felt very much like bait sitting there alone. It didn't help when some well-meaning observer would mention he'd seen some fins outside and behind me that I never knew were there. Sometimes it got exciting. That was when the waves were huge and the white water was enough to make a real wave after it passed over the reef. I was even able, once, to ride from the outside all the way to the beach by working the break all the way in from 200 yards or so outside.

But sometimes I got lucky. The whole time I'd surfed at Punaluʻu I'd never seen a real quality wave like the ones in the surf movies. Except for one day. By then I could leave my board with a friend and ride my dirt bike to the beach to check the surf. One day, I couldn't believe my eyes. Somehow the tides, the swell, and the wind had conspired to produce a three-to-four-foot swell breaking in the middle of the bay that was far better than anything I'd ever seen at Punaluʻu. It was all perfect—snappy little curls that didn't close out and real walls to work. Best of all, I had it all to myself. I surfed until it was dark when I paddled in exhausted and happy. The next day I raced to the beach on the same tide, but no dice—same old wave. I never had it that good again, but that one day was enough.

There was also a one-to-two-foot wave on the left side of the bay, on the inside near the boat ramp under the wharf ruins. It was small, but it could be interesting. This break was caused by an underwater berm or breakwater near the wharf, which formed little waves when the swell from outside hit it—usually not very big, and certainly not long, but still kind of fun. It was drop in, stand up and turn, ride until the wave closed out, then straighten out and ride up onto the sandy beach.

Normally the surf was small but there were times when it got very interesting. Every time there was a hurricane the surf was brutal. I mean really brutal. The times I saw it, the wind had pushed the water into the bay where there were huge swells. Unrideable, dangerous, but fun to watch. But one day in the late '60s a storm brushed by the bay that was a little different.

That day I didn't have my board, but there was a six-to-seven-foot shorebreak on the left side of the bay near the boat ramp. So, a friend and I jumped off the wharf and bodysurfed for about two hours until we were tired. It wasn't much—mostly taking the drop, ducking under the wave, and swimming back out with the backwash for another wave—but it was surfing, and it was fun. Afterward we were standing on the wharf, watching the swell come up over the top of the old wharf, then sinking down almost to nothing, over and over, up and down. So, after watching and timing the waves for a while, I stepped off the wharf into the crest of a wave, rode the swell down, swam a little outside, then on the next swell rode the swell up and stepped back onto the top of the wharf. It was so cool. We did that for hours until it got too rough and we had to leave.

There was one other incident at Punaluʻu that taught me a valuable lesson. One year at Christmas Pop had given me a brand-new and shiny waterproof Waltham watch. A Waltham watch with a Twist-O-Flex watchband to boot. It didn't get any better than that. So, the next day I tooled to the beach with my brand-new watch so I could flash it and know the time while I was surfing. I jumped into the water as usual and started to paddle to the outside. Then *bam*. Something came out of the gloom and tore the face off my watch, then vanished. All that was left was the case and the Twist-O-Flex band. It didn't help when I asked the old man if he would replace it. Not a chance, he told me. Not that I really expected he would. But at least I learned a valuable and lifelong lesson. From that day forward, I never wore anything shiny in the water. Still, it could have been worse—I could have lost my hand.

I surfed alone until 1965, when another surfer moved to Pāhala whose father also worked for the plantation. Rusty and his family had just finished cruising from California to Tahiti. Unlike myself, he looked like a surfer, which he happened to be—actually a much better surfer then I was back then. He was in my class at school, had a board, and had surf bumps. Go figure—it seems like I've always been a little behind. We had a great time while he lived in Pāhala. We surfed Punaluʻu when we had to, but most of the summer we surfed in Hilo. Every morning we rode with his mother to Hilo where she worked. Then Rusty, who had a driver's license, and I would take her Volkswagen and look for surf at the various Hilo breaks, staying out until we had to pick her up for the ride back to Pāhala.

There were other spots to surf in Kaʻū. One was Kāwā, about four miles down the road from Punaluʻu toward Nāʻālehu. It was a small, very rocky break that was not easy to get to since it involved parking off the main road and hiking through the kiawe about a mile to the beach. The break was in the middle of a smallish bay with a heiau up on a cliff to the left of the break. I didn't surf there often; somehow the place was very ominous and scary. It was at the end of a low spot in the road where the road flooded often. There was a ford up from the beach that sometimes was up to two to three feet deep in water from the hills. As a result, the water offshore there was always murky and really dirty. I never saw the bottom even once when I surfed at Kāwā. I always thought it was sharky, even though I never saw one, but it was just too threatening. I was always looking over my shoulder there and felt like that bay just didn't want me around.

Honuʻapo, on the way to Nāʻālehu, also had waves, both out on the point and inside. I never had the guts to ride the point, especially after hearing about the resident tiger sharks that lived in the area. The old-timers told us the tigers used to attack the cattle as they were swum out to the interisland steamers when the wharf was still there. I stuck to the smaller two-to-three-foot break on the inside in the shallows.

But it wasn't very safe there either. One of my classmates was spearing manini in the shallows under a ledge in about three feet of water. The way I heard it, the light coming in from outside the ledge was reflecting off the manini and the guys were just taking turns spearing them until they got enough. But it went sideways when it was my classmate's turn. He was under the ledge laying on the bottom, waiting to take a good shot, when his friends suddenly saw his legs vanish into the gloom. They jumped down off the rocks, grabbed his feet and legs, and pulled him out—with a puhi on his hand up to his wrist. They had to cut the eel off at his fingertips and take him to the hospital to have the rest of it cut off. The way I figured it, the eel saw something flash and just engulfed it. After that I kind of stayed away from the rocks there. I saw his scars. It had to be a huge eel to run that far up his arm—and once there, it wouldn't have been able to let go. That's why we mostly never went to the ocean alone.

One of the best, but most difficult to reach, surf spots in Kaʻū was Kaʻaluʻalu Bay, off to the left on the way down to South Point, at the end of many miles of dirt roads and jeep trails.

I first visited Kaʻaluʻalu when one of the groups on the plantations from Pāhala and Nāʻālehu threw a big weekend picnic at the bay. While we were there, Ron and I noticed a very clean hollow point break that was kind of big. It was just off the left of an old wharf used to ferry cattle from shore to ships offshore. There was also a smaller but really nice break toward the left of the middle of the shallow bay. We tried to bodysurf the break in the bay, but it was too slow for that kind of surfing, so we watched it for hours, trying to figure out how we could get there again and get into some waves when we were older.

Later on, I got my chance. It was when I was about seventeen and had acquired a Chevy Corvair station wagon from a friend's father for about $100. What a deal! It ran, it was air cooled, the radio worked sometimes, and I never really cared about the hole in the floor on the passenger side. I know the Corvair wasn't Ralph Nader's favorite vehicle, but that car had one feature that was priceless. It had a rear engine and lots of weight in the back, which meant it was *almost* impossible to get it stuck and it could go pretty much anywhere a Jeep could.

It got even better when one day I was leafing through a car parts catalog and saw some spring expanders, a cheap way to lift a car further off the road. They were dead simple and really neat. They were selling metal blocks that fit inside an expanded spring to keep the spring open, an inexpensive way to raise the bottom of the car. Naturally I had no money, so I made my own spacers out of old kiawe wood, which wears like iron. They were cheap, easily replaced, and I could do my own adjustment on the height. Wonder of wonders, they worked like a charm! In fact, I never broke a pair, ever. That's when it hit me. I could now reach Kaʻaluʻalu. All I had to do was jack up the back of the car, insert the spacers, and I'd have plenty of clearance to avoid the high spots on the jeep trails.

Jeep trails, or trails built for four-wheel-drive vehicles, are kind of interesting, and it takes some finesse to drive on them. Mostly back then, people had surplus military Jeeps. There were other makes of four-wheel-drive vehicles, but we called them all Jeeps. Basically, jeep trails are two deep ruts in the ground, with high ground in between that's still lower than a Jeep's clearance but higher than a car's. There were two ways that I used to successfully negotiate them. If the ruts weren't too deep, I'd just follow them. If they were really deep, I'd drive with one tire in the middle and one on the opposite side straddling the rut. Believe me, it worked better than it sounds.

Anyway, once I figured out how to get there and back, my younger brother and I surf safaried to Kaʻaluʻalu. The surf was great—glassy head-high waves breaking off the cattle chute in deep, clear water. Just two of us and the waves. We had a great time and left sunburned, tired, and surfed out. I guess about eight hours in the water without a break will do that to just about anybody. I was the first person I ever heard about who took a board out there.

After that first successful session, I would make occasional forays to Ka'alu'alu, and aside from the time investment to get there, it was great. But it was a dangerous place to surf. Not because of the surf, but because of the sharks. Not the rumor of sharks, not the urban legends of sharks, but real sharks, tiger sharks, the kind that bite. I learned this one day when I was out thrashing, island style. I had seen a fisherman on shore waving at me, but the waves were just too good for me to leave, so I just kept going until I was tired. When I went in, the fisherman walked over to me. I thought he was going to compliment me on my surfing, but instead he asked if I was crazy staying out there with sharks in the water. I hadn't seen a thing, but he told me there were two or three huge fins just outside the break the whole time I was out. Chicken skin moment! I asked my younger brother, who had been watching for sharks while I surfed, if he had seen them; of course he had, he wasn't blind. When I asked him why he hadn't told me, since I'd been riding in and paddling out for hours, he said he didn't want to scare me. Right. I guess he forgot he couldn't drive.

On another trip, I didn't even get into the water for a paddle out. When I got to the bay that day, it was horrific. There were cattle carcasses washing back and forth in bloody water, with tiger sharks chomping them up. It was incredible to watch; each tiger rushing into shallow water and taking huge bites out of the cattle, shaking and thrashing until the meat broke loose. Then it would circle back out and another one would have a turn. Just chilling, especially for a nearsighted surfer who was deathly afraid of sharks. I never did find out what got the cattle into the water. Someone speculated they'd stampeded for some reason and headed into the water, where some of them broke their legs and couldn't get out again. I guess I'll never know, but I took a long break from surfing Ka'alu'alu after that.

I did take a guy from California out to the bay one day. We surfed the smaller break in the middle, but he was pretty skittish and kept looking out for sharks. He wasn't reassured when I told him I'd be more worried about the kākū, or great barracuda. Things got very real for him when a huge barracuda skipped across the water and jumped over the front of my board. He screamed, "What's that?" I told him it was a barracuda, a big one, but that he shouldn't panic since it wasn't unusual to see them skipping like a stone across the surface before disappearing into the depths. But he left the water when I told him I wasn't going in and that I was way more worried about the sharks—but I figured we were in shallow water and if we were going to get bitten it would have already happened, so why worry now? He went in very quickly after that, and I had to take him back to Hilo. At least I wasn't surfing alone for once. But you know I didn't tell him about the cattle incident before we got in the water.

CHAPTER 57

Honoli'i Pali

Of course Ka'ū wasn't the only place to surf on the island. Honoli'i is where I really learned to surf. The break is about five miles outside of Hilo, alongside a cliff and under a huge bridge fronting a river mouth.

At Honoli'i, there were two main breaks we surfed: the point, which broke on the left side of the river and channel, and the bay, a break on the right side of the river. They both broke toward the middle of the river in very dark and scary water. Because of the river, the water at Honoli'i was always cloudy. The point, when it was breaking, was bigger, faster, and more critical. They both broke toward the river mouth in very dirty water. Not contaminated, just dirty.

Getting to the beach in those days meant that we had to carry our long, heavy boards down the cliff on a narrow, muddy, and slippery footpath worn into the near vertical face of the cliff. There was a better way, but the residents of the house with this access really didn't like surfers, so we struggled with the cliff.

Once at the bottom the "beach" was nothing more than a very narrow stretch of dark sand and slippery boulders that shifted under our feet when we went into the water. Sometimes there was sand at the end of the shoreline towards the river mouth. That was usually the best place to paddle out, since the flow of the river eased paddling and waves didn't break often in the river's deeper water. But that's where locals said the tiger sharks hung out, waiting for their next meal to come downriver.

I never saw a shark at Honoli'i—maybe because I was so nearsighted, or maybe I was just lucky. But I know they were lurking about. I knew because I saw a board a tiger had bitten out at the point, while the surfer was sitting in the lineup waiting for a wave. The board was yellow, and the tiger just appeared out of the water, ignored the surfers, and gently chomped down on the board, then released it and disappeared again. The bite went from one side of the board to the other. Wiser heads than mine estimated that this shark was more fourteen feet long.

I surfed a lot at Honoliʻi with Ron. We would go to the beach together, but he would paddle out to the point and I would go the other way. We rarely surfed the same break because we were looking for different kinds of waves.

Ron never took to board surfing. He tried it and did okay, but never liked it as much as paipo boarding. At first, he started out with the same board he used at Punaluʻu, but when he found out that didn't work at Honoliʻi he upgraded to plywood.

Then he tried to make his own paipo board by copying a commercial plywood board. It had an upswept nose and curved down in the back on both sides. Such boards were fast, really fast, and pretty maneuverable. Most of the best paipo surfers at the time used them.

But Ron was different. He was a minimalist, and that popular paipo design was a large board, difficult to work with when it wasn't on a wave. Ron wanted just the bare minimum needed for speed and maneuverability. He also wanted something that would duck under waves easily when paddling out so he could punch through the big sets. Accordingly, he designed and built his own, with a notch in the front for his hand and a curved section in the back that tucked against his belly.. He handmade and adjusted all of his boards to fit just the way he liked to surf.

He could really ride those little boards. He could carve waves from one-to-two-foot ankle snappers to eight-to-ten-foot point tubes. On the larger waves he would take off late, in the tube, and carve to the bottom, make a turn, move up the face of the wave, then slow down and let the wave catch up, and there he was, locked into the tube. Then he would push down on the front of his board, accelerate out of the tube and carve a cutback, then a bottom turn that took him from the bottom of the wave up and over what was left of the wave.

I wasn't that good. I finally got okay on a board. I could catch waves, stand up, take the drop, turn either way, and do all the neat things like nose rides, cutbacks, head dips, quasimodos, coffins, and other moves with those peculiar and unique surfing type names.

While all this was going on, I was also immersing myself in what I thought of as surf culture, with all its trappings—in my own somewhat skewed and inept way, but with boundless enthusiasm. I bought some custom canvas surf shorts with "competition stripes." Not that I ever wanted to compete—rather, it was the "cool" factor. Of course, I didn't listen to the seamstress and had her make them to fit and didn't allow for shrinkage, even though she kept telling me they would get smaller after washing. At least they kept me thin. I also got some mail-order *huarache* sandals from Mexico (too small, even after soaking in hot water and wearing until I just about couldn't walk), and I let my hair grow out. Pop got mad and made me get a haircut, but that was okay—I was a surfer.

What wasn't okay was that I lusted for surf bumps but was never able to grow them. Surf bumps are calcium deposits on a surfer's knees that build up from knee paddling a surfboard; they are the badge of the dedicated surfer. No matter how hard I tried, I couldn't knee paddle and therefore couldn't grow bumps. Such is life.

There were a couple more surf breaks near Hilo. The first, I rarely surfed; it is called Bayfront because, of course, it fronts Hilo Bay. It broke best off to the right of the metal bridge, but it also broke on the left side. It was the longest wave near Hilo and probably on the island, but it was at the mouth of the Wailuku River and, like Honoli'i, very dark and scary. Not many surfers rode the break off to the left, which was short and gnarly. Most rode the main break off to the right of the river. When it was breaking, there could be up to ten-foot walls ("old style") and incredibly long rides. But the paddle out was not for the faint of heart, and sitting out there always made me feel like a couple of leg sticks waiting for a shark.

I need to explain that when I refer to wave height, I use what we call "old style," which means that we measured wave height by looking at the wave with a surfer on it and then estimating how many surfers would fit from the bottom to the top. They say this purposely underestimated waves. Could be. It's just the way I learned and, despite the whines, it was easy. You looked, you estimated, and that was it. Now they measure the face of the wave from the trough to the crest. It adds about one-third more to the height, so a ten-foot wave would now measure thirteen or so, and a four-foot wave would measure five feet, I guess. Kind of confusing to me so I stuck with the old style. I liked it and that's what I use. After all, it's my story.

We also surfed one of my favorite spots, Richardson's, which has three different types of breaks: the main break directly out from the parking area, which breaks just off to the left of a small, board-eating island; a point break on the other side of the island; and a small reef break in the middle of the bay on the right side.

The takeoff at Richardson's is kind of dicey on a big day. You have to paddle straight at the island until you catch the wave, then turn away from the island down the wall until the wave closes out. The trick is to take the drop, make the turn, and ride along the wall until just before the wave breaks, then pull out or straighten out, and hope there isn't a bigger wave outside, because there is nowhere to go.

I haven't mentioned that—save for one exception that I'll get to later—just about every wave I surfed on the Big Island ended up in the rocks. We had to walk over rocks to get to the surf, walk through the rocks to get out, and surf around rocks in the breaks. That meant if we lost our boards they got dinged, every time. I spent a lot of time patching my board.

The other two breaks at Richardson's were on the other side of the small island. I mostly surfed the smaller break in the middle of the bay. It was quite fun; the wave broke over a shallow reef into deeper water. We could take off, make the turn, run the nose, then move up as far as we could on the nose to bury it and use our momentum to stop.

But there were also poignant moments fraught with danger at Richardson's. One day, one of the professors from the college in Hilo came down on a big day. He had been there the day before and apparently had been held down by a closeout set, which is never a fun time. But on this day he had a plan to keep himself safe: He wore a ski belt to give him floatation. It sounds like it would work because people do not float in foam; we sink and can't breathe. Good plan, bad idea. It all went pretty well until he started to paddle out, then he got caught inside in front of a closeout set. He didn't panic; he bailed out per his plan and tried to dive under the wave that was breaking right on top of him. No dice, didn't work at all. Every time he tried to dive under, we could see his feet go up, then down a little, then back up again, just in time to get pounded by the next wave of the set. Good thing there were only five to six waves in that set. By the time he finally got back to the rocky shore, he unbuckled the ski belt, threw it away, and jumped up and down, cursing it quite thoroughly. Meanwhile, we had jumped in and rescued his new board, mostly before it hit the rocks, and gave it back to him. It had a couple of dings from the rocks. To our credit, none of us even snickered about his misfortune. He was a good guy, and no one wanted to hurt his pride. But no more belt for him. After that he took it in the chops just like the rest of us did all the time.

CHAPTER 58

Hāpuna

Later, when I was working on the plantation and I had a car, I would sometimes camp out at Hāpuna Beach on the weekend with a bunch of friends. Hāpuna is up the coast on the other side of Kaʻū, toward the uppermost part of the island. Hāpuna was mostly a bodysurfer's dream, and one place where the waves didn't end in the rocks. There were big, crystal clear waves on a north or northwest swell, and lot of other things to do, but normally it was a bodysurfing beach. But one day, one perfect day, I had one of the best days of surfing in my life. We had drunk a couple of beers the night before and camped out on the beach (I was old enough and not driving).

As usual, at the crack of dawn I was up checking out the surf. I couldn't believe it. The beach break was peeling perfect tubular six-to-seven-foot waves both ways, rights and lefts, off a section of rocks near the middle of the bay. It was just before the sun came up and I could hear the roar of the waves as they broke and see the mist in the still air.

The waves were breaking in water that was about one to two feet deep just off the beach (that's why it was normally a bodysurfing beach). Most times, the whole wave pretty much broke on the beach all at once. But this time the waves were peeling down the beach, real fast and hollow and just unbelievably perfect. I grabbed my board and paddled out.

On that day, in that place, I was a surfing machine. At first nobody else was out, so I had the place all to myself for about an hour, until a couple of other surfers riding shortboards joined me in the water. Not many guys wanted to paddle out; it looked real gnarly from the beach. I guess it was, because they didn't do very well. They just kept taking off and getting pounded. But I had the only longboard, so I could sit outside, line up, and catch the waves much earlier, which made the difference between fun and pain. That meant I could pick the biggest waves in the sets, which turned out to be the best waves to ride, since they broke a little further off the beach and were probably a little safer. It was so unbelievably cool. I'd line up at a little bit of an angle, take two to three strokes, drop in, turn under the curl, move up to the front of the board to gain speed, then stand or crouch in the tube or on the wall and ride a screaming left until the wave jacked up and broke right on the beach in a foot or two of water. But, just as the wave was closing out, I'd move to the front of the board, grab the left rail, and lean into the wave and let it pass over me, then I could pop out the back of the wave unharmed. I'd paddle back out and do it again. Over and over and over. It never got old. As I said, what a rush. Even now, I still get chicken skin remembering that day. As it got a little lighter and the bodysurfers started swimming out, I got out of the water. I didn't want to hurt anyone, and it was only fair they got a turn. I'd had mine. The whole time I surfed that morning, I never wiped out or made a mistake. I made every wave I paddled into. It was just incredible.

Every surfer should have a couple of hours, days, or waves like that. A time when everything comes together and it all works the way we always dream it could. I did, and I treasure those times; for me they were few and far between. When I surfed, I was a proficient but not great surfer. But still, there were times when I surfed greatly.

I really can't explain how or why, but I'll always be grateful for those moments. Those were the times when I somehow was able to combine everything I was and what I could be, and pull it all together.

I believe that somewhere deep inside is the person that I've always struggled toward and wanted to be. And sometimes, when everything lines up, something bigger than I am gives me a taste. Not of what I am, but the best I can be, and it feels damn fine when it happens.

This wraps it up for surfing on the Big Island. I did go on to other surfing adventures on Oʻahu, but those are tales for another time.

CHAPTER 59

So What Does It All Mean?

I started to write my recollections of my time in Pāhala to pass something down to my daughter, and now my granddaughter. I felt it was something I needed to do before the stories and the way I grew up were lost. When my father and Ron died, I felt that what we had experienced together and remembered so fondly began to slip away. But those memories deserve to be preserved and passed on to others.

As I wrote, I discovered something I didn't realize before I put pen to paper. I found that the experiences I had—the good and not so good—mixed together into a large part of my story and are the reason I became who I am now.

I never started to write to get revenge or pick on anyone. I know now that most people are just doing the best they can, and they, like me, don't always get it right. So I hold no grudges, and in the end I feel like I gained much more than I ever expected or realized. It wasn't all good, but that's okay. It certainly wasn't all bad.

But I did have to decide whether to leave those parts in or take them out. In the end, I left them most of them in. It's not very comfortable and it was a hard decision. But I decided I had to tell the whole story, or most of it, if I was going to be honest. Otherwise, it would have been only a part of the story, when there would have been so much more to tell. I have purposely not used names and tried not to identify specific people because it just didn't seem fair. No doubt they probably saw things a little differently than I remembered.

I found something else out. As I wandered through my memories, I realized that Pāhala was more than just a name or a place. It was alive, just as alive as I was, and it was a part of my family that encompassed all the people and places that were part of that place and time. Even though

I knew I would leave, I never felt like I was running away from Pāhala. Looking back now, it feels like Pāhala had given me what it could, and what I needed in order to move on, and was letting me go. But I knew I would always take some of it with me. I just didn't realize how much I had been given and how much I would take away.

The town and people in it also gave me something else. I've always believed that everyone should live by a code, but until I started looking back, I never realized I had absorbed my code and most of my resiliency, optimism, and sense of humor from my early days in Pāhala.

Mine is a pretty simple code; it's not always easy to follow, but I try to stick to it and don't have many regrets. Except that pig; I still wish I hadn't sent that ball bearing downrange. I'm not going to write my code out, but I think you can find it in what I wrote. Just like I did, you'll have to find one of your own. Just make sure you can live by, and with it, as you go forward in life.

One last thought: I could never have made it through my childhood to being the person I am today without friends. I've heard a lot of people give lip service to friendship, yet many of them never understand that friendships naturally grow and shrink, ebb and flow, as we move through our lives.

For me, in my life, there have been pretty much three levels of relationships, aside from family, which is out there all by itself.

There are acquaintances. Mostly those are people I don't mind hanging out with or doing things with who drift in and out of my life. Not the kind of person I avoid, but not the kind I would confide in or ask for advice either.

There are friends. Those are the people I mostly associate with. They share the same kind of interests, and somehow it seems that they live by the same kind of code I do, so I feel comfortable with them and like to have them around. I hope they feel the same about me.

Then there are true friends. I'm not sure how to explain the difference between a friend and a true friend, but the difference is there and it is profound. Think about it and I think you will know what I mean. If I had to say, I guess for me it's a person who I know always has my back, and for whom I would do the same. They accept me for who I am, without judgment, as I do them. But they also can call me out when I'm wrong about something, without making me feel the fool, and help me figure out how to make things right. There is a balance in true friendship. It doesn't mean that anyone's keeping score, but somehow, and without discussion or effort, the give and take of true friendship keeps things even and in balance.

I've always felt luckier than most. I have true friends and I've had them for most of my life. No doubt my life is richer, more rewarding, and safer for having them there.

Finally, there are some last, last thoughts that aren't mine, but that seem only fitting to pass on to you, the reader.

When my father was suffering from terminal cancer, he moved in with me for his last months, and we had a chance to really talk to each other. We never seemed to before: I guess the time had never been right. In one of our last conversations I asked him what he felt was the most important thing to him, considering his situation and the inevitable outcome. Without a pause he told me, "Family and friends." He didn't have to explain. I got it. I hope you do as well.

A while back I went through a divorce. That's okay, those things happen, but going through it wasn't real fun. It wasn't a bitter or contentious separation, but it was a big change I didn't want and wasn't really ready to make. I guess sometimes we don't get to decide our destinies. But when I talked to my mom about it, she always said, "Things work out for the best." Turns out she was right, and I found out that sometimes it's better to take the long view instead of focusing on an unhappy situation. She was spot on. That time, it did turn out for the best.

My mother-in-law was one of the kindest persons I ever knew. She could be blunt and to the point, but somehow we always knew that she was on our side and wanted the best for us. But what I remember most fondly is what she used to say and what she lived by. She always said, "It doesn't take one cent, not one single cent, to be nice to people," and that's the way she lived. She hit that nail on the head.

Epilogue: Ron

Right around 1992 Ron left us. After he'd come back from Vietnam things were a little rough for him for a long time. We didn't always get along—that's life—but when I needed his help the most he was there, and I don't know what I would have done without him. Taking care of Pop when he was dying of cancer, working, and going to school were a little more than I could handle, but Ron left his job, came over to Oʻahu, and stayed with me until Pop died. During that time we let go of anything negative that we'd had between us. What was left was two brothers who respected, appreciated, and loved each other. Ron was killed by another Vietnam veteran who also had PTSD, who then killed himself when he realized what he had done. The way I see it, they were both victims and it was a sad time. I always expected to grow old with Ron and tell these stories together, but that wasn't in the cards.

I tried to find a way to express who Ron was, but somehow whatever I came up with fell short of the person I knew. But my daughter knew him and, in the end, she said it better than I ever could. So, with her permission, here is a poem she wrote for Uncle Ron.

Peace and Comfort for My Uncle Ron
by Jessica Walters

I don't remember much of you.
I've forgotten your face,
I'm losing your smile,
and time promises
to erase all the little details
I manage to tuck away.

Listen, the *kōlea* fly across the sky.
Their wings beat a furious tattoo
across the fragmented blue.

At night pueo pull obake
From graves dug into lava.
Watch from your favorite thinking stone
They come, like a damp yet fine mist;
they pull life, layer upon layer,
and fly as years segment like a pomelo
split for the moonlight.

Under a fractured sky, flocks of nēnē cry
Tears of Pele flow as you march
through the forests of your memory
Lose the fever of visions,
wash away the muddied waters,
the tension of spent bodies
torture for the caring.
Wind through the ferns like *makani ikaika* breathe an escape.

Do not look as they chip a space for you,
As they scatter you into the ocean.

Let the waves pick up your bones,
swim away from this house, from your pain,
from his pain and his rage.

Gather yourself and hide like *honu*.
Carry your carvings, your poi pounders,
and come out of the stillness left by war.
Come out of imposed dark silence
and sleep under the *hōkū*,
think of the ocean and rest
easy in the symphony
of remembrance.

About the Author

John G. Walters ("Waltah Boy") grew up on sugar plantations on the Big Island of Hawai'i, including plantations in Hilo and Pāpa'ikou. But the place closest to his heart is his last home on the Big Island—the town of Pāhala.

John graduated from Ka'ū High School and earned a Master of Social Work degree from the University of Hawai'i. He retired as a social worker after twenty-five years with the State of Hawai'i Department of Human Services. He has also worked as a supermarket manager, beer salesman, and deckhand on an interisland tugboat.

John lives with his wife, Sheila, on the island of O'ahu, where he very much enjoys spending time with his daughter and her family. He also enjoys diving for tako off O'ahu's south shore and making custom knives from recycled concrete cutting saws. In his younger and more agile youth, he completed four marathons, was a volunteer group leader at the Honolulu Marathon Clinic and also completed the Waikīkī Roughwater Swim and several triathlons.

www.ingramcontent.com/pod-product-compliance
Lightning Source LLC
Chambersburg PA
CBHW071956110526
44592CB00012B/1106